follow ... in

German Inten... it

The evidence available sugg...

operations may soon be expecte...

(with the Germans attacking) ; ...

no means clear whether this w...

mean a relaxation of pressure

In view of the relatively weak...

Britain in the Mediterranean...

quite probable that pressure in...

may be maintained simultaneo...

LEES, formerly chief geologist...

Iranian Oil Company, now wor...

petroleum department, states tha...

organisation in Iraq is chaoti...

CLASSIFIED!

THE ADVENTURES OF A MOLEHUNTER

CLASSIFIED!

NIGEL WEST

Biteback Publishing

First published in Great Britain in 2024 by
Biteback Publishing Ltd, London

ISBN 978-1-78590-853-8

10 9 8 7 6 5 4 3 2 1

A CIP catalogue record for this book is available from the British Library.

Set in Minion Pro and Trade Gothic

Printed and bound in Great Britain by
CPI Group (UK) Ltd, Croydon CR0 4YY

FSC
www.fsc.org
MIX
Paper | Supporting responsible forestry
FSC® C171272

CONTENTS

INTRODUCTION

By the age of fourteen, in 1965, I had acquired a reasonably comprehensive understanding of the role and structure of the Security Service, MI5, and some knowledge of its sister organisation, the Secret Intelligence Service, MI6. This was unusual in those days, but there were two reasons for my interest. Firstly, in August 1960, my family had been drawn reluctantly and unexpectedly into what became known subsequently as the Profumo affair. My father, who had sat in the Commons since October 1959, had been appointed John 'Jack' Profumo's parliamentary private secretary (PPS) when Harold Macmillan had promoted him to Secretary of State for War from the post of Minister of State in the Foreign Office. Profumo and his wife Valerie Hobson were among my parents' closest friends, and they often brought their two boys, Mark Havelock-Allan and his half-brother David Profumo, to stay at our holiday home in Bembridge, on the Isle of Wight. Indeed, on the fateful day in August 1961 when Profumo broke off his short-lived affair with Christine Keeler, he promptly caught a train from Waterloo and joined us on the Isle of Wight. At that time, my parents had no knowledge of the brief relationship, although they had met Keeler, who had accompanied Claus von Bülow to one of their parties.

Thereafter, as rumours of Profumo's indiscretion circulated in Westminster, my father became increasingly preoccupied by what he regarded as unjustified speculation, even persecution, by Fleet Street, fuelled by the personal animus of a spiteful political opponent, George Wigg MP. A former wartime colonel in the Educational Corps who had represented himself to the Labour Party as a great expert on army matters, Wigg always participated in the army debates, and in 1961, when Iraq threatened to invade Kuwait, Wigg had advised the Labour Party that Britain would be powerless to honour our defence treaty and mount an effective defence of the tiny, oil-rich, pro-British Gulf state. Being in opposition, he was unaware of the detailed contingency plans that had been drawn up at the War Office and knew nothing of the strategy of deterrence that had been adopted by Cabinet. Both infantry and artillery were flown into Kuwait from Bahrain, and a squadron of tanks had been shipped from Aden, bolstered by an airborne brigade sent direct from Britain. These measures proved very effective and achieved the desired result in Baghdad, where they hurriedly decided against an invasion. In his memoirs, *Ringside Seat*, my father explained Wigg's hostility towards Profumo:

> All continued to go well, but unfortunately two clueless servicemen in a truck ignored signs to keep away from the frontier and drove straight into Iraq, where they were arrested and accused of spying, prompting the inevitable Parliamentary Questions. My task, as Jack's PPS, was to anticipate the likely supplementary

questions that would follow the main question: I expected that the worst would be something like, 'How well were these men trained?' In the event the supplementary question asked was, 'What were their orders?' and in reply Jack improvised, 'If they got lost they should return to their units,' but it took Wigg a full two minutes to see the joke.

The success of the Kuwait operation left George Wigg looking foolish as his predictions had not been realised. On the contrary, the War Office had taken the crisis in its stride, and had deterred aggression with considerable professionalism. Nevertheless, Wigg had demanded a debate, to insist that although the army had reached Kuwait just in time, it would not have been able to mount an effective defence against an Iraqi invasion. This left Jack an opportunity to be conciliatory to Wigg, and he agreed to a debate, but instead the wretched Opposition back-bencher was comprehensively savaged by Jack's junior minister, James Ramsden.

Wigg's technique had been to ingratiate himself with ministers by offering them excellent racing tips, and he believed he was very popular, although he was the only person who thought this. Nevertheless, he had received a leaked medical report revealing some dehydration among the troops despatched from England, and he had attempted to use this document to show that the men were unfit for combat. Ramsden contradicted Wigg on every point, making him look like a bad loser, thereby leaving Wigg convinced he had been let down badly by Jack.

Although we had regarded this as one of the occupational hazards of politics, where personalities are bruised in the

> rough-and-tumble of Parliamentary debate, Jack and I were unaware that these minor victories had been achieved at a price which would be exacted later.[1]

When the Secretary of State finally confessed to his wife, over the Whitsun weekend in Venice, he also broke the news to my father, ever his faithful supporter. As it turned out, Profumo had tragically misinterpreted an encounter with the Cabinet Secretary Sir Norman Brook, who had conveyed a request from MI5 for his assistance in entrapping the Soviet assistant naval attaché Eugene Ivanov. Profumo had thought Brook was warning him off Keeler and her companion Stephen Ward, and on the assumption that his love life had come to MI5's attention, promptly penned a short but unambiguous note to Keeler, which she later sold to the *News of the World*.

For years thereafter, my father was deeply troubled by what he perceived as MI5's interference in the political arena but grateful that his friend had never disclosed the full truth to him or sought his advice, which would have placed him in a difficult position. Mistakenly, he remained convinced, as did Profumo, that the Security Service had deployed Brook to deliver a subtle warning, but in August 1961, MI5 was only interested in persuading Ivanov to defect. It was a scheme that miscarried spectacularly.

It would take the unworldly Master of the Rolls, Lord Denning, to unravel the intricacies of the Profumo saga, but as I read our well-thumbed copy of his report in the autumn of 1963, I was intrigued to learn that the Security Service had no legal powers, that it operated in the never-never land of the royal prerogative and that Home Secretary Sir David Maxwell Fyfe's 1952 directive, which had set out the organisation's responsibilities and duties, had itself remained secret until Denning disclosed its existence.

The second reason for my fascination with intelligence was largely due to a Benedictine monk named Henry Coombe-Tennant, who had recently retired from MI6 and in 1961 had taken holy orders. Known by his monastic name, Dom Joseph, he had held a select group of boys enthralled as he regaled them with his adventures as an evading prisoner of war (PoW). As a Welsh Guards officer, he had been captured at Boulogne in May 1940 and sent to a camp at Warburg, Westphalia but had escaped in August 1942, with thirty other prisoners, by sabotaging the camp's fence lights and then scaling the wire with ladders built from duckboards. He spent two months walking to the Dutch border where he made contact with the local resistance and the COMET LINE, an escape network in occupied Europe. He was escorted across the Pyrenees to Spain and then was repatriated from Gibraltar.

Decorated with the Military Cross by King George VI, and promoted to the rank of major, Coombe-Tennant had joined Special Operations Executive's (SOE) planning staff with a very personal understanding of conditions in Nazi-occupied Europe. Soon after D-Day, having volunteered to join Operation JEDBURGH team ANDREW, he was parachuted into the Belgian Ardennes in August 1944 and remained behind enemy lines for the next three months, liaising with the local Maquis circuit, codenamed CITRONELLE, and harassing the enemy.

After the war, he returned to his regiment to be posted to Palestine and then joined MI6, which sent him first to The Hague and then to Baghdad in 1959, where he converted to Roman Catholicism. In 1961, he took early retirement from MI6 to be ordained as a priest and join the Benedictine order, and he fulfilled part of his vocation by running the school's shooting club. At that time, it was considered entirely reasonable for the boys who possessed shotguns to bring them to school and take the opportunity to participate in weekly rough shoots on the monastery's extensive estate during the Michaelmas term.

Coombe-Tennant's best friend in MI6 had been David Cornwell, now better known as the novelist John le Carré, who would occasionally drop in at the school on Friday afternoons as he drove from his house in Hampstead to his cliff-top home, Tregiffian Cottage, near Land's End. Cornwell had resigned from MI6 in 1965 following the unexpected success of *The Spy Who Came in from the Cold*, his cover role at the Hamburg consulate being impossible to sustain after his true identity had been revealed in the Atticus column of the *Sunday Times*.[2] Apparently, his chief, Sir Dick White, had offered him an alternative job but on the condition that he abandon his writing career, which was attracting so much attention. Cornwell opted for an author's life, and his resignation was accepted.

Cornwell was cordially disliked by most of his MI6 colleagues, and a tempestuous affair in Germany with the wife of an MI5 officer ensured that he had few friends in the Security Service, an organisation which has always prided itself on being very 'clubbable'. Cornwell's first experience of espionage had been his recruitment as an agent long before he went to Oxford in 1952. There he had spied on his fellow students at Lincoln College. Six years later, he made the unusual transition from MI5 agent to MI5 officer and then moved to MI6 in 1960. While Cornwell boasted of his brief time in MI6, he hated being reminded of his earlier career in the Security

Service. Indeed, when I was commissioned by Faber & Faber in 1992 to assemble an anthology, *The Faber Book of Espionage*, I asked Cornwell's permission to reproduce an extract from *A Small Town in Germany*.[3] He insisted on inspecting the biographical entry I had drafted. When he had read it, he telephoned me to ask my source for the assertion that he had worked in MI5's office in the Exhibition Road under Jack Bingham before he had transferred to MI6. I had also mentioned that his mentor Bingham had been the model for the spymaster in his books, George Smiley, although Smiley demonstrably had not shared 'Black Jack's' reputation as a lothario.

'Who told you that?' he demanded.

'Black Jack,' I replied.

After a long pause... 'Well... he shouldn't have.'

Cornwell conceded he had based Smiley on Bingham but refused me permission to quote from *any* of his books... *ever*!

Cornwell's talks to Coombe-Tennant's group of boys were held in private but undoubtedly influenced several of the attendees who later chose the clandestine world for their future. One of those was the Islamic scholar Sir Mark Allen who headed the school's falconry club, while others, such as Arthur Denaro, distinguished themselves in the 22nd Special Air Service regiment.

While still at university, I retained my interest in intelligence literature, limited as it was, and worked part-time as a researcher for two well-established authors, both with considerable experience of covert operations. The first, Donald McCormick, had served in the wartime Naval Intelligence Division before joining the *Sunday Times*. Over his long career, he wrote more than a dozen non-fiction books on intelligence, including *The Israeli Secret Service* in 1977 and a biography of Sir Maurice Oldfield in 1985.[4] The other was the delightful Ronnie Seth. With only minimal training, Seth had been transferred from the Royal Air Force to a section of SOE that proposed to exploit his pre-war knowledge of Estonia, where he had worked briefly as a university lecturer. In October 1942, Seth, codenamed BLUNDERHEAD, had parachuted into Silesia, and within forty-eight hours he had been betrayed to the Gestapo.[5] Sentenced to death, Seth escaped the gallows and experienced many adventures until he emerged in Paris in August 1944 wearing a Luftwaffe uniform, much to SOE's embarrassment.

Seth is the author of more than two dozen books on the subject of espionage, and in 1952 he completed his memoirs, *A Spy Has No Friends*.[6] This account, which described a harrowing escape from the gallows, a spell in a German PoW camp and even some service as a Luftwaffe officer in Paris, did not entirely conform with the official view taken upon his repatriation that he was a candidate for a court martial. While Seth protested that he was entitled to his back pay for the two years he endured in enemy hands, the British authorities assessed conflicting reports of a Briton matching Seth's description who had acted as a 'stool-pigeon' (informant) for the Germans in various different PoW camps.

Whatever the relative accuracy of Seth's recollections, he was a gifted writer who had led an extraordinary life. Characteristically, when the War Office balked at paying him the money he was owed, he lobbied Parliament and won his case. His encounter with SOE had left him with permanent poor health and a robust scepticism of what purported to be Whitehall's collective wisdom.

When I met Seth, he had been living in Malta for many years, and although he enjoyed the climate, which was essential for his health, he missed many of the facilities in the UK that had enabled him to become one of the most prolific authors of his generation. Based in Mdina, he was surrounded by a loyal group of expatriates, which included some MI5 retirees.

Among them was Joan Miller, who had been recruited to join MI5 by Maxwell Knight, a legendary agent-runner who had been responsible for penetrating the Communist Party of Great Britain (CPGB). It had been his key mole, Olga Gray, whom he had cultivated and placed in the British-Soviet Friendship Society, in the hope she would pick up some useful information. In fact, Olga had succeeded better than anyone could have hoped for and had become the confidante of Percy Glading, a senior CPGB activist and the party's former National Organiser. He was also at the centre of an espionage ring that was stealing secrets from the Royal Arsenal, and it was evidence from Olga, as a surprise prosecution witness identified only as 'Miss X', that ensured Glading's conviction and imprisonment in 1938. The coup proved the efficacy of planting long-term moles into target organisations, and Knight, known as the most mysterious man in MI5, attempted to repeat the exercise with Tom Driberg (later chairman of the Labour Party), whom he placed in the Young Communist League, and Joan Miller, who was dispatched to report on suspected fascist Archibald Ramsay MP and his connections to two shadowy pro-Nazi groups, The Link and the Right Club.

Seth also ran a sideline, selling his patented penis-enlarger by mail order under the name 'Dr Robert Chartham'. The sales were made through advertisements placed in British soft-porn magazines, and one of my duties as Seth's researcher was to visit kiosks in Victoria Station and buy the relevant titles, wrap them in plain paper and post them to Malta, where at that time the government enforced a strict ban on the importation of such dubious material. Thus, as well as undertaking routine research assignments for Seth, I was obliged to make a fortnightly tour of the top shelves in the station bookstalls so my employer could be sure his expensive advertisements had been published properly.

Thus, a combination of influences from Jack Profumo, Henry Coombe-Tennant, Donald McCormick and Ronnie Seth would act to push my career in one particular direction.

CHAPTER 1

THE VENLO INCIDENT

The irresistible combination of Cornwell and Coombe-Tennant triggered a deep-rooted fascination for espionage in me, but the school library had virtually nothing on the subject, apart from one memoir, *The Venlo Incident*, in which the author, Captain Sigismund Payne Best, described his experience as a British intelligence officer who, accompanied by his colleague Major Richard Stevens, had been abducted from the Dutch side of the frontier with Germany in November 1939.[1] He had spent the next five and a half years in concentration camps but had survived the experience.

As was the convention at that time, Best mentioned very few real names and concealed the true identities of his fellow professionals. However, according to Coombe-Tennant, Best's book was unique because no other wartime MI6 officer had ever written about their experiences. Released in 1950, *The Venlo Incident* appeared to break all the rules. But what had motivated Best to publish, and how had he got away with breaking one of the great taboos of the era? According to Coombe-Tennant, Best felt that he had been badly treated upon his return to England and had used the threat of publication as leverage against then MI6 chief, Sir Stewart Menzies, who had prevented Best's name appearing on a list of concentration camp victims who were entitled to compensation because of their incarceration by the Nazis. Evidently, Best had published his book but had been bankrupted anyway.

Until the early 1980s, there was a polite convention that books on the subject of espionage never used the real names of intelligence personnel. The tradition dated back to the conviction of Compton Mackenzie at the Old Bailey in 1933, charged under the Official Secrets Act for quoting from supposedly secret documents in his *Greek Memories*. Thereafter, discretion had prevailed. Virtually the only exception to the rule had been Best, a slightly Wodehousian figure who ran a successful business importing British Humber bicycles and had a penchant for wearing spats and a monocle. He and his MI6 colleague Stevens had been seized while waiting at the Dutch frontier for a Luftwaffe general who was alleged to be plotting against Hitler. In fact, the scheme had been an elaborate operation to entrap Stevens and Best, who spent the next five and a half years in Nazi concentration camps.

Although Best had not gone into much background detail in his book, the abduction of these two officers was to have a profound effect upon the clandestine war. The episode had scarcely been mentioned by the press, but its impact had been immense, for Stevens, the ex-Indian Army officer, had been the MI6 head of station in The Hague, and Best had been the local controller of a separate MI6 organisation known simply as 'Z'. The main MI6 operation in Europe was based upon MI6 professionals attached to British diplomatic missions in the guise of passport control officers (PCO). While ostensibly the PCO took responsibility for issuing visas and vetting travel documents, the majority of the PCO's staff was engaged on intelligence duties. MI6 regarded the PCOs as a very a convenient cover but there were two intrinsic drawbacks. The Germans had never been fooled by the transparency of the PCOs and because of their dependence upon official accommodation, they were vulnerable in the event of a collapse of diplomatic relations. Such an event would force a withdrawal, thereby effectively neutralising the PCO's local assets.

MI6 itself had belatedly recognised these two fundamental flaws. Soon after the annexation of Austria, the PCO in Vienna, Captain Thomas Kendrick, had been taken into custody temporarily by the Gestapo in August 1938, and over the two days of his interrogation, his captors had left him in no doubt about their depth of knowledge of his illicit activities. Kendrick had been released, but he had been powerless to assist his contacts, who had been rounded up and imprisoned. Thereafter, MI6 was painfully aware that an individual PCO's network, which depended upon the PCO to facilitate communications, would collapse the moment the host country was occupied. The second structural flaw was the universal nature of the cover. Wherever one was in the world, one could be certain that the nearest PCO was the local MI6 representative. While in some circumstances this might have been helpful, perhaps for an agent anxious to re-establish contact with the Service, it did make it easier for the enemy to mount counter-intelligence operations. As the Germans had demonstrated in The Hague, continuous surveillance of the PCO, his office and his home would eventually compromise every member of his network.

MI6's solution was the development of a parallel structure known as Z, which operated independently from the PCO and relied mainly upon commercial or journalistic covers. Its members were usually British expatriate businessmen and foreign correspondents who communicated directly to London, thereby insulating themselves from the insecurity of the local PCO. Thus, for MI6 to have lost someone as senior as one of its heads of station in an important European city was a terrible blow; the loss of the local Z representative too was a catastrophe. Enemy documents recovered after the war proved conclusively that the Germans had accumulated a vast amount of knowledge about the structure and personalities of the European Z and PCO networks, and the implication was that the data had come from Stevens and Best. In terms of its capability to sustain a clandestine organisation on the Continent, MI6 found itself severely handicapped when the Nazis overran France, Belgium, the Netherlands, the Balkans and Norway. The very few wireless sets that had been distributed quickly fell into enemy hands, and MI6 headquarters at Broadway was left almost completely blind, dependent upon neutral diplomats and reports reaching the remaining PCOs in Geneva, Stockholm, Istanbul, Madrid and Lisbon. The meagre preparations made before the war by MI6 proved totally inadequate to cope with Europe's new frontiers, and it is arguable that if SOE had not been created to foment resistance, and if Government Communications Headquarters (GCHQ) had not made its decisive and timely cryptographic breakthroughs, MI6 would have been lucky to emerge from the hostilities with any reputation at all.

The disaster at Venlo had occurred partly because of a misconceived directive issued to all MI6 personnel on the outbreak of war. The PCOs and the Z men were instructed to make themselves known to each other, and this meant Best revealing his clandestine role to Stevens – most PCOs only learned of Z's existence when they decoded the fateful signal. The result was to eliminate the secrecy which had isolated each of MI6's compartmentalised cells from the other. By ordering the two separate organisations to combine, apparently in the interests of avoiding wasteful duplication, MI6 had at a stroke undermined them, and it was this instruction, running contrary to all the rules of basic security and common sense, which Best had taken as the starting point for his autobiography.

From the enemy's viewpoint, the capture of Stevens alone would have been a marvellous prize. To have caught Best too must have been a source of jubilation, for each enjoyed a comprehensive knowledge of MI6's activities, not just in the Netherlands but into Germany and even further afield. Traditionally, PCOs avoided conducting risky operations in a host country where relations with the local authorities might be placed in jeopardy. Instead, the PCO concentrated his efforts on neighbouring states, thus allowing him a degree of plausibility if the moment came to deny MI6's involvement in a particular scheme. This convenient arrangement had meant that anti-Nazi operations were run mainly from Berne, Vienna, Prague and The Hague, the cities on the periphery of the Third Reich but out of the Gestapo's reach. Naturally, the Abwehr (the German military intelligence service), which had studied MI6's methodology for years, was fully aware of the disproportionately significant status of the MI6 station in The Hague and had made Stevens a priority target. Not surprisingly therefore, both men were subjected to intensive inquisition over many months as their interrogators sought to extract every item of interest from them.

When Best was eventually released from German captivity in the Italian Tyrol in May 1945, he was surprised to discover that MI6 regarded him as a traitor who had spoken too freely to his Gestapo interrogators. Both he and Stevens were blamed for the wealth of information the Germans had accumulated about MI6, and each of the men denounced the other as the Gestapo's principal source. Among the evidence against them was a document entitled *Informationsheft Grossbritannien*, a handbook intended for the use of the German invaders.[2] One chapter, *Der Britische Nachrichtendienst*, described in compelling detail the structure and personalities of MI6. What made the text so damning were the references, totalling seventeen, to Best and Stevens as the source for the material. An appendix to the book listed hundreds of people considered of interest to the invaders, among whom were dozens of MI6 officers and agents marked down for arrest. The contents were so accurate that even though it had been produced by the enemy, it was still regarded as highly sensitive even years after the end of the war, and my only opportunity to study it was at the Hoover Institution on War, Revolution and Peace at Stanford University, California. There I was given permission to copy the sections dealing with British intelligence, which enabled me to have the material translated. Based on my analysis of the captured material, there seemed little doubt that both Best and Stevens had been forced to help their interrogators. One passage was of particular interest because it assessed the two prisoners:

> Best is of a different opinion to Stevens. Unlike Stevens he is not a professional soldier. But he is superior to him as far as experience in the Intelligence Service is concerned, and as a result his attitude is more penetrating; these qualities he combines with considerable character defects and a complete lack of scruples. He is not a British officer like Stevens. He is a civilian who loves

> to live well and be a successful businessman. He may therefore see things in a clearer light in spite of a pretended lack of significance, or he may say more than Stevens.[3]

While Stevens accepted his fate and took a post as a NATO interpreter, Best became increasingly bitter, and *The Venlo Incident* was an unusual, if not unique, example of an MI6 retiree breaking ranks. The story of his clandestine contacts with what purported to be a cell of senior anti-Nazi officers was compelling, as was the tragedy of his abduction and incarceration. Stevens, who had attempted suicide while in prison in Berlin, died in Brighton in 1965, and in the same year, Best was declared bankrupt.

Although generally unrecognised as a book of disclosure, chiefly because of the author's unsensational style and the deliberate omission of his post-war humiliation, it was a tale that whetted my taste for intrigue, and it clearly demanded further research. Accordingly, as a starting point, I conducted a search of the bankruptcy records of the Chancery Division of the High Court, and my attention was caught by some apparently inconsequential correspondence with a lady in Church Street, Okehampton, Devon, who had been peripherally involved with Best in some unspecified way. When I visited the address, I learned that someone else, who lived at 18 Lickhill Road, Calne, had also expressed an interest in Best. This proved to be a tiny, terraced house, and it was here that I discovered Best on 4 June 1976. I had no expectation of finding him, let alone speaking to him, but when Best recovered from the shock of an uninvited stranger turning up on his doorstep and had replaced his dentures, he explained how MI6 had attempted to exclude him from the compensation paid by the Bonn government to victims of the

Nazi concentration camps and how he had tried to embarrass his former employers by declaring himself bankrupt. After making a thorough nuisance of himself in Whitehall, he had been awarded the paltry sum of £2,400 in 1968 as his part of the German compensation.

We were then joined by Best's third wife Bridget, who had returned from shopping. Initially very defensive and protective of her husband, she gradually relaxed when she realised I posed no threat to her husband and acknowledged that she had adopted her maiden name to gain access to his bankruptcy records.

Best vehemently denied ever having collaborated with the Gestapo but admitted that he had fabricated many of the pre-war MI6 agents he had claimed expenses for. With a wry smile, he recalled that his diaries, lodged with the Imperial War Museum and now relied upon by scholars, were really works of fiction, for all the agents to whom he had assigned codenames of household furniture, such as the redoubtable (but expensive) TABLE, CHAIR and LAMP, had existed only in his imagination and his cash ledgers. He had submitted dozens of false claims for the expenses incurred by his notional networks to the paymaster at MI6 headquarters, and they had all been paid.

Although he admitted to having been something of a rogue, Best resented the allegations made against him by Stevens and remained convinced that Stevens really had been responsible for the wealth of knowledge accumulated by their interrogators. He recalled that in June 1940, Stevens had slipped a note to Best in which he admitted he had been 'compelled to tell the truth'. 'Any other line would have been useless. They already knew too much … I was told that if I did not talk I would soon be made to.' Indeed, Best was emphatic that

Stevens had never had to endure the same degree of discomfort during his captivity, and he alleged that Stevens was 'a crypto-Nazi'. Best claimed that Stevens was supposedly intended to accompany the putative *Gauleiter* for England, Franz Six, to London after the Nazi invasion and that Stevens would have gone willingly.

In his book, Best described meeting a medical officer at Dachau who gave him news of Stevens, which was obviously intended to damn him:

> He said that Stevens himself was quite fit and that the conditions of his life were extremely comfortable; his quarters were roomy, he was allowed unlimited exercise in a garden which he shared with a number of other prisoners … and he was permitted to leave the camp in the company of a guard to play tennis, bathe, and even got to the theatre at Munich.[4]

Best died two years later, in September 1978, aged ninety-three. It was only much later I learned from Christopher Phillpotts, a very senior MI6 officer, that he had been innocent of the allegations made against him by Stevens. In fact, both men had resisted their interrogators, and neither had been informed that another high-ranking MI6 officer, Colonel C. H. 'Dick' Ellis, had confessed in 1966, while being questioned by tenacious interrogator Bill Steedman, to having sold MI6's secrets to the Germans pre-war. This was the material that the Gestapo had used to confront Stevens and Best in their separate interrogations, skilfully playing one off against the other to verify the data that Ellis had already supplied. Whereas Stevens and Best had endured ignominy during the post-war era, Ellis had returned triumphantly from his post in New

York, where he had been Sir William Stephenson's deputy, and had subsequently received senior appointments in Singapore and then London. Upon his retirement, he had returned to Australia where in 1952 he had played a central role in the creation of the Australian Secret Intelligence Service (ASIS).

Rather than face a scandal, MI6 had allowed the two elderly men to go to their graves embittered by a terrible sense of injustice. Best was a splendid old rascal who, being of mixed Anglo-Indian background, had also been a victim of racial intolerance. All too often, his contemporaries tried to explain that what they termed his deplorable conduct was a consequence of his mixed-race background and a chippyness about being a figure of some ridicule among the pre-war English expatriate community in The Hague.

While Best was still being vilified, Ellis was allowed to retire from MI6 and to escape prosecution for his crimes. Although he had officially retired in 1953 to take up a post with ASIS, Ellis had returned to London and had been employed at headquarters as a 'weeder', reading and discarding redundant files. In 1966, when MI6 was in the throes of a molehunt, various leads suggested that Ellis might have been an Abwehr source, and he was investigated. When confronted by Phillpotts and another officer, Theo 'Bunny' Pantcheff, Ellis had given a limited confession in which he had admitted to having passed MI6 material to the Abwehr before the war. Naturally, Phillpotts and Pantcheff had suspected that if Ellis had betrayed MI6 to the Germans, he might have done the same thing for the Soviets after the war. Ellis had denied the charge indignantly, citing his long opposition to the Bolsheviks, but his interrogators were reluctant to accept his assurances. In 1975, Maurice Oldfield, chief of MI6, had even made a final attempt to extract an admission from Ellis on his deathbed, but he refused to incriminate himself.

Ellis had displayed no remorse for his pre-war duplicity, and astonishingly, even tried to capitalise on his dismissal from MI6. As well as approaching the CIA for financial support, a plea that was interpreted as an attempt at blackmail, Ellis also reported to Sir William Stephenson that he had been dismissed from MI6 because he had been caught raiding the files on his behalf in 1963 and requested suitable compensation.

Stephenson had been the director of British Security Coordination (BSC) in New York during the war, and Ellis had remained in close touch with the millionaire businessman afterwards. In fact, Stephenson had commissioned Ellis to write his biography, and he had been engaged on this project until December 1960. His effort, *The Two Bills: Mission Accomplished*, had apparently been rejected by Stephenson, who hired Harford Montgomery Hyde instead.[5] Hyde, who had also worked for BSC during the war and was fond of visiting Stephenson at his home in Bermuda, had completed the project with the publication in November 1962 of *The Quiet Canadian*.[6] In 1976, Stephenson had collaborated with another author, William Stevenson, who produced *A Man Called Intrepid*.[7] What made this third book so remarkable was the inclusion of a foreword in the form of a 'Historical Note', written by Ellis. Although I did not realise it when I first read Stevenson's work, almost the entire book was a fabrication, and the material which appeared over Ellis's name was bogus and certainly never written by him. In fact, almost everything about the book turned out to be fraudulent, including the title. Actually, INTREPID had not been Stephenson's impressive codename but was BSC's official, publicly registered cable address in New York.

When I first met Stephenson in June 1979, he had few reservations about *A Man Called Intrepid* and had yet to learn that his trusted subordinate, Ellis, had been a traitor. Though not in the best of health, having suffered a stroke, Stephenson received me graciously at his modest bungalow in Paget, Bermuda and insisted that I view a videotape of the TV miniseries based on Stevenson's book, which starred David Niven and Michael York. I had not seen the film before and was surprised by it and also by Stephenson's dismissal of its many historical inexactitudes. When I queried an episode in which SOE agent Noor Inayat Khan was portrayed as having transmitted a radio warning from France on the night of the Luftwaffe's raid on Coventry, Stephenson had brushed aside the obvious chronological discrepancy. Khan had not reached France until June 1943, yet the attack on Coventry had occurred more than two and a half years earlier, in November 1940. This encounter with the man who liked to call himself INTREPID persuaded me that there was something very odd about the book. As it turned out, I was not, of course, alone in my disquiet. Hugh Trevor-Roper had denounced it in a review as worthless and Sir John Hunt had been equally scathing, but they had judged the book only on its value as an authentic historical record, while I was more interested in the possibility that this was not so much a case of an inaccurate biography but rather that it was something more akin to a hoax.

Soon after my return to England, I visited the Northamptonshire home of Jean Overton Fuller, an authority on the Abwehr's penetration of SOE and Khan's friend and biographer. When I mentioned the extraordinary episode in *A Man Called Intrepid*,

Jean revealed the extent of her involvement with the book's author. From her own knowledge of Khan, she was aware that Khan had never met Stephenson, and when she had read the relevant passages in Stevenson's book, she had been outraged to discover that a large part of Chapter 27 had been lifted from her own biography *Madeleine*, which had been released in 1952. She had complained to Stevenson's British publishers about the duplication, and they had instantly agreed to delete the offending chapter. However, Fuller had not realised that Stevenson had used a different publisher in the US, and that it had been the American edition, complete with all her material, that had been the basis of the series. What particularly aggrieved her was the collapse of the sale of her own film rights to *Madeleine*, as the story had already appeared in *A Man Called Intrepid*.[8]

Fuller's very serious charge of plagiarism, which she could not pursue in the American courts because she was time-barred by the statute of limitations, was the first proof that there was more to this book than met the eye. More evidence was to follow. One significant item, which I came across accidentally in the Public Record Office at Kew, was a letter confirming the appointment of Ellis as an assistant PCO in Berlin, in October 1923. This was effectively the moment Ellis had joined MI6, yet it contradicted what had purported to be Ellis's own recollection in the 'Historical Note' that he had already been 'twenty years in the professional secret intelligence service when in 1940' he had been sent to New York. According to the document at Kew, Ellis had only been in MI6 for seventeen years in 1940, and this seemed a strange mistake for Ellis to have made about his own career. This prompted a closer look at the Historical Note, and another inconsistency immediately struck home. Ellis asserted that Hyde's biography of Stephenson, *The Quiet Canadian*, had received official approval from MI6, which had been anxious to repair the damage inflicted by Kim Philby's defection: 'I can now disclose that the reason for the break in the silence about BSC in 1962 was the escape to the Soviet Union of Kim Philby.'[9] But, once again, the chronology was entirely wrong. Philby had defected in January 1963, two months *after* Hyde's book had been released. His escape could not have played any part in motivating approval for publication because *it simply had not happened yet*! This bizarre blunder served to undermine the credibility of the Historical Note, which clearly could not have been written by Ellis, and it drew my attention to the main body of the book. The more I researched *A Man Called Intrepid*, the more it appeared to be a compilation cobbled together from a dozen or so published books. However, I remained mystified by Stevenson's continuous references to the secret 'Station M' archives where he had allegedly uncovered a veritable gold mine of original documentation… and photographs.

A Man Called Intrepid had become a worldwide bestseller, and part of the book's undoubted attraction lay in the collection of forty photographs, which the author claimed had been recovered from 'Station M'. Some had obviously been gleaned from Hyde's books *Cynthia* and *The Quiet Canadian*, and a portrait of Khan had been lifted from Fuller's *Madeleine*, but fourteen in particular struck me as suspicious.[10] Ostensibly they were snaps taken of BSC agents undergoing training, and they all had the same fuzzy appearance. Was it likely that someone preparing to risk their life in enemy-occupied territory would be willing to have their picture taken? Surely this reckless behaviour amounted to a real threat to security? Working on the assumption that they were perhaps photos of something quite different, I had them copied and placed on blank sheets of paper without the captions, which I thought were probably fictitious. I then showed the mounted pictures to a Fleet Street picture editor who studied them and, without knowing what they were, suggested they might be movie stills. Scarcely believing that anyone could misrepresent movie stills as authentic photographs, I asked the Imperial War Museum's film archive to identify what I convincingly described as the war film from which the fourteen stills had been taken. In a very short time, there was a positive identification. The film was *School for Danger*, a feature made at Pinewood Studios just after the war. Far from being genuine photos snatched of agents departing on secret missions, they were stills that had been taken without consent.

Accordingly, I arranged for two *Sunday Times* reporters to view the entire film and have each of the fourteen frames frozen on the screen so a comparison could be made with the book illustrations. So there could be no absolutely no room for doubt, they then spoke to Stevenson at his home in London and asked for an explanation. His response was to threaten legal proceedings if the *Sunday Times* published a word of criticism. Unimpressed, the paper published an exposé, and even traced the actress who had played the part of a trainee agent, but Stevenson never sued. Instead, he left the country and declined to answer any further questions on the subject.

• • •

I had been prompted to take another look at *The Venlo Incident* after I had read Richard Deacon's *History of the British Secret Service*, which had been published in 1969, in the wake of a series of stories in the *Sunday Times* about Kim Philby, whose own autobiography, *My Silent War*, had caused such scandal the previous year.[11] Philby's notoriety and the details of his disappearance in Beirut in January 1963 came about as a consequence of another internal MI6 dispute, this time involving a retiree, Leslie Nicholson, who had joined MI6 in 1929. He served in Vienna, Prague and Riga before the war and afterwards was sent to Bucharest. Later, when his wife fell ill, Nicholson pleaded for financial support from his chief, Sir Stewart Menzies, but the request had been denied. Nicholson argued that he had been persuaded to leave his army career by the promise of a pension he would be able to commute, but Menzies was adamant.

Already embittered and an alcoholic stricken with terminal cancer, Nicholson took his revenge when his wife died by adopting the pseudonym John Whitwell to publish his memoirs, *British Agent*, in the US.[12] The Australian-born *Sunday Times* journalist Phillip Knightley, who did not share his colleagues' reverence for Whitehall conventions, tracked down the forlorn Nicholson to his chaotic accommodation above a seedy cafe in London's East End in 1968 and learned about how MI6 had protected Philby since 1951 and had kept silent about his defection to Moscow in January 1963. Philby's disappearance was all the more embarrassing because in October 1955, the then Foreign Secretary Harold Macmillan had been obliged to clear him publicly, in the House of Commons, of the accusation of having been the 'third man' in the defection of Guy Burgess and Donald Maclean. For the past five years, MI6 had discouraged anyone seeking to establish the details of Philby's mysterious absence from his post in Beirut. Knightley had the scoop that made his reputation, and Nicholson died in obscurity in

1973, consumed by guilt about his indiscretion, which had exposed Philby and prompted the traitor to rush out his own memoirs.

The chain of events that effectively terminated a long period of deference to the British security and intelligence establishment had been triggered, albeit inadvertently, by Nicholson and had led to the exposure of Philby as a long-term Soviet mole who had been able to skilfully manipulate MI6's instinct to protect him. Naturally, the KGB had sought to exploit the situation and rushed out Philby's memoirs, *My Silent War*, which were largely accurate and surprisingly only suffered one minor mishap. A British diplomat, Sir David Kelly, objected to the description of his wife as 'ugly' and threatened a libel action, so the offending words were removed from the proofs. Kelly had been the ambassador in Ankara when Philby had been stationed at the consulate in Istanbul, and there had been considerable antipathy between the two men.

Nicholson had also triggered a major KGB operation – although he never knew about it – involving another as yet undetected Soviet spy, James MacGibbon. Strongly suspected by MI5 of having been recruited by the CPGB in 1936, MacGibbon had joined the distinguished journalist Robert Kee in 1948 to start a publishing house, MacGibbon & Kee. Although the readers of *My Silent War* were warned by such critics as Hugh Trevor-Roper that Philby's memoirs were somewhat Macchiavelian, few realised the scale of the KGB operation, which inevitably had left MacGibbon at some risk of exposure. MacGibbon only admitted his role as a Soviet spy in February 2000, shortly before he died.

The KGB took elaborate measures to conceal the existence of Philby's manuscript, but MI6 was passed a copy by Graham Greene, whom Philby had approached to contribute a foreword. Greene, who had been handed the document in Paris, then tipped off the MI6 chief Dick White, who had sought advice about how to react from Felix Cowgill, then living in retirement in Wiltshire. Cowgill, whom I visited in March 1982, had been one of Philby's principal victims, unscrupulously outmanoeuvred and sidelined by his own subordinate, and he was outraged by the scale of Philby's betrayal. However, realising a ban would prove counterproductive and anxious to protect Greene, White opted for silent inactivity, much to Cowgill's frustrated fury. Cowgill had pioneered MI6's wartime cryptographic exploitation department, designated Section V, but had been replaced by Philby who had headed Section V's Iberian sub-section and had promoted the view that excessive caution in handling the Section's invaluable decrypts was proving counterproductive. Philby had stirred up discontent among the Section's 'customers', the recipients of Section V's vital intercepts, and when Cowgill was on a visit overseas to the US he replaced him.

Philby re-emerged in Moscow in December 1967 by giving an interview to Murray Sayle of the *Sunday Times* in the Minsk Hotel, the purpose of which was to float the idea that plans for *My Silent War* might be scrapped if two spies convicted in 1961, Morris and Lona Cohen, were released from prison in the UK. The proposal was firmly rejected in London, and the book's release in New York in April 1968 marked an all-time low point for the British intelligence community. Put simply, there were few wartime intelligence secrets unknown to Philby. However, although he had hinted at Bletchley Park's success in solving the U-boat cipher system and the control of enemy agents, he had not mentioned some other sensitivities such as the joint MI5–MI6 TRIPLEX project, which routinely violated the diplomatic pouches of foreign missions in London by distracting the couriers, or the Anglo–American VENONA programme, which decrypted wartime Soviet intercepts and would continue until 1979.

One of the reactions to the book's publication was a conscious effort to restore the reputations of MI5 and MI6 by mounting a counter-offensive, and the first opportunity was the Double-Cross System alluded to by Philby. Although somewhat garbled, details of how MI5 had established a secret interrogation centre at Ham Common, known as Camp 020, and had persuaded dozens of captured spies to switch sides and act as double agents to deceive their Abwehr masters had already been disclosed in New York by Nicholson to an American historian, Ladislas Faragó. The antidote, as advocated in Whitehall by Sir John Masterman – chairman of the Twenty Committee, which had run the Double-Cross System – was to publicise an authentic intelligence triumph and thereby push the Philby fiasco off the front pages. Of course, there was considerable resistance to his scheme, which centred on a copy of an official report Masterman had written for MI5 in 1945 documenting the entire project. He lobbied his two former Oxford students, Prime Minister Ted Heath and his Foreign Secretary Alec Douglas-Home, to authorise the declassification and release of the document, a copy of which he had been allowed to retain at the end of the war.

Masterman's persistence and determination paid off, and in 1972, an edited version of *The Double-Cross System in the War of 1939–45* was released in a race to trump Ladislas Faragó's *The Game of the Foxes*, which purported to be based on captured Abwehr archives.[13] Faragó was disadvantaged by his reliance on Nicholson, whose memory was imperfect, and on a collection of tin boxes at the US National Archives, which contained some files recovered from the

Abwehr's *stelle* (office) in Hamburg. However, Faragó had learned about the cryptographic work against the Enigma cipher machine conducted at Bletchley Park, references to which had been excised from Masterman's book. In his analysis of the Abwehr's network of spies in England, Faragó was intrigued by one particular agent who had parachuted into Cambridgeshire in September 1940 and had continued to communicate with his Hamburg controllers until the very last day of hostilities. He was known to the Germans as A-3701 and to his MI5 handlers as TATE, and he had lived under his alias 'Harry Williamson' throughout the war... and then had remained in England. According to the Munich-based historian Günter Peis, who researched the case for his *Mirror of Deception* in 1977, TATE was still alive.[14] There were three good reasons to believe Peis. Firstly, he had very good sources among Abwehr veterans, especially in Hamburg; secondly, the Viennese George Weidenfeld would have taken the greatest care in agreeing to publish *Mirror of Deception*; and thirdly, Peis's original German manuscript had been translated by Bill Steedman, an MI6 retiree. Steedman was something of a legend in the counter-intelligence world, having joined MI6 in 1949 and having served in Berne and (twice) in Bonn before retiring in 1969. Put simply, Steedman had effectively endorsed Peis's claim.

The impact of Nicholson, Philby, Faragó, Peis and Masterman on the public's understanding of how the secret intelligence war had been fought by the Allies is hard to exaggerate. The enemy's most sensitive communications, discreetly referred to by Churchill as his 'most secret sources', had been compromised with great professionalism. Thousands of cryptanalysts, technicians and linguists had been employed to intercept, read and collate Axis wireless traffic. A smaller group of case officers had successfully 'turned' the enemy's spies into double agents who had peddled the components of what came to be known as 'strategic deception'. Historians scrambled to engage in wholesale revisionism, acknowledging that there had been a massive missing dimension to the established view of how the war had been fought. Those who had been indoctrinated into this secret world, including Churchill and Eisenhower, had been successfully persuaded to exercise discretion on these topics. So, with the new revelations, over a very short period of years in the 1970s, there was a thirst for more disclosures and a demand for researchers to venture into this new field of study.

CHAPTER II

SPY!

For six years, I enjoyed a cordial relationship with Richard Deacon, the pen name of Donald McCormick, formerly a wartime naval intelligence officer and later the foreign news manager of the *Sunday Times.* During his lengthy newspaper career, McCormick had worked with Ian Fleming, the legendary Antony Terry and wartime MI6 officer Donald Darling. Undoubtedly, McCormick had some good sources and possessed a nose for some great stories. But he was always very secretive about his network of contacts and was always reluctant to allow me to read the proofs of his books. I also spotted several errors in his title *The British Connection*, which attributed some information to a single individual, an MI5 officer named as 'Saunders McCulloch', whereas I knew Miss Saunders and Miss McCulloch had been two quite distinct women.[1] In another chapter, he had referred to the 'late' physicist Sir Rudolf Peierls as having been investigated as a Soviet spy suspect, but he was still very much alive. However, years later when Peierls's very extensive MI5 file was declassified, it showed that McCormick had been right about Peierls having been investigated as a likely Soviet spy.[2]

In 1978, McCormick was asked by BBC TV's general features department to advise on a six-part drama-documentary series, *Spy!*. Due to pressure of work, he turned the offer down but recommended me instead. When I joined the production team at Kensington House, I found that the producer, Frank Cox, had already filmed one segment based on *Cynthia*, the biography of Elizabeth Pack written by Harford Montgomery Hyde, and another about Richard Sorge, which left a further four to be completed. My suggestions were the Venlo affair; the wartime double agent codenamed TATE; the honeytrapped spy John Vassall; and the Soviet assassin Bogdan Stashinsky, who had been deployed against Ukrainian nationalists living in West Germany.

When the filming was underway and we had accumulated a large quantity of research material, I obtained Cox's permission to suggest we release a book to complement the television series. An interview followed with Victoria Huxley of BBC Publishing, a senior editor who had been thinking along the same lines. Rather than discard our voluminous files, they could form the basis of a hardback release. The BBC owned the full rights to the television series, and to all the research that had been gathered but was keen to commission an author to produce a book which could be released as the series was broadcast. I volunteered to write it, and at a later stage, Richard Deacon was brought in to give the manuscript the professional polish my amateurish efforts needed. In its final form, *Spy!* was released with both names on the jacket and included much of the new information that had been acquired, though not some of the more controversial things we had uncovered.[3] A certain amount of tact was required for this project because an interview with Hyde at his home in Tenterden revealed that his book about

Pack, published in 1966, had been written during a visit to her chateau in the South of France when he had rekindled a wartime love affair. Although subtitled *The Spy Who Changed the Course of the War*, the book was largely fiction and, as historian Harry Hinsley has explained, the central story of Pack's theft of the Italian naval code from naval attaché Admiral Alberto Lais was nothing more than a cover story, invented to protect the cryptographic breakthrough achieved at Bletchley Park.

As part of my research, I had already met Hyde at his home in Kent for lunch in October 1978 because I had been keen to find out from him how much of the material that had appeared in William Stevenson's *A Man Called Intrepid* had originated in Hyde's *The Quiet Canadian*. A former Unionist MP for Belfast, Hyde explained that Stevenson's book 'had taken liberties' with very large quantities of his own material, but he had decided to do nothing about it because of his continuing friendship with Sir William Stephenson. During the course of our conversation, he mentioned that after the publication of *The Quiet Canadian*, which had included a chapter about the spy whom he had identified only as 'Cynthia', he had been surprised by a letter from her inviting him to make contact. He had responded and had been invited to stay with her and her husband at their picturesque chateau in the Pyrenees in southern France.

Best known as a BSC agent who had used her considerable charms to extract secrets from first the Italian and then the Vichy embassies in Washington DC, Pack had moved to France after the war and in 1946 had married Charles Brousse, the French diplomat against whom she had been deployed so effectively in 1941. Born in Minneapolis in 1910 as Amy Elizabeth Thorpe, she had married a British diplomat, Arthur Pack, in April 1930 and given birth six months later. To avoid embarrassment, the child had been dispatched to England to be brought up by foster parents while the Packs had moved on the diplomatic circuit from Washington to Chile, Madrid and then Warsaw. When, in 1940, Arthur had been posted back to Santiago, Elizabeth had stayed with him for only a short time before reverting to her maiden name, Thorpe, and returning to the US, where she had operated for BSC. There was some suggestion that she may have helped MI6 while she and her husband had been in Poland, but Hyde had not elaborated on this part of her career. His main concern had been to relate her adventures with BSC.

A former naval pilot, Brousse had been captivated by Betty when he had first encountered her in his capacity as press attaché in the Vichy embassy and as a patriot and an Anglophile, he had willingly given his lover access to the building late at night. According to Hyde's version, this was when the Vichy cryptographic material had been copied. Evidently, in the intervening years Betty had lost none of her allure, for Hyde confided that he had conducted a short affair with her and that the fruit of their collaboration had been *Cynthia*, which was published in 1966. Hyde revealed that he was not entirely convinced of the accuracy of everything his subject had told him but that he had felt an obligation to her to produce a manuscript that met with her approval. The book revealed her identity for the first time and was released three years after her tragic death from cancer, in October 1963. Brousse was heartbroken and died ten years later in what was thought to be an accidental fire at his home.

The first complication to have arisen had centred on Hyde's description of the members of the Vichy embassy in Washington DC in *The Quiet Canadian*. The former ambassador, Gaston

Henry-Haye, was still alive and had objected to the allegation that he had 'organised a kind of Gestapo in the Embassy to report upon the activities of supporters of the former French Government'.[4] Consequently, Henry-Haye had brought a libel action and had won substantial damages from Hyde.

The author, who was himself a barrister who had written extensively on the subject of libel, had also run into trouble over his assertion that 'Cynthia' had seduced the Italian naval attaché in Washington, Admiral Alberto Lais, and that in return for a bribe he had allowed her to remove a copy of the Italian naval cipher from his office. Although Lais himself had died soon after the war, his family had been infuriated by the suggestion that the admiral's indiscretion had led to the Battle of Cape Matapan in March 1941. The revelation that Admiral Cunningham's famous victory had been made possible by espionage had caused a sensation, and the admiral's family had brought an action under Italian laws of defamation, which allow a family to defend the honour of a member who has died. On this occasion, Hyde had declined to defend the litigation, seeking to avoid huge legal expenses in Rome, and consequently the court had found in favour of the plaintiffs. Hyde simply ignored the judgment, but the hearing had served to restore the admiral's tainted honour.

The background to Hyde's discomfort was extraordinary. The Battle of Cape Matapan, fought on 28 March 1941, was one of the great events in naval history. The Allies had confronted the Italian fleet and inflicted a decisive defeat in which 2,300 Italian seamen died and 1,000 were captured. Three cruisers, the *Fiume*, *Pola* and *Zara*, were sunk with a pair of destroyers. In addition, the Italian flagship, the battleship *Vittorio Veneto*, was hit by a torpedo.

The location and intention of the Italian fleet had been compromised by the interception and decryption of a series of signals transmitted in an Enigma cipher, which had been broken by Bletchley Park cryptanalysts. The traffic revealed a major naval operation designated 'Day-X' in the eastern Mediterranean, and an ambush was prepared by the British Mediterranean fleet. As cover for the cryptanalysts' discovery, a Sunderland reconnaissance aircraft was deployed from Malta to 'find' the Italians off the coast of Crete.

Alerted to the Italian task force, Admiral Sir Andrew Cunningham undertook several further deceptions to suggest that his aircraft carrier HMS *Formidable* was docked in Alexandria before making a secret getaway at night. In particular, Cunningham made his presence known in the port by visiting a local golf club, where he would be seen by agents of the Japanese consul general. They ploy certainly worked, for the Italians were taken completely by surprise and suffered terrible losses. On the British side, the losses amounted to just three aircrew and a single aircraft.

The Italians had no reason to suspect that their communications had been monitored, so Hyde's disclosure that their naval codes had been compromised by Lais was received badly in Rome. The evidence pointed to the fact that Pack's version of events was probably a convenient cover story to conceal the role played by signals intelligence. Hyde claimed that Lais had told his lover where to find the relevant codebook on the day he sailed home from New York on 25 April 1941 – but that was a month after the battle had taken place!

Quite apart from the defamation problems, I had become aware of another flaw in the *Cynthia* narrative. Its central proposition – that Vichy and Italian ciphers had been compromised by Pack's liaisons with enemy diplomats – in reality was nothing more than an elaborate cover story intended to provide a plausible reason for the cryptographic successes accomplished at Bletchley Park, which had remained a closely guarded secret in 1965, the year Hyde had made his sensational disclosures. Certainly, Pack had been employed to cultivate sources within the Italian and Vichy diplomatic missions, but the idea that she had purloined a copy of the Italian naval ciphers or had photographed the French diplomatic codebook was a plausibly embellished fiction. In the view of Harry Hinsley, who led the team of Cambridge historians writing the official history of British intelligence and who confirmed the doubts that surrounded Hyde's tale, it was without foundation, even if the participants had themselves believed it to be true. After all, it was not unusual for agents to be encouraged by their handlers with rather exaggerated assurances of what had been accomplished. The logic was obvious, for why would any agent take palpable risks with their liberty for what may prove to be nothing more than a minor exercise in deception?

Accordingly, my first painful duty upon joining the BBC was to break the news to the producer that the first programme in his series was not wholly accurate. He then received his first lesson in BBC economics: a budget of £100,000 had been agreed with the Dutch co-producers, and it would be too wasteful to scrap the preparatory work that had been undertaken already. Thus *Cynthia* – which was filmed in November 1978 in a house located on the outskirts of Brighton which looked quite like the embassy building in Washington – became one of the six documentaries, and I was informed that some work had already started on the background to the stories of Richard Sorge and Bogdan Stashinsky. These segments had been chosen tentatively, but I was invited to offer the production team the remaining three topics of the series, and to take responsibility for researching them.

The BBC, of course, preferred Hyde's version of events, but the consequence was that the Lais family sued the authors of *Spy!*. Since Lais's family had already won their libel action against Hyde in 1967, the second offence was all the more egregious since it had been confirmed already by the automatic referral to Court of Appeal in 1968, and led to a conviction for the more serious transgression of criminal libel, on the grounds that the two authors must have known of the courts' judgment.

The BBC was on stronger ground with John Vassall, who had been arrested in October 1962 for breaches of the Official Secrets Act and sentenced to eighteen years' imprisonment. His espionage for the KGB had begun during his four-year posting in Moscow where, as secretary to the naval attaché, he had been compromised in a homosexual honeytrap, and it continued after his return to the Admiralty in London in June 1956. The case still had wide appeal because little was known of how Vassall had been identified as the Soviet source in the Admiralty, and the tribunal that had been set up to review how the investigation had been run had imprisoned two journalists for refusing to reveal who had tipped them off to a scoop relating to the case. In addition, there was the political aspect to the scandal. Vassall had been befriended by a senior minister, Tam Galbraith, who had resigned from the Macmillan administration after rumours started to circulate about the contents of supposedly intimate letters he had written to Vassall. Predictably, Fleet Street had concentrated on Vassall's potential relationship with Galbraith, but in fact he was entirely innocent of having done anything except to have been hospitable to Vassall, who had never missed an opportunity to ingratiate himself with his minister. According to evidence submitted to the Vassall Tribunal, Vassall had been identified as a result of careful sleuthing by MI5, and after his arrest, proof of his espionage had been found concealed in his flat in Dolphin Square in the form of a camera and exposed films, which he had used to photograph classified documents. This was the line peddled during my interview with Colonel Roberts, director of naval security, an officer whose post had been created on the recommendation of an inquiry into another, earlier lapse, the Portland spy-ring case. Roberts met me at his office in Spring Gardens, by Admiralty Arch, and was suspiciously evasive. From his manner, I believed there was something very odd about the Vassall affair.

Vassall had pleaded guilty and had been sentenced to eighteen years' imprisonment. He was released in October 1972. At the suggestion of Lord Longford, who had visited him in prison, he had written an autobiography which had been published by Sidgwick & Jackson, the company of which the peer was chairman, and then he had disappeared from sight. In his candid memoirs, Vassall had described how he had been the victim of a honeytrap in Moscow, where he had served in Sir William Hayter's embassy. He had been photographed in a compromising situation, in bed with another man, and had been blackmailed into giving classified material to his KGB contact. Upon his return to London, he had continued to meet Russians operating under diplomatic cover and hand over secrets from the Admiralty, and over the years he had developed a curious rapport with the Soviets who had applied the pressure on him. Among my first tasks was to find him, and eventually, I learned that he had acquired a new identity and was working in a trusted position in the City.

The more I learned about the Vassall case, the more I realised that his cooperation was essential for *Spy!*. I had been told that the original tip to MI5 about the existence of a spy in the Admiralty had come not from brilliant detective work but from a Soviet defector who had virtually pinpointed the area in the Admiralty where Vassall had worked. Furthermore, I was assured that two clandestine operations had been undertaken to confirm the identity of the spy: a search had been made of every desk in the Admiralty in the dead of night, conducted by a couple of security officers, and Vassall's flat had been broken into in an attempt to find evidence against him. These disclosures were quite sensational, for apart from the obvious visual attraction of reproducing the illicit search of the Admiralty, the implication was that the search made *after* Vassall's arrest had been entirely superfluous.

Having established Vassall's new identity and home address in north London, I invited him to lunch at the Savoy Grill, which I knew he would be unable to resist, and teased him with the prospect of learning, for the first time, exactly how he had been caught. Predictably, Vassall took the bait and in November 1978 became a willing collaborator in the project. Now a devout Roman Catholic and a regular visitor to a monastery in Storrington, West Sussex, he consulted various friends about the advisability of participating in the preparation of the film. Some, he told me, had urged him to put his past behind him, while others had suggested he cooperate to ensure accuracy. In the end, after two further meetings and consultations with his Harley Street psychiatrist Dr Rose and his priest Father Ian McLean, he agreed to help. A conference with the BBC production team was held at the Great Eastern Hotel, near Liverpool Street Station, and we embarked upon the final draft of the script.

During the course of the research, we encountered the Security Service's sensitivity on the subject of break-ins and learned that the illicit search of Vassall's flat in Dolphin Square had been authorised by the permanent undersecretary at the Home Office, but any portrayal of this episode would endanger similar operations. There was also anxiety about the identification of Anatoliy Golitsyn as the KGB defector who had first alerted the CIA to a spy in the Admiralty, but it was soon realised that there was a greater danger with regards to defamation. The Vassall case had gone into the folklore of Fleet Street as an example of how journalists should behave when required to protect their sources. Brendan Mulholland and Reginald Foster had served six months' and three months' imprisonment respectively for refusing to name the source who had told them of a link between the Portland case and Vassall. Both men were regarded as heroes who had conformed with the code of silence demanded by journalists, but the truth was really rather different. They had gone to prison on a contempt charge, having declined to answer the Vassall Tribunal's questions on this topic and thereby ensured their martyrdom, but in reality, there had not been any source at all. They had concluded on their own that it was too great a coincidence to have two unconnected cases of Soviet espionage in such a short space of time inside the same government department and had written a story implying that Vassall had been caught as a result of leads discovered during the Portland case. There was no truth in this at all, but neither crime correspondent could admit to having manufactured the tale without destroying their reputations. Nor, for that matter, could the BBC pursue this aspect of the Vassall story without encountering strong legal objections from the two men.

Another consideration was the involvement of Fleet Street icon Percy Hoskins, who suggested in print there was much more to the story, hinting that items recovered at Peter and Helen Kroger's house in Ruislip indicated that the Soviet network extended much further and implicated other, as yet unidentified, espionage suspects. Naturally, this information was taken very seriously by the Radcliffe Tribunal, which raised the issue with MI5's director general, Sir Roger Hollis. He denied that MI5 had found such evidence.

Hollis was not asked about and did not disclose the full truth, which was that there had been a belief, articulated by MI5's Ronnie Symonds (a future deputy director general) that there was indeed another spy in the Admiralty. His suspicion had been based on the knowledge that Golitsyn had described having seen documents in Moscow that could not be attributed to Vassall. There was also the curious reaction of Nikolai Korovin and Nikolai Karpekov, who had been the subject of electronic surveillance at the time the arrest of the Portland spies was announced publicly. Neither the KGB *rezident* nor his deputy seemed to have reacted to the bombshell, which seemed very odd.

Symonds had also been advised by GCHQ that the clandestine wireless traffic that had linked spy Gordon Lonsdale and the Krogers to Moscow had continued to be transmitted, which rather suggested it was supporting another parallel spy-ring.

Paradoxically, the Security Service had developed a tendency to overreact to speculation surrounding the Admiralty spy trials because there had been an investigation into another leakage of information. The investigation had led to a senior naval officer being placed under surveillance and supposedly spotted visiting a basement flat in Notting Hill Gate, where a Soviet attaché was also spotted. The MI5 officer in charge of the case had requested permission to interview the suspect, but apparently Hollis had ordered the case to be abandoned for fear of the political consequences of a third security scandal in the Admiralty. Details of this episode only became known in 1977 when Gordon Brook-Shepherd named the suspect in the first edition of *The Storm Petrels* and found himself facing a libel action.[5] The book was promptly withdrawn from sale and the offending name, Admiral Colin Dunlop, removed from the subsequent editions.

Although the BBC's treatment of the Vassall case did not include everything that had been uncovered during the research and omitted references to the illicit entry of Vassall's flat, it did disclose how the CIA had supplied the original tip and recreated the late-night search of the Admiralty, which caused a small stir in the correspondence columns of *The Times*. Vassall himself was entirely satisfied by the programme and it was judged a success by the critics.

The Vassall case was still sensitive in 1978, partly because he had often hinted at his relationships with other men, some of them parliamentarians. Concerns about Vassall's contacts in Westminster led his MI5 investigator, Charles Elwell, to research Fergus Montgomery and Sir Harmar Nicholls. Montgomery had been elected to the Commons in 1959 and had served as Margaret Thatcher's parliamentary private secretary while she had been Education Secretary and Leader of the Opposition. Nicholls had worked as a barrister, elected to the Commons in 1950 and ennobled in 1975.

Both had known Vassall, but to what extent, if at all, had the relationships been potentially compromising?

Elwell was highly respected within the Security Service, not least because of his wartime incarceration at Colditz. He was fond of recalling how on a visit to the Polish officers' mess he had been astonished to find the floor covered by small model tanks, skilfully fashioned from discarded tins of condensed milk. However, he had been puzzled by their means of independent propulsion when wireless radio control had not been developed. His hosts proudly allowed him to inspect one of the miniature armoured vehicles and he found a mouse inside.

Elwell had run the interrogation of Gordon Lonsdale, the KGB illegal *rezident* in London arrested with the Krogers in January 1961, and his own experience as a PoW had enabled him to develop a considerable rapport with the Russian, who had offered to defect. Lonsdale had been exchanged back to the Soviet Union in April 1964 but had died there of a stroke in October 1970. The deal negotiated by Elwell involved Lonsdale returning to the Soviet Union and then defecting with his wife and daughter. In return for his resettlement, Lonsdale promised to reveal the names of the other spies he had handled in London, but the plan failed to obtain Whitehall approval, leaving Lonsdale to languish in Winson Green prison until his swap.

The penultimate episode in *Spy!* was to be the Venlo affair, and by luck, I discovered that two members of the MI6 station in The Hague at the time of the abduction of Stevens and Best were still alive. Coincidentally, Lionel Loewe, who had been sitting in the office of the director of the Dutch Military Intelligence at the moment Stevens and Best had been seized, lived close to the BBC offices in Brook Green, Shepherd's Bush and was extremely cooperative. As well as providing his own perspective, he was able to name all the other players on the British side. His subordinate, Rodney Dennys, had been a young man on his first MI6 assignment in 1939 and was now the Somerset Herald, with an office in the College of Arms on Queen Victoria Street. Like Loewe, he recalled the kidnapping all too well and agreed to check the BBC's research material to ensure accuracy. Unfortunately, the BBC's budget did not extend to filming abroad, so I spent a few days in The Hague and at Venlo taking photographs so a reasonably accurate film location could be reconstructed. The filming would eventually take place on a country estate criss-crossed by private roads in the flatlands of Suffolk that resembled the Dutch landscape.

On the day in question, in early November 1939, Stevens and Best had been driven from The Hague to the German border, where they had arranged to meet a senior anti-Nazi who they had been led to believe was a dissident Luftwaffe general. They had been driven by Best's chauffeur, Jan Lemmens, and had been accompanied by a Dutch military intelligence liaison officer, Lieutenant Dirk Klop. The Dutch authorities, with whom MI6 had excellent relations, had been informed of the planned meeting, and Loewe had been assigned the task of briefing General Johan van Oorschot, Dutch Military Intelligence chief. Britain had been at war with Germany for just over two months, but hostilities had not started in earnest. Nevertheless, in the neutral Netherlands, the atmosphere was tense and there were continuous rumours of German troops concentrating near the frontier. The four men were waved through the numerous military checkpoints as they approached Venlo, but when they reached the appointed rendezvous Cafe Backus, located on Dutch territory next to the German customs post, the situation appeared relaxed. As they arrived, they spotted one of their German contacts on the restaurant's veranda, so Best parked his American Buick in the neighbouring car park.

Moments later, a vehicle moving at high speed and carrying men armed with machine pistols on the running boards swept through the German side of the frontier and skidded to a halt beside the astonished pair of Englishmen. Best had stood gasping at the spectacle, while Klop had drawn a revolver and started running back towards the Dutch border, firing as he went. Several bursts of automatic fire followed, and Klop fell in the bushes, mortally wounded. Best, Stevens and Lemmens raised their hands in surrender and the armed SS men surrounding them frogmarched the disarmed trio swiftly onto German territory. The incident had lasted a couple of minutes, too short a time for anyone else present to react, and this was how the two Britons had found themselves in German custody. Loewe recalled that as the news was received by van Oorschot, panic had set in both in The Hague and in London. Dozens of people had witnessed the episode, which was widely reported, but the identity and nationality of Best and Stevens was suppressed until their fate had become known. The following day, the German press had announced their arrest, without describing the circumstances, and had blamed them for the attempt made two days earlier on Hitler's life in Munich. Apparently, the abduction had been ordered in retaliation for the bungled assassination bid, although neither Best nor Stevens, nor even MI6, had been involved.

For the purposes of the BBC's reconstruction, the story began in The Hague and described how Stevens had been duped into entrusting a wireless set to the German they had been in contact with, who claimed to be the intermediary acting for a group of disaffected, high-ranking officers. The film recorded Best's claimed reservations about the final rendezvous and repeated his charge that the inexperienced Stevens had been guilty of an appalling breach of security when he had compiled a list of agents whom he would have to evacuate in advance of a Nazi invasion of the Netherlands. This allegation had been made by Best in his book, and surprisingly, Stevens, who had been alive at the time of its publication and must have read it, had not sued him.

When it was broadcast, the Venlo programme was well received, but it prompted protests from the widows of both Best and Stevens, who insisted that neither man had been interviewed by the BBC. As head of department, Desmond Wilcox received the flak, and, fearing sloppy research, demanded to know every detail of the measures taken by the production team to ensure the film's accuracy. Although I was obliged to protect the identities of Loewe and Dennys, who had given their help on condition of confidentiality, he did produce in the BBC's defence the notes that I had made of my interview with Best at his home in Calne. These confirmed the accuracy of the BBC's portrayal of the incident, and Wilcox was able to use them as a trump card to silence the two vociferous critics.

CHAPTER III

TATE AND THE DOUBLE AGENTS

The publication in 1972 of Sir John Masterman's *The Double-Cross System in the War of 1939–45*, in the teeth of opposition from Whitehall, was a major milestone in the release of information about wartime Allied intelligence operations. Although the version released had been sanitised to protect the crucial role played by the cryptographic source designated ULTRA and to remove any hint of the true identities of the individual agents, the book was a revelation and, as intended, helped restore the somewhat tarnished reputation of both MI5 and MI6.

Another eye-opener, published around the same time, was *The Game of the Foxes* by Ladislas Faragó, who claimed to have stumbled across several footlockers filled with the microfilm records of the Abwehr's wartime intelligence operations and discovered the existence of numerous, previously undisclosed espionage networks in England and the US. Faragó had spent months studying and cataloguing the microfilms but had made the mistake of accepting their contents at face value. While in the final stages of writing *The*

Game of the Foxes, he had learned that many of the Abwehr's spies in Britain, which he had assumed had gone undetected after looking at the records, had in fact been under the continuous control of the Security Service. As his publication deadline had approached, Faragó had been obliged to hastily rewrite much of his book so as to take account of what was to become known as the Double-Cross System, the deliberate manipulation of the enemy's entire espionage organisation in Britain. Taken together, the books were a revelation, for they disclosed for the first time the extent of MI5's wartime successes, which hitherto had not even been hinted at.

Not long afterwards, there was a further landmark moment when, in 1974, Frederick Winterbotham gave an authoritative account of the cryptographic work undertaken at Bletchley Park in his book *The Ultra Secret* and described for the first time how the codebreakers had exploited lapses in the enemy's cipher system. Whereas previously there had been nothing more than vague, elliptical clues and undocumented hints at what GCHQ's boffins had accomplished, Winterbotham used his own first-hand experience to tell the story of how the cryptanalysts had solved many of the enemy's most strategically important messages, which had been enciphered on the Enigma machine, and how the course of the war had been influenced so dramatically by what Churchill had fondly called his 'most secret source'.

Winterbotham's controversial decision to shatter the secrecy that had surrounded GCHQ's activities for the past three decades had been prompted by the certainty that a journalist, Anthony Cave Brown, had learned of some aspects of Bletchley's achievements from a loquacious American war veteran and he intended to publish what Winterbotham regarded as a distorted and unreliable account, aptly entitled, in his view, *Bodyguard of Lies*.[1] Winterbotham, who had taken a tremendous dislike to Cave Brown during the course of an interview at his pig farm in Devon, was determined to pre-empt him and he did so with *The Ultra Secret*, albeit by only a matter of months.[2]

Together, Masterman and Winterbotham opened up an entirely new area of historical research. Doubt was suddenly cast on many of the accepted, contemporaneous accounts of the Second World War, which, necessarily, had omitted a vital component – the contributions made by the strictly classified weapons of deception by 'special means' and 'special intelligence'. One was the euphemism for misleading the enemy by manipulating his agents and the other a term for cryptographic success. This was not just an unprecedented opportunity for the revisionists to reassess the achievements of such established military strategists as Bernard Law Montgomery and Dwight D. Eisenhower, but it opened the field to historiographers and others whose research might shed new light on events that had gone unchallenged since 1945. Indeed, considering the passage of time and the fading of memories, it seemed positively essential to delve into the arcane sphere before its inhabitants had forgotten all their secrets.

The principal obstacle in the way of researching this unique topic was, of course, the ubiquitous Official Secrets Acts. I was especially aware of their scope, as it had been a legal failure on the part of one of my ancestors, Sir Harry Poland, that had brought the first Official Secrets Act onto the statute book. Poland had been Counsel to the Treasury in 1878, responsible for prosecuting a journalist, Charles Marvin, who had printed details of a secret Anglo-Russian treaty in *The Globe*. In the absence of any criminal law concerning secrecy, Poland had prosecuted Marvin under the Larceny Act, but the magistrate at Bow Street had thrown out the case and acquitted Marvin, who had deployed an ingenious defence: he had not stolen anything (as required by the terms of the Larceny Act) but instead had memorised every word of the treaty. He was able to demonstrate his phenomenal memory and prove that he had removed nothing from the Foreign Office, where he had worked on a part-time basis. He had simply strolled into *The Globe*'s offices and reproduced the entire document, word perfect. Marvin was triumphant, and Prime Minister Benjamin Disraeli and his Foreign Secretary Lord Salisbury were considerably embarrassed, especially as both had publicly denied the existence of such a treaty. As a direct consequence, the first Official Secrets Bill was presented to Parliament in 1888 and was passed into law the following year. Subsequently, the Act was strengthened to further inhibit the unauthorised disclosure of official information, and this led to a climate in which it was virtually impossible to research or write anything on issues deemed sensitive enough to be covered by the Acts.

Furthermore, there was an equally pernicious measure, which was not grounded in statute but was judge-made law, based on Public Interest Immunity Certificates (PIIC). These were directives, signed by ministers exercising Crown privilege, that could be deployed by the prosecution to prevent defendants from making disclosures deemed to be against the national interest. Originally intended to prevent the addresses of prosecution witnesses being revealed in open court, the PIIC soon became the weapon of choice to silence witnesses and deny defendants a particular line of defence, such as 'I was working for a secret government agency' or 'I was following instructions'. The use of the PIIC became commonplace, although the practice went unreported, and was invariably treated as a trump card by the bench. Indeed, in one example in 1992, a defendant changed their plea to guilty after having been served with a PIIC, which prevented any mention of a long-standing relationship with MI5. In reality, two of the company's directors had been acting for both the Security Service and MI6 and had acted under instructions. After several appalling miscarriages of justice, PIICs were downgraded to mere applications to a judge.[3]

The effect of this unfavourable environment was that precious little was ever published about Britain's intelligence establishment. Whenever an author tested the government's resolve, the Old Bailey was the inevitable scene for the conflict, and this situation dated back to the First World War and even covered fiction.

William Somerset Maugham admitted in the preface to *Ashenden*, a collection of short stories, that his book was 'founded on my experiences in the Intelligence Department during the war but rearranged for the purposes of fiction'.[4] When he tried to release a sequel entitled *Somerville*, Winston Churchill advised him to destroy the manuscript or face a criminal prosecution. Nor was this an empty threat: Compton Mackenzie was convicted at the Old Bailey in January 1933 for breaching the Official Secrets Act with *Greek Memories* and received a fine of £100.[5] His offence was to have given an accurate portrait of his work for MI6 in the Aegean and to have revealed the identities of dozens of his colleagues. Almost as heinous, he had confided to his readers that his chief had been known only by the single letter 'C'. All copies of *Greek Memories* were withdrawn from sale, and it was to be a further five years before an abridged edition was released. Years later, Mackenzie took his revenge with *Water on the Brain*, a wicked satire on the absurdities of British intelligence agencies.[6]

Captain Henry Landau, on the other hand, had avoided the risk of arrest by arranging for the three volumes of his war memoirs to be published in New York. The first, *All's Fair*, was distributed in the US in 1934, and in the preface the Secret Intelligence Service officer, who had supervised many of the Allied train-watching networks along the Western Front, explained:

> I have not attempted to conceal the identity of diplomatic representatives and public officials, and of some of the agents employed in neutral countries. As regards the agents in territory occupied by the enemy, I have only mentioned such names as were known to the Germans through the arrests they made; others I have either changed, or not mentioned at all. This I have done in order to protect former agents in the event of another invasion of Belgium or France during their lifetime. I am the best judge of what information would compromise them. I protected their lives during the War. I am, therefore, competent now to know what can be divulged. In short, nothing has been mentioned in this book which can do anyone harm.[7]

Landau followed *All's Fair* with *Secrets of the White Lady* in 1935, *The Enemy Within* in 1937 and *Spreading the Spy Net* in 1938.[8] All could be described as books of disclosure, revealing details of the author's wartime service with MI6, but he was not hauled before the courts for his trouble, although according to one of his contemporaries, MI6 contemplated taking some unspecified action against him.

In the years immediately after the Second World War there were very few attempts to breach the convention that MI5 and MI6 personnel should remain silent about their wartime work. More than 10,000 recruits contributed to the cryptographic breakthroughs achieved at Bletchley Park but all held their tongues. Many hundreds of others were seconded to intelligence duties with MI5 or MI6, but they kept their own counsel afterwards. Even the agents, who had endured so much and possessed such marvellous knowledge, succumbed to a code of silence worthy of an order of Trappists.

The first to deviate from the line was Eddie Chapman, whose story, written with a journalist named Wilfred Macartney, nearly appeared in a French newspaper, *Etoile du Soir*, in 1946. Chapman was a burglar who had been incarcerated in a Jersey prison when the Germans had invaded the Channel Islands. Taken to Germany and trained as a spy, he was parachuted into East Anglia in December 1942 to begin his programme of sabotage. However, always a reluctant Nazi spy, Chapman offered himself to the Security Service and returned to Germany in the guise of a successful agent. Incredibly, Chapman persuaded his controllers of his bona fides and was dropped back into England for a second time. His tale was quite unique, and when he was convicted of having sold the serial rights to his story, he persuaded his MI5 case officer Michael Ryde to appear and give evidence for the defence during the trial, which was held entirely in camera in March 1946. From the witness box, Ryde confirmed to the chief magistrate, Sir Bertrand Watson, that Chapman was the bravest man he had ever met, and so the professional safecracker and his collaborator, Macartney, were let off with a £50 fine and costs of £28.

Although the penalties imposed were insignificant, it was a manifestation of the determination on the part of the authorities to suppress any disclosures regarding MI5 and MI6. When George Blake had been convicted of spying for the KGB in May 1961, a D-Notice (publication ban) had been issued to prevent any mention of his MI6 role. Nor was there any public statement when Kim Philby fled to the Soviet Union in January 1963. Philby's autobiography, *My Silent War*, only emerged in 1968, a year after a team of *Sunday Times* journalists had produced a series of articles as a prelude to *Philby: The Spy Who Betrayed a Generation*.[9] These disclosures, which Philby claimed had prompted him to write his own account, must have given palpitations to Britain's intelligence establishment, for it broke the long-recognised convention that neither MI5 nor MI6 officers should be identified by their real names. Of course, in the context of Philby, who was then at liberty in Moscow, such an exercise was entirely pointless, but nevertheless the authors of *Philby: The Spy Who Betrayed a Generation* did go through the motions of conforming by omitting the identities of some of the key players in the drama. Similarly, when E. H. Cookridge came to write George Blake's biography, he managed to do so without revealing the name of a single one of Blake's MI6 colleagues.[10]

MI5 and MI6 took the closest interest in anyone digging into their past, and the very few, rather banal books written about the two organisations had been heavily vetted by the authorities. Broadly, intelligence literature could be categorised into three different groups: the personal memoirs which had been sanitised and approved by the appropriate agencies; the serious attempts made by outsiders at revealing more about secret operations; and the rather superficial efforts of journalists to exploit the market without any real consideration for authenticity. In the first category was Duško Popov's *Spy/Counterspy*, which was released in 1974, two years after Masterman's book.[11] Popov changed many names in his autobiography, submitting his manuscript to MI5 and MI6, and received official permission to publish.

In the second category was Hugh Trevor-Roper's *The Philby Affair*, which not only made a very determined attack on the conditions that had shielded Philby for so long but also planted some intriguing clues on related topics, such as a particularly teasing reference to Allied cryptographic success against U-boats.[12] In the third were the many books of authors such as Bernard Newman, Ronnie Seth and Bernard Hutton, who had almost monopolised the genre and had adopted no clear standards of accuracy. The works of Faragó, Cave Brown, Winterbotham and Masterman were an entirely new departure and opened the way for much more detailed analysis of operations that hitherto had been considered beyond reach.

Although the 1970s saw these dramatic breakthroughs in terms of the impact of intelligence operations on the conduct of the Second World War, there was a dearth of information when it came to the actual personalities involved in ULTRA and the Double-Cross System. Who were these remarkable men and women who had achieved so much? The tradition of anonymity for the inhabitants of the secret world was exceptionally frustrating, but not everyone accepted the need for discretion forty years later. Another big secret, as assessed by Whitehall, was the degree to which the Cambridge spies had successfully manipulated the establishment. Not a single book from that era mentioned that Guy Burgess's brother Nigel was a an MI5 officer, or that Donald Maclean's sister Nancy worked in MI5, or that Philby's sister Helena had been employed by MI6.

One of the programmes in the *Spy!* series was entitled 'Camp 020', the military designation of Latchmere House. Latchmere was a former mental institution which had been used to accommodate shell-shocked officers after the First World War and in the Second had been taken over by the Security Service as a secret detention facility. The BBC's objective was to explain how German spies who were interned there were persuaded to become double agents. The location of the hideous Victorian mansion, just outside the village of Ham on the outskirts of Richmond Park, had been revealed first by Faragó in *The Game of the Foxes*. Faragó, of course, had written extensively about MI5's success in 'turning' enemy spies, and Masterman had produced the definitive study of the phenomenon in *The Double-Cross System in the War of 1939–45*. However, neither had really explained exactly how MI5 had accomplished the extraordinary feat of transforming hardened Nazis into committed supporters of the Allied cause. Indeed, very little had appeared in print about MI5, surprisingly. The *Daily Telegraph* journalist John Bulloch had written a short history of the organisation but had devoted only two brief chapters to the Second World War, neither of which dealt with the subject of the BBC's interest. Curiously, despite the disclosures made by Masterman, there were only three books that had been written by the double agents themselves. One was Duško Popov's autobiography, *Spy/Counterspy*, in which he had recounted his adventures as the spy codenamed TRICYCLE by MI5. The second was *Secret Service Rendered* by Lily Sergueiew, though her original story, published first in France, predated Masterman by six years and clearly had been written from a very narrow perspective, the full scope of the Double-Cross System then being a closely guarded secret.[13] The third had been written by the splendid villain Chapman, codenamed ZIGZAG.[14]

Sergueiew had died in May 1950 and Popov had led a peripatetic existence in Germany and South Africa before settling in the south of France, so Eddie Chapman proved the easiest of the three to interview, as he divided his time between a health hydro he had founded in Hertfordshire and his flat, 512 Bunyan Court, in the Barbican. The reformed safecracker was characteristically enthusiastic about the BBC's project and put me in touch with Michael Ryde, who had been his MI5 case officer. Unusually, Ryde had allowed his agent to know his real name, and this disclosure had been made in connection with the latter's prosecution at the end of the war. Chapman remained grateful to Ryde for his intervention, and when I visited him at his flat, the jovial ex-criminal was delighted to recall his brief stay at Camp 020 after his arrival in Cambridgeshire in December 1942 at the end of an Abwehr parachute. My encounter with Ryde in April 1978 was also to prove beneficial, for he was being nursed through some ill health by a newspaper journalist, Marjorie Eaton-Jones, who knew nothing of his MI5 connections. She had sat in on the interview and during a drive back into London from Long Ditton, she suggested that when the BBC's project was nearer completion, the *Daily Telegraph* would be keen to publish an article. The producer welcomed the chance to publicise the *Spy!* series, but regrettably, owing to some administrative oversight, the article which appeared as the cover story in the *Daily Telegraph* magazine had not been cleared with the head of department, which led to another bitter wrangle with Desmond Wilcox.

Because there had never been any complaints regarding treatment at Camp 020, the research team concluded that some subtle mental techniques had been employed, and I interviewed the leading criminal psychiatrist of the era William Sargant at his consulting rooms in Hamilton Place, just off Piccadilly, to find an explanation. He told me that the regime at Latchmere House had been developed by a respected colleague, Dr Harold Dearden, and I had little difficulty in tracing his widow to her farmhouse near Hay-on-Wye. Although she could shed little light on the detail of her late husband's work for MI5, apart from confirming his long-standing consultancy for the Security Service, their son had inherited a unique collection of wartime photographs, taken by his father at Camp 020. Amazingly, the 020 staff had known that Dearden was an enthusiastic amateur photographer and had not objected when he had produced his camera. As well as snaps of the building itself, his collection included a series of pictures of a downcast man in civilian clothes being escorted by military personnel in a field, examining a parachute. It was later determined that this was the sole photographic record of the German spy Karel Richter returning to his landing site in Hertfordshire, accompanied by his MI5 captors. Although MI5 had been keen to let Richter join the other Abwehr agents who had undergone the turning process, he had been hanged. The BBC also identified Camp 020's feared commandant, Colonel Robin 'Tin Eye' Stephens, his deputy Colonel Stimson, a Special Branch detective and some other MI5 officers.

A visit to Latchmere House showed that it was still under the authority of the Home Office as a remand centre. Having obtained official permission to tour the main house and the prison wing built in 1940, the BBC heard from the staff about the microphones that had been found concealed in the ventilation system of the cell blocks. One of the prison officers also showed me a harrowing letter retrieved from behind some pipes during restoration work that had been written by a Belgian who evidently believed he was about to be executed for espionage. He protested his innocence but acknowledged that his future was bleak.

The BBC realised early on in their research for the programme that very few of those who had worked at 020 were willing to discuss their experiences. Colonel Stephens was dead, and his deputy Colonel Stimson, whom I found living near Maidenhead, seemed very reluctant to discuss anything to do with the place. Most 020 veterans cited the Official Secrets Act, but finally, one double agent who had been codenamed TATE proved to be more forthcoming.

TATE had landed in Cambridgeshire in September 1940 and, having been 'turned' at Camp 020, had spent the rest of the war transmitting to his Abwehr controllers in Hamburg under MI5 supervision. Historian Günter Peis had referred to him as A-3701 and named him as 'Hans Hansen' but had also mentioned the fact he had remained in England after the war and become a respected breeder of canaries. These and other clues led me in April 1978 to 55 Leggatts Wood Avenue, a modest semi-detached house in north Watford, where I called on 'Wulf Schmidt', who corrected me by introducing himself in a heavy German accent as 'Harry Williamson'. I explained that I was looking for a Dane from Aabenraa in Denmark who had come to England in 1940. After some prevarication, Harry admitted his true identity and asked me to wait in the kitchen while he telephoned 'the office'. Some minutes later he reappeared and explained that he had just spoken to the Security Service and had been advised to say nothing and show me the door. Despite this discouraging start, Harry seemed keen to chat, and a couple of hours later, we had agreed to meet again to discuss his extraordinary, as-yet untold story. It was the story of a Nazi spy, arrested within hours of landing by parachute, who became the longest-serving double agent in the wartime UK, finally transmitting his last signal just as Allied troops entered Hamburg.

Harry's account was sufficiently complete for the BBC to devote the programme to him. He recalled how he had been placed in solitary confinement and then had been interrogated in the ground floor reception room of the main building by a 'board' of well-informed officers in military uniform who had sat behind a long, baize-covered table. TATE had stood alone in the centre of the room, the only other person present being a secretary who had taken shorthand notes of the proceedings.

Initially, TATE had explained that his decision to switch sides and help MI5 had been motivated by self-preservation and an understandable wish to avoid the gallows. He told me that he had been visited in his cell by Dr Dearden, who had sat on the end of his bed and shared a bottle of whisky with him and that he had been treated well by his captors. Only later did he confide that during his first interrogation by the board, which had been chaired by Colonel Stephens, he had been required to stand stark naked, an experience that had been intended to humiliate him in front of the demure MI5 secretary who seemed entirely oblivious to his fear. He made me promise not to include the scene in the programme and also said that on a single occasion he had been assaulted by an MI5 officer.

TATE's almost reluctant admission that he had been maltreated explained in part the obvious reluctance of those who had worked at Camp 020 to say anything about the regime imposed by Stephens, who had been universally disliked. Only after TATE had told me about having been beaten did one officer give the explanation. A single MI5 officer, who had not been attached to the permanent 020 staff, had been responsible for the attack on TATE. The individual concerned had been disciplined and transferred overseas. It was the only occasion of its kind, although Stephens had been court-martialled after the war for maltreatment of prisoners at an interrogation centre in Germany. TATE himself expressed no bitterness about what had happened to him. Indeed, he had been grateful for the opportunity to escape execution, and he had remained on good terms with his case officers and the radio operator who had supervised his wireless transmissions.

Although TATE's experience was not representative of how the other Abwehr agents were handled, it was decided to include a scene in which his interrogator struck him. Of course, this had the effect of undermining the widespread belief that although Stephens had run Camp 020 very strictly, he had never been brutal, and predictably, the incident provoked letters of protest to the *Daily Telegraph*, signed by ten women who had been on 020's secretarial staff, when the programme was broadcast in January 1980.

TATE himself had no complaint about the programme and was pleased that the scene in which he had endured naked humiliation had been excluded. The fact that a promise had been kept, despite grim warnings from his MI5 contact, was to prove a key step in gaining his trust and his cooperation for a further project, a history of the wartime Security Service.

• • •

While researching the background to MI5's work on turning enemy agents, I had approached Sir Dick White for an interview. He had by then retired as the Cabinet Office's intelligence coordinator, and he seemed the best-qualified person to give guidance about Security Service operations. He had joined MI5 before the Second World War and had established his reputation in the counter-espionage division. Later, he had risen to the post of director general and in 1956 had been switched to head MI6. As the only person in the history of either organisation to have held both top jobs, he was widely regarded as something of a legend.

Originally a teacher at the Whitgift School in Croydon, White had joined MI5 in 1935, having been recruited by Malcolm Cumming on a ship sailing to Australia. One of his first cases before the war was the anti-Nazi diplomat Wolfgang zu Putlitz, who worked at Joachim von Ribbentrop's embassy in London and maintained almost constant contact with the former press attaché, Klop Ustinov. Zu Putlitz provided invaluable political information, which was handled at the Foreign Office by Sir Robert Vansittart, and a wealth of counter-espionage tips about German agents paid by the embassy, which he passed to Klop acting as a 'cut-out', or intermediary. Although in theory the careers of professional intelligence personnel are not dependent on the performance of their individual agents, White was the exception in every way. He was widely credited with his deft handling of the somewhat temperamental zu Putlitz, and his name circulated in Whitehall because of his association with the embassy source. He was also a university graduate, at a time when MI5 was almost entirely staffed by the director general's army friends. During the war, he positioned himself as Guy Liddell's protégé, advocated the development of strategic deception peddled to the enemy by double agents, and personally indoctrinated selected case officers in the Middle East into the signals intelligence material codenamed ISK and ISOS. These top secret decrypts gave MI5 a huge advantage, thus enabling double-cross committees to be established across all counter-intelligence theatres, including Cairo, Algiers, Beirut, Damascus and Baghdad. When White retired as MI6's chief in 1968, a new post of intelligence coordinator to the Cabinet Office was created so Whitehall did not lose his unrivalled experience. He had finally retired in 1972.

When I telephoned White at his modern home near Arundel in April 1978, he readily agreed to discuss the principles of handling double agents. A meeting a fortnight later, which I had anticipated would be short, grew longer and longer as White lectured me and indoctrinated me into the ways of the clandestine world. Over coffee, a vegetarian lunch and finally tea, he gave a compelling picture of how he and his colleagues had transformed a small, moribund group of intelligence officers and had effectively taken control of the Abwehr's operations. He spoke of the first, hesitant recruits into the Double-Cross System and how skilful handling of controlled enemy agents allowed them to develop a comprehensive understanding of the Abwehr's structure and methodology. He described how, after the war, the examination of captured documents had proved the extent of their success. White also explained that Masterman had necessarily drawn a veil over the vital contribution made by ULTRA, which had enabled MI5 to verify the enemy's reaction to every move made by the Security Service and had prevented the interlocking tapestry of deception from becoming unravelled. Now that Fred Winterbotham had revealed ULTRA's origins, there was little left to keep classified, apart from the personal details of the participants. By the end of the afternoon, I had realised that the very little that had been published about MI5's wartime activities was wholly inadequate, and if even a fraction of what the retired director general had said was accurate, there was plenty of material for a proper history of the Security Service. When I suggested this to White as we parted, he gripped my hand firmly and told me that no one would *ever* be able to write such a book for publication.

In retrospect, White's vehemence on this issue is entirely understandable. These were uncharted waters, and quite apart from any other considerations, the legal climate seemed quite unpromising.

On my journey home to London, I mulled over White's remark, and I concluded that I had been challenged to research a wartime history of the Security Service. The idea of writing one alone had simply never occurred to me, even though I was then working on the book of the television series. My instinct was to persuade another author to write the book, and I offered my services as a researcher to Professor M. R. D. Foot, the historian who had completed *SOE in France* for the Cabinet Office.[15] Foot's most recent contribution to the literature was *MI9*, an official account of the wartime escape and evasion service, and this seemed an ideal model upon which to base a book about MI5.[16] Foot was sceptical that there was enough material available for a book and over lunch at the Savile Club in September 1979 made a counterproposal. If I really believed a wartime history of the Security Service was practical, he would introduce me to his publisher, Barney Blackley at The Bodley Head, and recommend that I be given a contract. This is indeed exactly what happened, and two days later, I was commissioned to produce a comprehensive history of MI5 within three years.

My signature on the contact coincided with the BBC's decision to commission a further six-part series entitled *Escape!*, based on the success of *Spy!*. The topics to be tackled for the drama-documentary series included the rescue of the newspaper editor Donald Woods from South Africa, the Houdini-like adventures of Alfie Hinds, who was then something of a legend in the underworld, and the rescue of the passengers hijacked on a Lufthansa flight in Mogadishu. As had happened on the previous series, I was invited to suggest some suitable subjects and came up with the disappearance of Kim Philby from Beirut in January 1963, the removal of five Israeli gunboats from Cherbourg on Christmas Eve, 1969 and a much more recent incident, the vanishing act performed so completely by Lord Lucan.

Following a conversation with the Israeli naval attaché in London, it became clear that the Cherbourg project was doomed. The Israelis considered the matter closed, and the French remained deeply embarrassed by the removal of the embargoed missile boats. An alternative was needed, so I proposed the extraordinary story of Else Krüger, Hitler's secretary, who had not only escaped from the *Führerbunker* in Berlin during the very last days of the war but had subsequently married the British intelligence officer who had interrogated her. She had been taken into custody by the British because she had also worked for Martin Bormann, and in the immediate post-war period the Allies had not been sure he had died. Krüger had fallen in love with her inquisitor, who had subsequently pursued a very successful academic career and had been appointed a professor. To my surprise, and hers, she was found to be living in Cambridge, but she was reluctant to play any part in what the BBC had in mind, namely a reconstruction of her last hours with Hitler and her arrest by the British occupation authorities. Respecting her privacy, the project was dropped. The next alternative, which turned out to be quite the riskiest of the projects, was the murder of an Arabic-speaking schoolteacher, John Cartland – the escape being that accomplished by his son Jeremy from a murder charge in France in 1973.

When I first met Jeremy Cartland, who had moved to Powis Square in Brighton, I was surprised by his willingness to cooperate in a reconstruction of what must have been for him an extraordinarily painful episode, not least because of his near encounter with the death penalty. Jeremy's father, for whom he had worked at his language school in Brighton, had been bludgeoned to death outside the caravan the two men were sharing in Provence, and the local police had been convinced from the outset that Jeremy was a murderer. According to Jeremy, he had been attacked by unknown assailants in the middle of the night, and his father had been killed with an axe before their caravan was set alight. The police maintained that Jeremy had argued with his father, killed him in a drunken brawl and then fabricated the evidence which supported his version of events. His knife wound had been self-inflicted, claimed the police, and the fight with a mysterious thief, who allegedly had been disturbed while rifling their car, had been invented. What had caught my attention had been the speculation about Cartland's motive for being in Provence. Jeremy insisted they were visiting land they intended to buy, but there were rumours that his father had suffered the same fate as Sir Jack Drummond, another Englishman who had been murdered as he had camped beside a main road in Provence in August 1952. The similarities between the two killings were striking. Drummond, who had been a nutrition expert at London University and the Ministry of Food, had known Cartland briefly in Brussels after the war. Both had enjoyed vague, unspecified intelligence connections and were rumoured to have been silenced by former members of the resistance, perhaps to protect consignments of gold parachuted into the south of France during the war. The murders had taken place within thirty-five miles of each other. An elderly local farmer named Gaston Dominici had been convicted of Drummond's murder, but Jeremy had been the only suspect in the second incident. He had been released into British custody by the French police, but the Director of Public Prosecutions had announced that there was insufficient evidence to press charges. Jeremy had returned to Brighton to run the Kate Bush fan club and write an account of the whole grisly business, *The Cartland File.*[17]

Press reports of John Cartland's career concentrated on his double first at Oxford, his work for the Italian section of the Political Warfare Executive, which had been based at Woburn Abbey during the war, and his post-war travels to the Arabian Gulf, perhaps on behalf of MI6. One rumour suggested that Cartland had been silenced to stop him disclosing details of the Nazi archives he had liberated in Belgium in 1945. Others linked him to French collaborators and resistance traitors. What was the true story? Surprisingly, Jeremy agreed to cooperate with the BBC film, and those involved in the programme came to the conclusion, separately, that he had known more about the killing than he had admitted and that collaborating with the BBC's research had been a cathartic experience for him. After the broadcast, his family registered a complaint with the BBC about how he had been portrayed, but it was not pursued, and Jeremy Cartland died in Brighton in June 2014 at the age of seventy.

The Philby episode in the *Escape!* series initially depended upon two sources: Philby's son, John, a joiner who was an acquaintance of a friend in the racing world, and Miles Copeland, the legendary CIA veteran who had already written about his adventures in an autobiography and had been quoted extensively about his friendship with Philby. A committed Anglophile who had made his home in Oxfordshire, Copeland had operated across the Middle East long after his formal departure from the CIA and had retained strong ties to its stations in Cairo and Beirut. Of particular interest to me was his recollection of the events that had led to Philby's sudden disappearance, for most of the accounts that had hitherto been published of this episode had been quite vague. It was known that Philby had been confronted by an MI6 officer in Beirut and that a few days later he had mysteriously failed to turn up at a dinner party held by British diplomat Glencairn Balfour Paul, but virtually nothing else had been written on the subject. Copeland gave two important clues: firstly, he identified the MI6 head of station in Beirut as Peter Lunn, son of the skiing pioneer Arnold Lunn, and he also named the MI6 officer who had confronted Philby as Nicholas Elliott, son of the former headmaster of Eton.

With these two important pieces of the jigsaw, the BBC was able to reconstruct more of what had happened to Philby on the night of his flight, but we heard from Moscow, through Philby's son, that the man himself was not interested in cooperating. Although not entirely unexpected, the news was a disappointment, for his acknowledged help would have been an astonishing journalistic coup. However, his refusal did serve to encourage the BBC in the belief – correctly, as it turned out – that there was rather more to Philby's disappearance than had been suspected. For instance, we had been told by one well-briefed informant that Philby might have been whisked away from Beirut by the KGB, who could have been worried about Philby taking advantage of an offer of immunity and returning to London. Another source suggested that Philby might have explored the possibility of moving back to London, and a third even flew the kite that he had always been a loyal MI6 asset.

Although we did not realise it at the time, the topic of Philby's escape to Moscow was still a matter of some sensitivity because the vital ingredient in the tale, which had hitherto remained undisclosed, was what exactly had happened when the donnish Elliott, with his thick, heavy-rimmed spectacles, had confronted the traitor. Clearly, the encounter must have been filled with drama, but what exactly had happened at the meeting, and why had Philby fled? Much later, we learned that the issue was considered highly delicate because Elliott had travelled to the Lebanon armed with a formal offer of immunity from the Attorney General, Sir John Hobson, for Philby, and *it had been accepted*. Allegedly, Philby had exchanged Hobson's immunity for a written confession, which he had handed to his friend, but this document was to give rise to the suspicion that the spy had been tipped off in advance of Elliott's arrival. Apparently, Elliott – who was characteristically discreet about his brush with history and not entirely pleased to have been identified by Copeland – had written his own version of events but had not yet received permission to publish. Given the atmosphere of secrecy then prevailing, it seemed unlikely that he ever would, but he was later to release two collections of amusing anecdotes, *Never*

Judge a Man by his Umbrella and *With My Little Eye*.[18] Years later, I found Philby's typed confession (unmarked as such) in the MI5 file on Arnold Deutsch, the People's Commissariat for Internal Affairs (NKVD) illegal *rezident* in London who had recruited Philby in 1934. I would also learn from Arthur Martin, the MI5 officer who had negotiated Philby's immunity, that Philby most probably had neglected to mention the immunity to his KGB handlers.

Philby's persistent duplicity may have been the reason why he had not mentioned the immunity or his acceptance of it in his 1968 memoir *My Silent War*, but why had he also omitted any reference to VENONA, the cryptographic source that had been so beneficial to so many post-war counter-intelligence investigations? That omission, in Martin's opinion, was probably a reflection of the KGB's embarrassment about the flaws in its cipher system, which had caused so much damage to its networks. However, there was no reason for the KGB to be coy about the immunity, unless, of course, Philby had never mentioned it. It would not be until 1999, more than a decade after Philby's death, that KGB retirees admitted he had never disclosed the immunity deal.

• • •

The prospect of finding out enough about MI5 – arguably Britain's most secret branch of government – to satisfy a demanding publisher was difficult enough, but the task of avoiding the Official Secrets Act was daunting. Although never formally employed by any government department, I was, like everyone else in the country, subject to the provisions of the Act. In their ignorance, many people believed that the Act only applied to those who had been required, by the nature of their jobs, to go through the signing of the Act. However, its signing is really nothing more than an acknowledgement that you had read the terms of the Act and were fully aware of its provisions and penalties, the acknowledgement of which could then be used against you in any subsequent prosecution. My intention was to declare to the Security Service at the earliest opportunity my plan to write a serious book, in the hope that at worst, no obstacle would be placed in my path and that at best, I might receive a degree of cooperation. Accordingly, an appointment was made to see the secretary of the D-Notice Committee, Admiral Bill Ash, and he listened to my offer to submit my draft manuscript for clearance before publication with an air of bemused disdain. He concluded a rather frosty meeting in his tiny room in the Ministry of Defence by saying that he really saw no need for him to read the manuscript. 'You won't find anything out, and there is no chance of anyone speaking to you,' he added, full of confidence. When we next met, two years later, he was to make a very determined effort to delete 194 names from the first draft and to eliminate one entire chapter.

While researching the book, I remained intrigued by the complexities of MI5's wartime double agents. Although I had spoken to a couple of retired MI5 officers, the one subject they refused to discuss was the identity of their agents. Duško Popov, Eddie Chapman and Lily Sergueiew were the exceptions, for they had written accounts of their activities. Sergueiew had died years earlier, but I traced Popov to his wonderful home outside Opio, in the south of France, and learned from him the names that he had concealed in his book, *Spy/Counterspy*. In the comfort of what had been the bishop's palace, he recalled that after his arrival in the UK in

December 1941, under MI6's sponsorship, he had been assigned an MI5 case officer whom he had known as Bill Matthews.

The case officer's role, as defined by Masterman, was to supervise every aspect of the double agent's life, thereby ensuring that the deception remain undetected for as long as possible. The case officers, who sometimes had more than one case to handle, reported to the head of the MI5 section designated B1(a), Colonel T. A. 'Tommy' Robertson, a much-respected figure who had developed an impressive talent for obtaining the very best from all his loyal subordinates and agents. Even the recalcitrant Lily Sergueiew, whose temperamental behaviour had belied her MI5 codename TREASURE had been entranced by Robertson and persuaded by him to give greater cooperation. Whereas Robertson's name appeared in the books written by Sergueiew, Popov and Chapman, none had known the true identities of their case officers. Robertson's staff was never more than a dozen officers, but because case officers had adopted aliases for handling each agent, B1(a) had appeared rather bigger than it really was. As I later discovered, Billy Luke also took the surnames Matthews, Marks and Johns, and Christopher Harmer called himself Palmer. Only Michael Ryde, who had been Chapman's case officer, had allowed his agent to know his real name, and, as previously outlined, only because he had insisted on supporting his former agent by giving evidence for him as a character witness at the Old Bailey.

The case officers had been a key but hitherto unrecognised component in the success of the Double-Cross System. The system had been well established before Masterman had chaired the first meeting of his Twenty Committee, which oversaw operations, in January 1941 and so called because of the number twenty in Roman numerals – XX, a double cross. In the published version of his book, Masterman had not identified any of the case officers individually, but each had enjoyed experiences almost as fascinating as their agents, and some felt that their roles had not received sufficient recognition from him. Thus, when approached for their own accounts of the system, their recollections neatly dovetailed with the official version but were a lot more colourful.

According to Masterman, TATE had been but one of more than forty double agents, and I set myself the task of tracing them all. Duško Popov was of enormous help in the quest because, as his codename TRICYCLE implied, he had worked with three others: BALLOON, GELATINE and DREADNOUGHT. With his help, I found Dickie Metcalfe in retirement at his home in Waltham St Lawrence, interviewed Friedl Gaertner at her sister's house in north London and spoke to Dr Ivo Popov – Duško Popov's brother, who had also been an agent – at his beachside apartment outside Nassau. Metcalfe (BALLOON) and Gaertner (GELATINE) had been disappointed by Duško's memory of them and were delighted to have an opportunity to give a more balanced account of what they had accomplished. In particular, Gaertner's story was of some significance, for her sister had married Stewart Menzies's younger brother, so there had been some rather curious wartime weekend house parties which had been attended by the chief of the British Secret Intelligence Service, his younger brother and his younger brother's wife, who was, after all, an enemy spy.

BALLOON and GELATINE had been recruited by Duško, and he was also in touch with a network ostensibly run by his brother Ivo, a physician who had stayed in Belgrade during the war while Duško had made good his escape to London. Duško was able to put me in touch with Eugn Sostaric, codenamed METEOR, a Yugoslav Air Force officer who had taken up residence near Como in Switzerland and FREAK, the Marquis Frano de Bona, with whom I talked at length at his flat overlooking the Adriatic. Neither FREAK nor METEOR were anxious to have their real identities disclosed during their lifetime, so I promised them confidentiality, an undertaking that later I was to be released from.

While FREAK and METEOR had their own reasons for preserving their anonymity, which I suspected had more to do with their post-war activities than their work for MI5, MUTT and JEFF wanted to have their stories told. My hunt for MUTT, whose true name is John Moe, took me to Sweden, where I found him living with his young son in a quiet town near Malmö. Coincidentally, he had been thinking of writing his memoirs, and he willingly allowed me to tape several hours of his story, starting with his recruitment by the Abwehr in Oslo in 1941 and his flight across the North Sea in a Luftwaffe amphibious aircraft to Scotland, where he and his companion JEFF, real name Tor Glad, had landed as spies in a rubber dinghy. They had both endured a short spell at Camp 020 and, having been able to prove their credentials, had been enrolled as double agents under the supervision of Christopher Harmer.

MUTT had spent the remainder of the war as a successful double agent and later had joined the Norwegian Army. JEFF, however, had not been so lucky, as Moe explained. Glad had resented the restrictions imposed on their movements by MI5 and disobeyed the curfew by sneaking out of the safe house in which they had been accommodated and meeting girlfriends at West End nightspots. This was regarded as very risky behaviour by the Security Service, which was always concerned that a breach of the accepted tradecraft might allow word of an agent's duplicity to filter back to the Abwehr, thereby jeopardising the entire double-agent system. Accordingly, Glad had been detained in an internment camp for enemy aliens on the Isle of Man, an experience that had given him acute depression. Worse still, at the end of hostilities, he had been repatriated to his native Norway under military escort and accused of collaboration with the enemy. Fortunately, the charges had been dropped following MI5's belated intervention, but the episode had blighted his career because many of his colleagues had assumed there must have been some substance to the allegation that he had assisted the Nazis during the occupation.

Moe had not kept in touch with Glad, but with his help, I found Glad working for a Norwegian television station. I flew to Oslo to meet him, and once his initial reservations about reopening painful memories had been overcome, Glad realised that I represented a chance to set the record straight with his friends and colleagues who still harboured suspicions about his war record. Thus, MUTT and JEFF were persuaded to join ZIGZAG, TRICYCLE, GELATINE, BALLOON, DREADNOUGHT, METEOR and FREAK to help with the chapters in the book devoted to the management of double agents. Furthermore, both MUTT and JEFF agreed to travel back to London to appear in a television programme and even visited Camp 020. Moe's own story, *John Moe: Double Agent*, was later written by a Swedish journalist, Jan Moen.[19]

As the double agents disclosed their stories, it became obvious that Masterman's summaries of their contributions had been woefully superficial and had not begun to do justice to the extraordinary adventures experienced by these remarkable spies.

Perhaps the most frustrating story from the double agents was that of BRUTUS, a Polish Air Force officer who in October 1942 had pretended to escape to London in order to spy for the Germans before turning himself in and working as a double agent for the British. He had operated on the staff of the Polish headquarters. I had few clues to BRUTUS's identity, so an attempt to trace the personnel based at the Rubens Hotel in Victoria, where General Władysław Sikorski – Prime Minister of the Polish government-in-exile – had been accommodated seemed the best place to start. At that time, there was still a Polish government-in-exile in London, and I was directed towards the émigré administration's Minister of Information, Roman Garby-Czerniawski. After the war, he had remained in London, and he now ran a small printing business in Fulham Broadway, less than a mile from my London home. As I arrived, Garby-Czerniawski asked if I had read his war memoirs *The Big Network*, in which he had documented his work with the French resistance in 1940 and 1941, prior to his arrest by the Gestapo.[20] We agreed to meet again after I had read his book, which had ended with his escape from prison in Paris and his arrival in England… in October 1942. Evidently, I had found BRUTUS, as was later confirmed by his case officer, Hugh Astor.

The publication party for *MI5: British Security Service Operations 1909–45* was held at the Hyde Park Hotel in November 1981. Both Wing Commander Garby-Czerniawski and Hugh Astor came to the event, together with all the other surviving case officers led by Tommy Robertson. The hotel had been selected because before the war it had been the location of Sir Vernon Kell's private dining club, the 'IP' Club. Depending upon whom he invited, the first director general of the Security Service claimed that the initials stood for 'Intelligence Person' or 'Important Person'.

The occasion was marked with a photograph subsequently published in *The Observer*, in which many of the guests agreed to appear. One exception was Harry Williamson, who had attended the event in defiance of the advice given to him by his current MI5 handler. He maintained a discreet distance on the far side of the room but otherwise celebrated *MI5*'s publication with enthusiasm.

During the three years it had taken to research *MI5*, there had been several moments when the project looked in jeopardy. The first problem to arise was a letter signed by a senior Security Service officer, who threatened to terminate Robertson's pension unless he withdrew his offer to write a foreword to my book. Robertson had protested that he had avoided giving away any sensitive information, but it was argued that his association with me would add credibility to the book, and this might be interpreted as some official endorsement. In those circumstances, we decided to scrap his contribution.

An attempt was also made to persuade the publisher to revoke my contract. It so happened that Barney Blackley had also contracted one of his schoolfriends, Stephen Watts, to write his memoirs, *Moonlight on a Lake in Bond Street*.[21] Before the war, Watts had been the *Daily Express* theatre critic, and in early 1943 he had been transferred from the Army Educational Corps to act as a liaison officer between MI5 and the Supreme Headquarters Allied Expeditionary Force (SHAEF). Watts was asked by Blackley to read my manuscript and assess my progress, but instead he made a copy, which he passed to MI5. On instructions, he advised Blackley to cancel my contract, but Watts had not counted on Blackley obtaining a second opinion, which was far more favourable. When confronted, Watts admitted he had 'taken advice' about my manuscript and had no personal knowledge of any inaccuracies. If anything, this episode proved counterproductive, with Blackley reassuring The Bodley Head that *MI5* was a controversial book but authentic.

MI5: British Security Service Operations 1909–45 represented a considerable milestone in the way historians dealt with the intelligence community. Hitherto, a culture of deference had discouraged external comment or criticism (of the Security Service in particular), but this toxic atmosphere had been transformed by the Philby affair and then by the disclosure in November 1979 that a former wartime MI5 officer, Professor Sir Anthony Blunt, had spied for the Soviets… and had been granted immunity from prosecution back in April 1964. Prime Minister Margaret Thatcher's statement to the Commons on this subject had astonished even the most hardened supporters of the security establishment and had encouraged me to approach Blunt for an interview, on the basis that his wartime experience had been highly relevant to any objective account of the organisation's history.

To my surprise, Blunt invited me to his sixth-floor flat in Portsea Hall, just off the Edgware Road, and told me that he had been deeply offended by an accusation in the *Sunday Telegraph* that he had been responsible for the betrayal of SOE agents in Holland to the Nazis during the war. The story, published three days after the Prime Minister's statement, had been based on a misunderstanding about the alias 'Major Blunt', which had been adopted by an officer named Charles Blizzard. Anthony Blunt, who had never been involved with SOE, wanted the record put straight. According to the mistaken *Telegraph* article, Blunt had headed SOE's Netherlands section and had been responsible for the deaths of forty-nine agents who had been victims of the German counter-intelligence operation *Englandspiel*, which had effectively taken control of the British networks in Holland. The front-page headline, which did not have a byline, was part of wider coverage, including an article by Joan Clements who repeated that 'Blunt was head of the Dutch Section of Britain's Special Operations Executive' during the two years the losses were incurred. Another item, credited to Ivan Rowan, described 'The World of Anthony Blunt', detailing 'the spy and the cover-up'.[22] However, the really damaging piece was a contribution by the respected biographer Kenneth Rose, who purported to provide the background to the 'wartime catastrophe' of Blunt's espionage.[23] He described it as 'a story of unmitigated disaster' and claimed 'the entire network remained in the hands of Blunt and his colleagues'. Insufferably pompous, Rose stated that he knew 'the role he played in wartime intelligence. I can shed light on it'. Rose not only directly accused Blunt of responsibility for the Dutch debacle but revealed that some of the SOE agents had tried to warn London of the developing disaster and 'Blunt failed to act on the warnings'.

Alone, Blunt was supposed to have declined to participate in the post-war Dutch parliamentary inquiry into the fiasco, with Rose stating, 'Blunt himself, in command during the crucial years 1941–43, did not appear and apparently the Foreign Office found this not at all odd.' Of course, Blunt had not been invited to attend the post-war investigation conducted in London and The Hague for the obvious reason that he played no role in the tragedy, but the *Sunday Telegraph* carried considerable weight. Rose was considered an establishment commentator of some gravitas, and the paper was edited by Sir Peregrine Worsthorne, whose father, Alexander Koch de Gooreynd, had been a Belgian general officer. Another member of the family, Peter Koch de Gooreynd, had served as personal assistant to MI6's chief, Stewart Menzies, during the war.

Blunt had consulted his solicitor Michael Rubinstein over these calumnies, who had explained that as a self-confessed traitor, he had no reputation to defend so a legal action for defamation was not an option. In these circumstances, Blunt wanted it known, perhaps through my forthcoming history of the wartime Security Service, that he had never been in SOE. I was content to do so, for Blunt may have been guilty of many crimes but not that particular one. Indeed, on 21 November, three days after the offending feature, Thatcher elaborated on her statement made in the Commons the previous week:

> Professor Blunt has said that during his period in the Security Service from 1940 to 1945 he regularly passed to Russian intelligence anything that came his way which would be of interest to them. We do not know exactly what information he passed; we do know, however, to what information he had access by virtue of his duties. There is no doubt that British interests were seriously damaged by his activities. But it is unlikely that British military operations or British lives were put at risk. Further, the story that he jeopardised the lives of secret agents in the Netherlands is without foundation; he was never in the Special Operations Executive.[24]

My first meeting with Blunt on the morning of 27 May 1981 proved to be a strange encounter, with the disgraced art historian tentatively probing to find out the limits of my knowledge. A month earlier, I had flown to Rome to interview John Cairncross, so I had some understanding of the network known as the Cambridge Five. Over a long lunch in the Hotel Hassler's rooftop restaurant, Cairncross had revealed that he had confessed to MI5 during an interview conducted in Cleveland, Ohio in February 1964. More recently, Cairncross had been tracked down by Barrie Penrose of the *Sunday Times* and had admitted having spied for the NKVD during the war. This information was inserted into a postscript in *MI5: British Security Service Operations 1909–45*, which was intended to deal with the then-hot topic of Soviet penetration of the wartime (and post-war) British intelligence community. Having been advised not to return to England, Cairncross had been quite forthcoming about stealing secrets from Bletchley Park and from his subsequent post in MI6's Section V. Cairncross claimed that he had not known Philby was a spy, even when they had worked in the same Section V office in St Albans, although he had always suspected that Blunt had been the person who had talent-spotted him at Trinity College, Cambridge. He had disliked Blunt, but it had been James Klugmann who had invited him to drop his Communist Party membership and work for Moscow. Aware that I had recently spoken to Cairncross, Blunt agreed to talk.

At my second meeting with Blunt the following week, we discussed how the dominos had fallen after the defection of Guy Burgess and Donald Maclean in May 1951. Cairncross had resigned from his post in the Ministry of Supply in the same year, after he had been compromised by an indiscreet, handwritten letter found in a suitcase abandoned under the bed in Burgess's flat. This item had been traced to Cairncross, who had been confronted but allowed to resign. Penrose had been tipped off to the resignation of an espionage suspect and had scrutinised the *Civil Service Yearbook* to produce Cairncross's name. During our conversations, Blunt mentioned another Soviet spy, a source he had recruited and run personally, who had served in MI14, the wartime German order-of-battle unit. Eventually, he identified his agent as Leo Long, another Cambridge graduate, but by the time Blunt gave up the name there was insufficient time to research his case and find him.

After my initial skirmishing with Blunt, I felt almost physically unwell at his cold-blooded attitude to his treachery, which, as he admitted, had resulted in the death of at least one British source in Moscow. He seemed unaffected by the betrayal and adopted the position of a ruthless intelligence professional who would be diligent and loyal… for as long as it was expedient to remain so. He saw himself as the absolute professional, now willing to assist the Security Service after having served the KGB with the same detachment.

Blunt explained that he had told his MI5 contact about my request for an interview, and the officer concerned had raised no objection but had asked that I should telephone him in Tasmania. This was my introduction to Peter Wright, with whom Blunt was on the friendliest of terms. Accordingly, I called Wright and agreed that I would report to him everything Blunt told me. We would have many conversations, and at least some of these were discussed with the Security Service in London, with whom he was in regular contact.

Wright made no comment about Leo Long and would not explain why, if Blunt had been the only spy to receive immunity from prosecution as Thatcher had asserted in November 1979, Long was still at liberty in north London, having retired from a career in the film industry? These and other issues that emerged from my exchanges with Blunt would have to wait, as I was under pressure from The Bodley Head to return the proofs and meet the agreed publication date. My solution was to complete the postscript as best I could but leave some unexploded bombs for future detonation. One would be Leo Long, to whom I concealed a message in the book. My convoluted signal, intended to indicate to Long that I knew his name, read:

> The second, another Cambridge CPGB member who had 'gone underground', admitted having once been a Soviet agent but assured MI5 that he had long since abandoned Marxism. He had held a sensitive post in military intelligence during the war but had long since ceased to have access to secrets.[25]

The insertion of these ostensibly clumsily phrased sentences had the intended effect, and when the *Sunday Times* called on him on publication day, he answered the door... with a copy of the book in his hand. He made no denial and said he had been expecting this moment for years. He asked only that he should be given time to break the news to his wife, who was unwell and knew nothing of her husband's past espionage.

At a press conference hastily called at the Hilton Hotel in Park Lane, Long confirmed he had been recruited by Blunt and revealed that he had been assured that he would not be prosecuted. This disclosure caused a political storm, and Thatcher addressed the issue on 9 November 1981:

> In 1964, Leonard Henry Long was named to the Security Service by Mr. Michael Whitney Straight, the United States citizen who

identified Mr. Anthony Blunt, as someone else whom Mr. Blunt might have attempted to recruit as an agent for the Russian Intelligence Service. When Mr. Blunt made his confession in April 1964, he admitted to having recruited Mr. Long before the war and controlled him during it.

Mr. Long was then seen by the Security Service. He asked for immunity from prosecution; this was refused, but he was told that he was not likely to be prosecuted if he co-operated in the Security Service's inquiries. He then made a detailed confession.

Mr. Long was an undergraduate at Trinity College, Cambridge, and a member of the Communist Party, before the Second World War. While at Cambridge, he was recruited by Anthony Blunt as a potential Soviet agent. From 1940 to 1944 he served in MI 14, the section of the War Office responsible for analysing German military intentions. He had access to analyses based on intelligence derived from secret sources, but not to the sources themselves. He passed information obtained from these analyses to Anthony Blunt, knowing that Mr. Blunt would pass them to the Russians. He has said, and there is no reason to disbelieve, that he passed information obtained from official documents but not the documents (or copies of the documents) themselves, and that he passed all his information to Mr. Blunt, who was his controller.

After the war, from 1945 until his contract expired in 1952, Mr. Long was an intelligence officer in the Control Commission in Germany. He has all along said that he did not pass information to the Russians during this period. He left the public service in 1952, and has had no access to classified information since then.

Neither the Attorney General nor the Director of Public Prosecutions was consulted before Mr. Long was interviewed in 1964.

It has to be remembered that he had been out of the public service for twelve years; that, in the wake of Mr. Blunt's confession, the Security Service's main concern was to obtain as much information as it could about other possible spies, and in particular about any that might still be in the public service and have access to classified information; and that Mr. Long could not have been expected to co-operate in the Security Service's inquiries if he had believed that he was likely to be prosecuted if he did so.

It is true that a confession obtained as a result of the sort of indication given to Mr. Long would be inadmissible as evidence for the prosecution in court; but the Security Service did not have any other evidence which could be used against him and which would be likely to secure a conviction. There was thus a good deal to gain and little to lose from obtaining Mr. Long's co-operation in the way that was done.

As my right hon. and learned Friend the Attorney-General told the House in the debate on 21 November 1979, the only person who has been granted immunity from prosecution if he confessed to espionage activities and co-operated in the Security Service's inquiries is Mr. Blunt. I am aware of only one case other than that of Mr. Long since the beginning of 1964 (records are not available before that) in which someone suspected of espionage offences was or may have been induced to make a confession by an indication that he was unlikely to be prosecuted if he co-operated in the Security Service's inquiries. My right hon. and learned Friend the Attorney-General referred to this matter in his reply of 20 November 1979.

I am satisfied that the present procedures of the Security Service would prevent anything of the sort happening today without the knowledge of the prosecution authorities. In my speech in the House on 21 November 1979 I set out in some detail the procedures for applying the principles governing the relationships between the Security Service and Ministers.

I can assure the House that a person suspected of an espionage offence would not now be interviewed by the Security Service on the basis that he need not fear prosecution unless the case had first been referred to the Attorney-General and permission had been given for the interview to be conducted on that basis.

In the wake of Mr. Long's public admission of his treachery, a number of people are being named in the press as having been suspected of being involved in espionage activities or as having been interviewed in the course of the Security Service's inquiries. I believe that we have to be very careful to avoid the risk of creating a climate of guilt by association. The contacts of those who are known to have acted as agents of the Russian Intelligence Service have been extensively and exhaustively investigated; and many people have been interviewed over the years.

As I said in my statement in the House on 26 March, the fact that somebody has been the subject of investigation or has been interviewed does not necessarily or even generally mean that he has been positively suspected. Many people have been investigated simply in order to eliminate them from the inquiry. Others have been interviewed not because they themselves were suspected but for any information they might be able to give about those who were.

I felt able to make a statement about Mr. Blunt because his guilt was known and admitted, and because there was no question of

> prosecuting him. I have been able to give this answer today about Mr. Long because he has publicly admitted his guilt.
>
> As a general rule, however, it would in my view be totally wrong for me, under cover of Parliamentary privilege, to name people who were suspected but against whom the evidence available was not sufficient to justify a prosecution; and it would be no less wrong for me to name people who were interviewed in the course of the Security Service's inquiries, when to do so might be held to suggest, often erroneously, that they had themselves been suspected. I do not therefore propose to comment on, either to confirm or deny, the stories which have appeared in the press recently.
>
> Nor have I seen anything in those stories which in my judgement calls for a new inquiry into the events of the past, which have been very thoroughly investigated. None of those named or implicated in recent allegations is still in the public service, and most of them have long since retired or died. We need to concern ourselves with the future, and with making sure that the arrangements for guarding against penetration are as good as they possibly can be. That is the purpose of the review which the Security Commission are now conducting.[26]

A week earlier, on 2 November 1981, Long had participated in a television interview with the BBC's Tom Mangold and acknowledged his past commitment to communism and his decision to pass classified information to Blunt. He also admitted that he had confessed to MI5 in 1964, after he had been exposed by Blunt, but he lied when he denied having continued to spy after the war when he was deputy director of the British Control Commission for Germany's intelligence division.

One of Blunt's remarks seemed to have had quite an impact on Wright. The art historian had recalled that in late 1944 he had been offered a permanent post in MI5 but instead had decided to return to academic life. Anticipating resistance to this plan from the Soviets, he had tried to enlist Guy Burgess's support but had been astonished when his NKVD contact had not even attempted to dissuade him. Blunt, who had joined the Courtauld Institute the following year, concluded that the Russians must have had another source in the Security Service, with at least his seniority and access. It was a chilling thought, especially when one considered that from April 1943, Blunt had enjoyed unrestricted access to everything so that he could draft MI5's monthly report to the Prime Minister.

The possibility that MI5 might have misled the Prime Minister in 1979 when John Jones, the deputy director general, had drafted her somewhat flawed statement on Blunt sparked a feeding frenzy in Fleet Street, where journalists were eager to find yet more traitors.

In retrospect, one can see that Thatcher's statement in November 1979 had a profound effect on the public's attitude to the security authorities. It had triggered widespread suspicion that there had been relief in Whitehall when Philby had fled to the Soviet Union in 1963 and suspicion that the offer of immunity to Blunt the following year was part of a pattern of behaviour which had also benefitted Cairncross and Long. Indeed, some in the intelligence community became convinced that this unseemly record might be something more sinister than sheer expediency.

My own role in exposing Long went largely unnoticed, but I took care to consult my editor, Venetia Pollock, who had been hired by my publishers to knock my manuscript into shape. I quickly learned that her sister was married to a senior MI6 officer, Michael Wrigley, who had been one of that organisation's legendary 'robber barons', running high-risk operations across East Asia from his station in Bangkok. I would later learn that Venetia had also edited Fred Winterbotham's *The Ultra Secret*, which had received MI6's unofficial blessing. My impression was that if I kept 'the Friends' informed, I would avoid unpleasant surprises.

CHAPTER IV

MI5 AND *A MATTER OF TRUST*

The call had come from my publisher at The Bodley Head, Barney Blackley. He had been approached – via one of his old schoolfriends Stephen de Mowbray, who had served in MI6 – by a recently retired MI5 officer who wanted to talk to me. The name he used initially was 'Miller', but within a few minutes of talking to him at his flat in Belgravia, I knew who he was: a molehunter who had devoted much of his career to the investigation of suspected Soviet spies. To meet Arthur Martin, as I did for the first time on 1 December 1981, and discuss the Blunt case with someone who could truly be described as an authority was a tremendous experience and served to fill many of the gaps left in my discussions with Anthony Blunt and Peter Wright.

Martin's name had been disclosed publicly in 1968 by Philby, who had recognised the molehunter as a shrewd and dangerous adversary.[1] He was married to Joan, who had been Dick White's secretary and sat in on our first meeting. Although crippled with painful arthritis in her hands, her prodigious memory was unimpaired, and she would occasionally intervene in our discussion to add some point of detail. Martin was impressed by some of the information I had extracted from Blunt about his Soviet handlers and accelerated a scheme that he had been formulating for some months, in order to get to the bottom of the issue of hostile penetration of the Security Service. His plan was to extract a deathbed confession from the sole remaining suspected Soviet mole, Graham Mitchell, who had retired as MI5's deputy director general in 1963.

As Martin filled me in about Mitchell's background – a pre-war journalist on the *Illustrated London News*, who had specialised in counter-subversion, studying fascist political extremists, and had been promoted to head the counter-espionage branch with absolutely no experience of that particular field – I began to grasp the scale of the challenge that so burdened Martin. Mitchell's wife was the sister of James Robertson, the senior MI5 case officer who had supervised the investigation of Donald Maclean.

Mitchell may not have had any first-hand knowledge of counter-intelligence but he knew plenty about how the Security Service worked and as deputy director general had chaired the weekly session to assign the 'Watcher' section its targets. He had also undergone the counter-surveillance course and habitually wore slightly tinted spectacles, which could be used as a mirror to detect anyone following. In other words, Mitchell was never going to be caught by conventional techniques but might succumb to an element of social pressure.

Martin believed that I had a good chance of persuading Mitchell to incriminate himself in return for my promise not to tell anyone until after his death, an event that Martin had been told was not far off. Martin appeared to assume that he was himself exempt from my pledge and that I would report everything to him. Naturally, Martin accepted that if I was willing to undertake the task and was to be deployed against Mitchell, I would require a good understanding of all the cases he had handled.

My initiation into the detail of Blunt's treachery had been conducted by Richard Deacon, who had always been suspicious of the art historian's dubious connections with Guy Burgess and Kim Philby. He had instructed me to mention Blunt's name to Dick White to see what kind of a reaction it caused, apparently certain that the respected academic, who had been Surveyor of the Queen's Pictures, had also been a Soviet spy. Having examined Blunt's unsurpassed career, and heard his name mentioned as one of the more distinguished wartime members of the Security Service, I simply could not reconcile his good name with that of a traitor. The definitive point, in my assessment, was that Blunt had been knighted in 1956, five years after the defections of Burgess and Maclean. Surely, I had reasoned, if Deacon was right and Blunt had been mixed up in that episode, the establishment would have closed ranks to prevent him receiving the honour? No British government would have connived in such a travesty, so either Deacon's chronology was wrong or he had chosen the wrong person.

I had been terribly reluctant even to raise the topic of Soviet penetration of the Security Service to White. The idea, at that time, was on the face of it quite ludicrous. It was not just a sensitive subject, but I thought it was probably close to insulting. Thus, I had waited right until the end of my first interview with White, held at his home in May 1978, to mention Blunt's name. I had eased the conversation around to it gently by broaching the subject of Soviet espionage and then putting it into the context of hostile penetration of MI5. I had expected White to erupt in fury, but instead he asked me calmly whom I had in mind. My first response was to offer the name of Graham Mitchell, a senior officer whose early retirement had caused some speculation within the intelligence community. Instead of protesting Mitchell's innocence, White thought long and hard, presumably trying to assess the depth of my knowledge, which he may have miscalculated as being rather less superficial than it was, and then gave a classically convoluted Whitehall reply: 'I do not know Mitchell to have been anything other than a loyal servant of his country.' This was an astonishing response. I had suggested the name of a former deputy director general of the Security Service, someone who had spent twenty-five years working either for or with White, as a possible mole. Yet, instead of descending into justifiable rage, he had given Mitchell a less-than-fulsome endorsement and had then asked if I had any other candidates in mind. Recognising that there must be substance to Deacon's belief that the Soviets had planted a spy into MI5 at a senior level, I gave Blunt's name. Once again, White thought for a few moments and then said, 'That, of course, is quite different.'

According to my interpretation of these proceedings, White had given very lukewarm support for Mitchell and had then as good as condemned Blunt as a Soviet spy. I was mystified and perplexed. Why should White seek to mislead me and was there any possibility that he might be telling the truth?

These exchanges had occurred eighteen months before Thatcher's statement in the Commons in November 1979, in which she described how Blunt had admitted his espionage on behalf of the Soviets to MI5 in April 1964 and how he was to be stripped of his knighthood. Although I reported White's strange remarks to Deacon, who had been working along parallel lines to the radio journalist Andrew Boyle, it had not been until I heard the Prime Minister's words over the news bulletin that I could accept that White, for whatever motive, had been telling the truth about Blunt.[2] In that case, I pondered, how should I judge his damning comments about Mitchell?

The bombshell presented by Martin was just as explosive. He told me that in his estimation, Mitchell had been working for the Soviets over a long period. He had been unable to prove the case conclusively, and in fact, his career had suffered because of the reluctance of some of his colleagues to accept his unpalatable verdict. Nevertheless, he remained convinced, apparently as were the majority of the other professionals who had studied the case, that Mitchell was the culprit. Martin's thesis rested on two central themes. One was that there were a number of incidents that could only be explained in terms of Soviet penetration of MI5 at a high level up to around mid-1963 and the second was that of the candidates available, Mitchell remained easily the best suspect. My objective, Martin suggested, was to obtain a confession from Mitchell.

The case made by Martin for Soviet penetration of MI5 was utterly compelling and was based on the so-called 'serials' developed by the joint MI5–MI6 committee of experienced molehunters assembled to study the problem. Between 1947 and the recruitment of Oleg Lyalin in 1971, MI5 failed to attract a single Soviet intelligence defector. Of those that went to the US, all reported that the British services had been heavily penetrated, and Yuriy Rastvorov, who had switched sides in Tokyo in 1954, had given harrowing anecdotal evidence of the story of a colleague who had made contact with MI6 in Moscow but soon afterwards had been entrapped by

KGB officers masquerading as MI6 personnel. Without doubt, the tentative approach had been betrayed in sufficient time for the KGB to take the appropriate countermeasures. The tale was chillingly reminiscent of the fate of Konstantin Volkov in 1945, whose intention to defect in Turkey with vital information had been reported to Moscow by Philby. Volkov had last been seen being bundled aboard a Soviet aircraft, only days before Philby had arrived to negotiate his defection.

According to Martin's catalogue of mishaps, MI5 had also failed to run any successful double-agent operations against the KGB. Almost uncannily, the KGB had backed off every time a case started to develop, almost as if the Soviets knew instinctively that the game was afoot. How could the London *rezidentura* have acquired such clairvoyancy? Even worse, between 1945 and 1973, MI5 did not catch a single spy on its own initiative. In almost every case, the original tip had come from a defector who had been received by the CIA. This was true of Alan Nunn May in 1946, compromised by Igor Gouzenko; Klaus Fuchs, identified in 1949 by VENONA; John Vassall, identified by Anatoliy Golitsyn in 1961; Harry Houghton, Ethel Gee and Gordon Lonsdale, compromised by Michal Goleniewski in 1961; and Douglas Britten, denounced by a long-term FBI source inside the Soviet Main Intelligence Directorate (GRU), Dmitri Polyakov, in 1968. The single exception was the arrest of William Marshall, who had been caught by MI5 in 1952 without the benefit of a tip from a defector. However, close analysis of the case revealed that Marshall had been unlucky in that he had been spotted by chance during a surveillance operation on a known KGB officer in London. His meeting with Marshall in a suburban park had been observed, and when questioned, the young radio operator, employed by the Diplomatic Wireless Service, admitted that he had succumbed to a KGB recruitment pitch. In other words, the statistics showed that MI5 had failed in its primary function, that of counter-espionage.

Martin believed that this appalling record of disaster was symptomatic of penetration, and the more he looked, the more persuaded he became that sheer bad luck and coincidence could not account for so many catastrophes. Alan Nunn May had avoided attending three meetings arranged for him in London in October 1945, where MI5 had intended to trap the scientist and his Soviet contact and under interrogation, he admitted he had been warned to stay away. Who had tipped him off? May claimed he had no idea who had alerted him. In 1951, John Cairncross had evaded MI5's surveillance on a west London tube station where he had been supposed to rendezvous with Yuri Modin, a member of the KGB *rezidentura*. Years later, Cairncross had confirmed to Martin when he interrogated him in America that he too had been warned that he had come under suspicion and should break off contact.

When Martin had looked at the wider picture, it showed a disturbing trend. The KGB was always one step ahead of the molehunters, and the big fish always seemed to escape. Burgess and Maclean had made good their exfiltration over a weekend in May 1951, hours before Maclean had been scheduled for a hostile interrogation. Much the same thing had happened with Philby, who had been confronted in Beirut, having accepted immunity from prosecution, and then simply disappeared to Moscow, leaving behind a fabricated confession that, upon close scrutiny, turned out to be entirely deceptive. Even though Blunt had finally confessed to Martin in April 1964, his admissions had, with the benefit of hindsight, seemed less than comprehensive. Had all of this been orchestrated by the KGB? Martin had concentrated on the Cambridge Five network but was aware that the CPGB had been equally active at Oxford, yet MI5 had never made any headway in researching the candidates for recruitment who might have been members of an Oxford spy-ring.

Of course, MI5 had been handicapped by its lack of any formal investigatory powers, its inability to pull in members of the public for questioning and the need to meet a very high standard of proof before even contemplating a criminal prosecution. Even when there appeared to be overwhelming evidence of espionage, as happened with the physicist Dr Giuseppe Martelli who was acquitted in 1965, the difficulties in bringing a case to trial were substantial. A confession, as supplied by Alan Nunn May, Klaus Fuchs, John Vassall and George Blake, was almost essential, while repeated denials left MI5 impotent. Martin and Wright had pursued dozens of suspected spies, including Bernard and Peter Floud, Christopher Hill, Jenifer Hart, James Klugmann, Bob Stewart and Edith Tudor-Hart, but none had cooperated. Some suspects, including Ursula Kuczynski, Wolfgang zu Putlitz and Bruno Pontecorvo, had simply left the country to live abroad, out of jurisdiction and far from MI5's reach. But was this a manifestation of incompetence, or an occupational hazard or perhaps a pattern of something much more sinister?

One of the reasons Martin and Wright became convinced of the existence of high-level penetration of the Security Service was the admission made by Blunt that when he had told his Soviet controllers he intended to leave MI5 in 1945, they had made no effort to persuade him to remain. Blunt then had been a talented, respected professional closely associated with Guy Liddell, the most experienced man in the organisation who was an obvious candidate to become a post-war director general. Blunt too was probably destined for the top, and he certainly had exploited his almost-unrestricted access to agents, files and office personnel. So why had the Russians been so relaxed about the departure of their star agent inside MI5? Martin and Wright concluded there was only one logical explanation: the Soviets must have had someone else in the organisation who enjoyed equally good access as Blunt. On this basis, the molehunters narrowed the field to three prime candidates, all senior officers: Malcolm Cumming, Roger Hollis and Graham Mitchell.

While on the one hand it seemed unthinkable that someone at director level could be a traitor, it was equally true that the Soviets had succeeded in penetrating MI6 at a high level. Quite apart from Philby and Blake, MI6 had purged Andrew King and Donald Prater, both former communists who had failed to disclose their youthful adherence to the CPGB. If, as was known, covert communists had succeeded in penetrating every corner of Whitehall, why had there been only a single case, apart from Blunt, of a CPGB member worming their way into MI5? In that sole example, Ray Milne, a secretary employed in the registry, had been detected through an indiscretion caught by the technical surveillance on the CPGB headquarters in King Street in 1941, and she had been fired but not prosecuted. Obviously, MI5 would have been a significant target for the Soviets, so it was reasonable to assume that some penetration had taken place, but none had been recorded.

Of the trio of Cumming, Hollis and Mitchell, the molehunters eliminated Cumming almost instantly. He qualified as a candidate only on the grounds that he had sufficient access, but in every other respect, as a former Rifle Brigade officer, he failed to fit the profile of an ideologically motivated spy. In contrast, both Hollis and Mitchell had traits that could have marked them as university-recruited agents, and much effort was expended on detecting any clues to their disloyalty. In the end, the verdict was inconclusive. Ever the bureaucrat, Hollis had no explanation for the shortcomings of his organisation while he had been director general, and he seemed an improbable spy, despite his long-term affair with his secretary and his rather exotic pre-war experiences in Shanghai and Moscow, about which he was always reticent.

Mitchell, on the other hand, had known Burgess well, was exceptionally bright, played world-class correspondence chess and never offered an explanation for his request for early retirement as deputy director general in September 1963, just as he had come under close scrutiny. While Hollis was known to have blocked MI5's investigations into some potentially embarrassing cases, such as the alternative spy in the Admiralty, he had always been very conscious of political sensibilities and very aware of his service's long-term interests within Whitehall. But for Mitchell, there were no convenient excuses. He had discouraged further research on VENONA, arguably the best and most reliable access into the NKVD's operations, and had supervised counter-espionage over a period when MI5 failed to entrap a single Soviet spy. Damningly, Mitchell had also overseen the final drafting of the notorious 1955 Burgess and Maclean White Paper, which contained so many half-truths, deceptions and outright lies that it was hard to imagine it could have been written by anyone other than a fully-fledged traitor.

Martin was a formidable counter-intelligence officer, who had started his career as, according to him, 'the world's worst intercept operator', assigned to a special wireless group in North Africa monitoring enemy radio traffic. At the end of the war, having been indoctrinated into the secrets of signals intelligence, he had transferred from the Royal Corps of Signals to GCHQ and in 1947 had been posted to MI5 headquarters as the custodian of the 'Y Box Files', a special compartmented registry which handled the VENONA material. He had been the guardian of the NKVD telegrams which compromised Klaus Fuchs and had acted as the liaison link between the MI5 case officers chasing up leads in the HOMER investigation into Maclean, and the highly classified vault at GCHQ's office.

Anxious to keep the VENONA secret as tightly held as possible and aware that Martin was indispensable to the molehunt for the spy codenamed HOMER, MI5 arranged for Martin to transfer permanently onto its staff, where he would remain for the next sixteen years. In December 1951, he was tasked to collate the evidence against Philby, which was presented effectively by Helenus Milmo in a confrontation that left Philby unable to defend himself or his first wife, Litzi. Martin's assiduous research and highly professional brief effectively demolished Philby, and no one present at the interrogation was left in any doubt about Philby's guilt or Litzi's pre-war role as a Communist International courier. In a theatrical moment reminiscent of Perry Mason, Milmo had cross-examined Philby about the couple's supposed abject penury while living in London in 1935 and had been told that they had lived on his father's charity. Milmo had then tossed Litzi's British passport onto the table and demanded an explanation for the many border stamps it contained, indicating her frequent travel across the Continent. Philby was rendered silent in what was interpreted as an admission of guilt.

When the Malayan Emergency was declared, exposing serious deficiencies in the local security apparatus, Martin was selected in 1954 first to conduct a review of the Special Branch there and then, as the security liaison officer in Kuala Lumpur, to supervise a wholesale restructuring of the counter-insurgency intelligence scene. Upon his return to London in 1958, as part of MI5's legendary 'Malaya Mafia', Martin continued his pursuit of Soviet assets who were thought to have burrowed deep into Whitehall. When Martin needed technical support during the PETERS inquiry into Mitchell in 1963, he was assigned a scientific adviser, Peter Wright, who hitherto had not been indoctrinated into such delicate operations. During his MI5 career, Martin would extract confessions from Cairncross, Michael Straight, Leo Long and Blunt. It was only after he had negotiated Blunt's immunity from prosecution and after his focus on 'office penetration' that he would be considered disruptive and be exchanged for an MI6 officer, Terence Lecky. As MI5's ace molehunter, Martin had ruffled more than a few feathers.

Martin was undeterred by his enforced transfer to MI6 and subsequent retirement. While he worked as a House of Commons clerk, Martin recruited me to pursue Mitchell, who was in failing health but still living at his family home in Chobham, where he would die in November 1984. The original investigation, codenamed PETERS, had lapsed, and the inquiry into Hollis, known as DRAT, had also run into the sand. Martin remained determined to get at the truth and agreed to adopt me as a pupil in return for my commitment to offer Mitchell the opportunity to make a deathbed confession. The result was months of briefing to acquaint me with all the evidence and with the case histories of all the relevant examples of Soviet espionage. We met regularly on neutral territory in Farringdon, midway between our respective homes in the country, and the notes taken by me during this period became the basis of my second volume of MI5's history, *A Matter of Trust*, tracing the course of the organisation between 1945 and 1972. I did not tell Martin that I intended to write a book based on his briefings, but I would have if he had asked. He certainly knew that I was taking prodigious notes, and the first half of each session usually involved clearing up any issues that had arisen when I had, as homework, written up my version of each case. After three months of intensive tutoring, I asked my literary agent to find a suitable publisher for the book I planned and informed the D-Notice secretary that I intended to deliver an advance copy of the manuscript, which was a sequel to *MI5: 1909–45* and would cover the post-war era.

Martin's ambition to finally close the PETERS file fell apart in April 1982 when, entirely without warning, I was served at home one evening with an injunction obtained by the Attorney General alleging 'breach of confidence'. The document alleged that the author had received highly classified information from an unnamed individual who had not been authorised to disclose it, and this was clearly a reference to the briefings given by Martin. Far from acting on behalf of MI6 or MI5, Martin had been freelancing, or so it was alleged in the affidavit served on behalf of the Crown in support of the High Court order preventing me from taking *any* step to further the publication of *A Matter of Trust*. Attached to the injunction was a penal clause, authorised by a judge, which warned that I would be subject to immediate imprisonment for contempt if I did anything to further the manuscript's publication. To obtain this additional, draconian measure, the attorney had filed an affidavit which certified that the contents of the book were true, were highly classified, had never been disclosed previously and would inflict immense damage if made public.

Luckily, a complete draft of the manuscript was already in the hands of an American publisher, Stein and Day, and the threat of an unexpurgated version being released in the US, outside the jurisdiction of the High Court, prompted MI5's legal adviser Bernard Sheldon to open negotiations at a meeting convened at the Westminster chambers of the Treasury solicitor, Sir John Bailey.

It had been the maverick New York publisher Sol Stein who had bought the North American rights to *A Matter of Trust*, and as soon as he received a copy of the injunction, he saw an opportunity to rush out the book with a new title, *The Circus: MI5 1945–72*. Far from being deterred by the government's unexpected intervention, Stein saw the entire exercise as a marketing strategy that would probably be strengthened if the author wound up in a prison cell. When I suggested that the blatant misuse of the title *The Circus* might annoy John le Carré, Stein was delighted at the prospect of further controversy that would generate further media interest… and sales.

The impasse required a settlement, and Sheldon found himself under a deadline threatened by Stein, who claimed that he was ready to print and distribute without delay. Thus, MI5's position, initially as the aggressor, turned into a disadvantage, with the book being given even greater notoriety and credibility. The compromise offer was that in return for a formal consent to proceed with publication in New York, the author agreed to use his best endeavours to delete certain sensitive passages from the text in the US. Grudgingly accepting this settlement, Stein had decorated the dustjacket of his edition with an extract from the Attorney General's affidavit, complete with facsimile seal, confirming the sensitivity and accuracy of the information contained in the book. 'What better endorsement of authenticity could an author wish for?' asked a delighted Stein. Under the terms of the agreement, the codename VENONA would be replaced by 'U-traffic' and Peter Wright's name would be changed to 'Peter W'.

In retrospect, these two items seem faintly ridiculous, but Sheldon insisted that VENONA was still top secret, and so was the identity of the MI5 officer who had handled Blunt since his confession in 1964. When I protested that Wright had told me that he had already written an account of his MI5 career and had entrusted it to a bank vault, Sheldon insisted that this was quite impossible, stating that Wright was utterly loyal to 'the office' and would never contemplate behaving in the way I had described.

The publication of *A Matter of Trust* put to rest any remaining chance of settling the issue of whether Mitchell had been a spy, but a few years later, when Oleg Gordievsky defected to the UK in 1985, orthodoxy dictated that there never had been a high-level traitor inside MI5. As a senior officer of the Third Department of the KGB's First Chief Directorate, and fully briefed on past operations in Britain, Gordievsky was said to have averred that he had never come across anything to support the proposition that MI5 had suffered penetration after Blunt's departure from MI5 in 1945. This view was reinforced seven years later when the KGB's archivist Vasili Mitrokhin defected with several suitcases of documents copied from the KGB's records, none of which indicated the existence of a spy inside the Security Service. But does the necessarily incomplete knowledge of Gordievsky and Mitrokhin mean that Martin and Wright had been deluded? Only time will tell.

CHAPTER V

THE HUNT FOR GARBO

Few historians, politicians or military commentators would dispute that one of the greatest gambles of the twentieth century was the decision taken by President Roosevelt and Winston Churchill to begin the liberation of France in the summer of 1944 with an Allied landing in Normandy, rather than in Calais. The element of risk was multiplied because the logical, most direct route to the heart of Nazi Germany was through the Pas-de-Calais where several ports were located that could be captured, which would enhance the supply of materiel to the combat zone. Orthodoxy dictated that taking the shortest route across the Channel increased the likelihood of delivering the troops in good fighting condition and offered the greatest opportunity to maximise air superiority, with ground-attack aircraft to support the troops. The enemy's military analysts also understood this and were agreed that the Allies would opt for the twenty-three miles between east Kent and the French coast.

Significantly, the German strategists included in their deliberations a factor that, as yet, had not been appreciated in London. The Wehrmacht High Command's intelligence staff, based at the

Château de La Roche-Guyon, knew about Hitler's 'vengeance weapon', the V-1 rocket, with which he intended to bombard London. The planned onslaught – an attack of up to a thousand buzz bombs a day, each armed with a warhead of 850 kilos of high explosive – had the political objective of flattening the capital and thereby creating a political crisis for the British government. The development programme was intended to become operational in October 1943, but Allied air-raids that focused on the assembly plants in Germany and the launch sites in France delayed the offensive until the middle of June 1944. Due to the V-1's limited range of 160 miles, the distinctive catapults, which in Allied aerial reconnaissance imagery resembled a 160-foot ski pointed at London, were concentrated in the Pas-de-Calais region. Accordingly, having been persuaded by their own propaganda, Field Marshal Erwin Rommel's advisers had attached great weight to the military and political importance of this particular part of the French coastline and adhered to the mistaken belief that Churchill's war Cabinet would demand that attacking the area should be a top priority.

The British planners, on the other hand, had only a limited grasp of the doodlebug threat and had instead been preoccupied with innovating some ingenious solutions to the difficulty of landing on the Normandy beaches, building two prefabricated harbours to be floated across the Channel and creating an underwater fuel pipeline to connect a pumping station at Shanklin on the Isle of Wight to a distribution terminal at Querqueville. Two harbours, codenamed MULBERRY, would be constructed off GOLD and OMAHA beaches, and the PLUTO fuel link obviated the need for dozens of tankers to deliver their cargoes across a stretch of sea that was likely to be infested with U-boats and minefields.

The decision to opt for Normandy had been taken at the QUADRANT meeting in Quebec in August 1943 on the advice of Lieutenant General Freddie Morgan, who had become an advocate of a concept – then still in its infancy – known as strategic deception.

The principle behind the objective of misleading the enemy about Allied strengths and intentions had been laboratory tested in the Mediterranean theatre by imaginative staff officer Colonel Dudley Clarke, who had been authorised by his commander-in-chief, General Archie Wavell, to exaggerate the strength and deployment of forces across the Middle East and to distract the Axis from Allied priorities. Initially, Clarke and his small staff, grandly entitled 'A' Force, employed rather primitive methods such as false radio signals to convey the deception. However, the arrival of an established MI6 double agent codenamed CHEESE in Cairo in July 1941 completely changed the situation and gave Clarke a conduit through which he could send his bogus information straight to a clandestine Abwehr receiving station in Bari. CHEESE was actually an Italian Jew named Renato Levi who held a British passport and had acted for the Service de Renseignements as a double agent prior to the occupation of Paris in 1940. Known to his Abwehr controller as ROBERTO, Levi was a playboy whose mother was a celebrated Italian actress, and whose father was a well-known boat builder and the owner of a large shipyard in India. Levi's mission, assigned by his German handler Kurt Knabe, was to travel to Egypt and recruit a spy-ring to replace the networks that had collapsed in May 1940 after a policy of internment of enemy aliens was introduced by the British authorities in Cairo.

Clarke embraced CHEESE but initially his British case officer, *The Spectator* critic and West End impresario Evan Simpson, was sceptical. This is reflected by his choice of pseudonym for the radio operator for the CHEESE network, who was described as 'a Russian of Syrian extraction' named Paul Nicossof ('pull knickers off'). Astonishingly, the Abwehr asked no more about Nicossof. On the rare occasions the Abwehr complained about some information turning out to be inaccurate, CHEESE responded that unless he was supplied with more money to fund his organisation, he could not afford to pay top level sources. CHEESE also acquired a fiery Cretan girlfriend, and gradually the CHEESE network expanded, feeding 'A' Force's falsehoods directly to the Abwehr. Specifically, Clarke invented non-existent military units, such as the 15th Armoured Division and the 7th Infantry Division, exaggerated the strengths of genuine formations and reported that the 9th Army, which was actually no greater than a corps, had been transferred to Syria.

Under normal circumstances, it is generally quite difficult to make a valid judgement about the success of a deception campaign, but the opportunity presented itself in August 1942 when commandos participating in the ill-fated raid on Dieppe plundered the town's military headquarters and recovered a classified handbook, *Das Britische Kriegsheer*, which was a recently circulated assessment of the entire British order-of-battle. Much to the delight of the deception planners, the book listed several notional divisions and brigades including Clarke's favourite, the elite parachute force 1st Special Air Service Brigade, which had existed only in his imagination. The CHEESE network would score numerous successes, such as providing cover for the convoy that broke the Axis siege of Malta, and it was responsible for the loss of German U-boat *U-372*, sunk off Haifa as it tried to deliver a courier carrying funds for the network.

The success in Cairo, subsequently corroborated by more captured enemy documents as the Allies moved into Italy, set the scene for BODYGUARD, the overall scheme that would mislead the German High Command in Europe over the place and date of the D-Day assault. Sub-components of BODYGUARD were FORTITUDE NORTH and FORTITUDE SOUTH. The former was intended to promote the idea of an amphibious attack on Norway and the latter to provide the enemy with confirmation of its opinion that the main D-Day landings would take place in the Pas-de-Calais.

In retrospect, it's safe to say that the issues at stake over D-Day were truly momentous. Some of the planners were burdened with the thought that if the operation failed and the Allies suffered a defeat on the beaches, the outcome predicted by Rommel and Hitler, the consequences would be grave indeed. It would be impossible to launch a second invasion later in the summer, and that implied that the war would continue for at least a further two years. That amount of time would allow the Wehrmacht to switch troops and reinforce the Russian front and perhaps give the opportunity to Berlin to develop its new wonder weapons, such as the Me 262 jet fighter, the Henschel guided missile and perhaps a 'dirty' uranium warhead for the V-2 ballistic missile.

Taking such conjecture a step further, it is unlikely that, following a tremendous victory in Normandy, there would have been any appetite in the High Command to make an attempt on Hitler's life on 20 July 1944. If the war had dragged on into 1947, the possibilities would have been grim indeed. In short, there was a lot riding on the Battle of Normandy.

Just as Clarke had relied largely upon CHEESE to convey the deception material to the Abwehr, his deputy, Colonel Noel Wild, was posted to Norfolk House in London to exploit MI5's double agents. Several were in communication with their apparently unsuspecting handlers, usually through neutral Spain and Portugal, but only three were equipped with wireless transmitters and thus able to communicate with their German handlers on a daily basis. Of the three, TATE had been operational the longest as he had been parachuted into Cambridgeshire in September 1940. His cover story, developed after he had been 'turned' at Camp 020, was that he was employed as a farm labourer on an estate at Wye in Kent. While this placed him in the middle of a supposed assembly area for American troops waiting for D-Day, his movements were very restricted, so he was of only marginal importance to the Germans. An attempt was made to find TATE a notional girlfriend who worked as a secretary in Whitehall. This would supposedly give him access to some Admiralty information, but the scheme bordered on the implausible and was eventually abandoned.

Another problem for TATE was that his radio signals were sent direct to Hamburg, and then relayed on a landline to Berlin. This made him unique in MI5's stable of double agents, whose traffic was often re-enciphered and relayed to Berlin from Madrid. By intercepting the radio channel between the outstation and Berlin, the Security Service could monitor the Abwehr's reactions and respond accordingly. TATE's route offered no such opportunity, so there was a lingering doubt in London that perhaps the Abwehr suspected TATE was under British control and his handlers were only maintaining the contact in an effort to help him survive.

The second spy in radio contact with the enemy was Roman Garby-Czerniawski, the Polish pilot who had come to London from Paris in October 1942. Codenamed BRUTUS, he reported to his German handler in Paris that he had acquired a transmitter and radio operator and then signalled that he had been posted as a liaison officer to the US Army, where he was to be employed on drafting leaflets that were being printed for eventual distribution in France. This tale was completely untrue but it achieved two important objectives simultaneously. Firstly, BRUTUS identified his new unit as the First United Sates Army Group (FUSAG) which was an entirely made-up formation supposedly commanded by General George Patton. BRUTUS's posting added credibility to FUSAG's existence, which had already been mentioned in the newspapers when Patton's promotion had been announced. Because of his impressive reputation, established earlier in the war in north Africa, German analysts had expected Patton to be given a senior command role in the coming invasion. Courtesy of BRUTUS, the Abwehr learned that FUSAG would be based around Ascot until embarkation. Its location in the south-east of England was interpreted by the enemy as further evidence of a build-up of troops in areas conveniently close to the Kent ports. According to BRUTUS, the Americans were confined to their camps for security reasons, which was his explanation for the absence of American uniforms in the area.

BRUTUS's fabricated role with FUSAG was intended to convey a very specific message to the enemy. The only reason why American forces in France would need to communicate in Polish was if they anticipated operating somewhere with a large Polish population – namely, Lille, at the heart of the Pas-de-Calais, which accommodated the largest expatriate Polish community in France.

The danger of having BRUTUS so closely associated with FUSAG was obvious. He would be expected to respond instantly to awkward questions and there would be some issues, such as embarkation orders, that he would be expected to know. MI5's ingenious solution was to separate BRUTUS from his radio operator with the claim that he could only leave the camp occasionally, so his messages were invariably two or three days out of date when they were received by the enemy in Paris.

The third and demonstrably the most important of the double agents working with the deception planners was a Spaniard who had spent eight months in Portugal fabricating information that he sold to his Abwehr controller based in Madrid until he was brought to London in April 1942. Known to the Abwehr as ALARIC, he had told the Germans in July 1941 that he had reached the UK, recruited a network of sub-agents codenamed ARABEL and had persuaded a KLM airline pilot to smuggle his letters back to Lisbon, which was the explanation for the Portuguese postmark on his messages. He was unaware that the Germans had relayed his messages on an Enigma-enciphered radio channel to Berlin and that his traffic had been monitored by British cryptanalysts, who had informed MI5 of a hitherto undetected enemy spy-ring. The Security Service knew from the Madrid decrypts that ALARIC was held in high regard by his handlers and so quickly seized the opportunity to take over the fictional ARABEL organisation. MI5 also helped ALARIC – codenamed GARBO by the British – to buy a radio transmitter and supplied him with an experienced operator to signal Madrid daily.

This was the origins of what became known as the GARBO operation and it continued until the end of the war. The details were disclosed by Sir John Masterman in his 1972 history, *The Double-Cross System in the War of 1939–45*.[1] The published version had been sanitised to protect ULTRA (which would not be made public for a further two years) and GARBO's true identity. Masterman, as chairman of the Twenty Committee from its inception in January 1941, was commissioned at the end of hostilities to write an account of the agents who participated in the operation and assess what they achieved. He obtained permission to retain a copy, on condition that he kept it securely in a safe and showed it to no one. Even under these terms, MI5's post-war deputy director general Guy Liddell had been very reluctant to allow the copy off the premises. In comparing the agents, Masterman observed, 'Connoisseurs of double cross have always regarded the GARBO case as the most highly developed example of their art.'[2]

In strategic terms, GARBO accomplished a great deal, some of which he was unaware of. For example, he never knew that MI5 had other double agents under control. Nor was he allowed to learn about the extraordinary cryptographic advantage he bestowed on British intelligence. As previously mentioned, GARBO's daily messages, having been drafted and approved by his MI5 handler Tommy Harris, were transmitted to Madrid where they were re-enciphered on an Enigma machine and relayed to Berlin. This channel was monitored by the Radio Security Service (RSS), a dedicated interception organisation, and cryptanalysts, already in possession of GARBO's original plain text, were able to reverse engineer the cipher text and reconstruct the 'key' or settings, which changed daily. Significantly, the Abwehr's daily key was employed on all the Abwehr's radio circuits, so thanks to GARBO, the RSS were able to read the traffic transmitted on dozens of their circuits. This was a potentially war-winning advantage of inestimable value to the Allies.

The fact that GARBO and his stable of two dozen (notional) subagents were well established across the entire country, from Glasgow to Dover, meant that there was no need for the Abwehr to send over more agents, which in turn gave MI5 some comfort. If the enemy needed a spy to visit a particular airfield in Norfolk, or observe rolling stock passing through Ashford, GARBO would simply deploy one of his ARABEL subordinates and transmit the report the same day. With such an efficient organisation immediately available to undertake the Abwehr's requests, there was no point in taking the risks associated with dispatching an agent on a mission. This confidence also enabled MI5 to concentrate their resources in the counter-intelligence field, rather than counter-espionage.

In strategic terms, GARBO was assigned three specific tasks, the first of which was to supply the enemy with reports in support of FORTITUDE SOUTH, which required agent sightings of troops massing in south-east England, close to the embarkation ports in Kent. This was relatively straightforward, but as the picture was painted, there were several artistic flourishes, such as the farm machinery that was converted to emulate the distinctive tank tracks that could be photographed by Luftwaffe aerial reconnaissance missions. Such missions were discouraged along the south-west's coastline but made easy in the airspace over East Anglia, where plenty of bogus landing craft and gliders were on display. These tactical deceptions were not unsophisticated and included the local broadcasts of military radio traffic associated with major troop movements and exercises.

GARBO's second task was to persuade the enemy that the Normandy landings were a mere feint to draw the Axis forces away from the Pas-de-Calais, which was the true objective of an assault scheduled for a fortnight later. Once again, the Axis was predisposed to swallow this particular falsehood because, when the Normandy beachhead was established, none of the Allied prisoners captured were from units that were part of FUSAG. The implication was that FUSAG had been retained in its holding areas, in anticipation of the second, principal landings in the Pas-de-Calais. This deception proved so successful that it was not until September that the Abwehr asked GARBO why the Allies had not made the expected attack. GARBO's plausible explanation was that the Normandy landings had gone much better than expected, so the much-anticipated second attack had been abandoned!

Supreme Commander of the Allied invasion General Dwight Eisenhower gave his personal approval for a message transmitted to Madrid at midnight on 5/6 June in which ALARIC declared that the Normandy assault, then already underway, could be safely ignored because the main Allied thrust would occur further north. Confirmation of FORTITUDE's efficacy became manifest when intercepted radio traffic indicated that the 1st SS Panzer Division, which had started to roll westwards for a major counterattack, was ordered on 11 June to return to its garrison at Turnhout. Similar instructions had been received by the 85th Infantry Division, the 16th Luftwaffe Division and the 1st Panzer Division, all of which had been north of the Seine. Astonishingly, a month *after* D-Day, the German High Command was still so fixated on GARBO's advice that the strength in the 7th Army area, north of the Seine, had actually *increased* from fifteen to eighteen divisions.

Without question, GARBO had shouldered the lion's share of the deception campaign that had ensured the enemy was taken completely by surprise. Those writers who had mentioned GARBO after Masterman's revelations – among them Dennis Wheatley, Tom Sefton Delmer, Ladislas Faragó, Anthony Cave Brown and even Kim Philby, who had described GARBO as 'one of the most creative intelligence operations of all time' – were all agreed on the extraordinary contribution made to the Allied cause by the anonymous Spaniard, but nobody seemed to know his true name or when he had died.[3]

As I began to research *MI5: British Security Service Operations 1909–45* in 1978, I took the opportunity whenever I met a former officer to ask about the GARBO case. Invariably, they offered words of praise for the double agent and his handler, Tommy Harris, but then repeated like a mantra, 'Tommy would know… but he was killed in a car accident in 1964 near his home in Majorca. His wife Hilda died soon afterwards. The need-to-know principle meant we avoided picking up really sensitive information.' A year before Masterman's disclosures, the veteran *Daily Express* journalist Tom Sefton Delmer released *The Counterfeit Spy*, taking care not to reveal anything relating to GARBO's true identity, except to say that after the war 'he set up a prosperous public relations firm along with an import-export business' in Angola, but 'suddenly in 1949' he had 'succumbed to another bout of malaria. And this time it killed him.'[4]

Delmer's assertion that GARBO was dead seemed improbable, but he said nothing further on the subject before his own death in September 1979, and his son Felix assured me he had not left any relevant papers. The question that remained unanswered related to Delmer's sources. What had persuaded him to write the semi-fictional *Counterfeit Spy*, and where had he acquired his information? Discreet enquiries suggested that behind the scenes there had been a row in Whitehall over the book because of a suspicion that Delmer had based his book on his unauthorised access to the Cabinet Office's copy of *Fortitude*, the official history of the invasion deception campaign which had been written at the end of the war by Roger Fleetwood-Hesketh. As it turned out, the person responsible for leaking *Fortitude* was Noel Wild, Dudley Clarke's deputy at 'A' Force. Somehow, Wild had acquired a copy of Fleetwood-Hesketh's report and passed it to Delmer, who had focused on GARBO – renamed CATO for the book. When Fleetwood-Hesketh complained to the Cabinet Office that his material had been looted by Delmer, the Treasury Solicitor pointed out that the Crown owned *Fortitude* and not Fleetwood-Hesketh. The final compromise was that Delmer agreed to acknowledge his source in future editions and Fleetwood-Hesketh received permission to publish a sanitised version of *Fortitude*, a copy of which was sent to him – Whitehall being unaware of the fact that Fleetwood-Hesketh had secretly retained two copies of his original report.

Convinced that my search for GARBO would only help his own prospects of finding a publisher for the final version of *Fortitude*, Fleetwood-Hesketh wanted to help and supplied all the passages that had been excised from the original version. Although this yielded plenty of fascinating secret material, it did not include GARBO's true identity. Nevertheless, Fleetwood-Hesketh felt if he could prove that, contrary to Delmer's assertion, GARBO was still alive, this news would enhance the value of his own book. His view was endorsed by his son-in-law, the publisher Anthony Blond, and we undertook an analysis of the censored passages.

Whereas much of *Fortitude* had escaped relatively unscathed, references to MI5's double agents had attracted a great number of cuts. In particular, references to GARBO, his wife and son, and the fact that he had returned to Madrid at the end of hostilities, where he had been welcomed by his former Abwehr handler who evidently had never suspected his agent's duplicity. I also noticed that the name 'García' had been removed, and this suggested that he may have used this as a name while he had been in London. The only reason for demanding the removal of this material was surely to protect GARBO and his family, which rather implied that he was probably still alive.

Unfortunately, this took me no closer to establishing GARBO's identity, and while researching *MI5*, I mistakenly identified the wrong person as GARBO. My first candidate was Spanish journalist Luis Calvo, who had been named by Kim Philby as an Abwehr spy in his memoirs, *My Silent War*.[5] Certainly, Calvo had lived in London during the war, but most of his time in England had been spent in custody at Camp 020. I tracked Calvo down to Santander, but when I interviewed the former editor of the Madrid daily *ABC*, I realised that I had found the wrong man. I knew from Masterman and Fleetwood-Hesketh that GARBO had not arrived in England until April 1942, yet Calvo had been the press attaché at the Spanish embassy in London since 1940. He had returned to Madrid briefly in January 1942 but had been arrested when he arrived back in the UK in mid-February 1942 and had remained incarcerated at Camp 020 until the end of the war, when he was deported to Spain. None of this fitted with what little there was already known about GARBO.

Having rejected Calvo as a candidate, I considered another Spanish journalist, an anti-fascist named Felipe Fernandez who wrote a column under a pen name for *La Vanguardia*. Not only did Calvo believe that Fernandez was GARBO, but he also felt certain that Fernandez had been responsible for denouncing him to MI5.

When I spoke to Fernandez in Madrid, he seemed enchanted

with the idea that he had been GARBO. He explained that he had been a close friend of Tommy Harris and at the end of the war had received a British decoration, the King's Medal for Service in the Cause of Freedom (which was not the MBE that Masterman had mentioned GARBO had recieved). The Central Chancery of the Orders of Knighthood at St James's Palace confirmed that Fernandez had received the King's Medal, a medal awarded to foreign nationals who had assisted the British war effort. However, it turned out that I had stumbled over another agent run by Harris's MI5 section, designated B.21, but not GARBO.

In May 1981, during the course of several long conversations with Anthony Blunt, we talked about GARBO. I had raised the topic because during his wartime employment with MI5, he had been the one person in the St James's Street headquarters who had deliberately ignored the 'need-to-know' rule and had set out to discover everything he could about his colleagues and their work, so he could report all to his Soviet contacts. He also had the excuse, from April 1943 onwards, of collecting information for the monthly bulletin on MI5's current activities that he compiled for the director general, Sir David Petrie, who handed it to the Prime Minister. The document, usually three pages in length, summarised every source, operation, double agent plan, counter-espionage investigation and incident of subversion or sabotage that involved the Security Service. It was not duplicated, and neither Churchill nor the Cabinet Office were allowed to keep a copy. Once the task of drafting the monthly report was assigned to Blunt, he became one of the best-informed officers in the entire country and thereby an asset of immense value to Moscow. He had the power to walk into any MI5 section and use Petrie's authority to find out what its staff were up to. Every operation, every recruitment, every investigation were confided to him. Who better to ask about GARBO?

Blunt was especially well qualified to talk about GARBO as he had been one of Harris's closest friends. Indeed, he had contributed an introduction to an exhibition of Harris's art at the Courtauld Institute, in which Blunt described Harris's participation in what Blunt called 'the greatest double-cross operation of the war'.

Blunt had a prodigious memory and recalled having dined with Harris and GARBO in the Garibaldi Restaurant in Jermyn Street in September 1944. When I told him that I knew GARBO's surname was García, he nodded and recollected that 'his first name was Juan or José'. I was another step closer to GARBO.

Unfortunately, since the names Juan García or José García are not uncommon in Spain, I had to wait until 1983 for another opportunity to advance the search. In that year, *MI6: British Secret Intelligence Service Operations 1909–45* was published as a companion volume to *MI5*. One of the officers mentioned was a Section V counter-intelligence expert who had been based in Gibraltar and for a period had worked alongside Kim Philby in the Iberian sub-section. Trained as a mining engineer, Desmond Bristow had been a wartime recruit and had been persuaded to remain in the Service. He sought me out because he had resigned in October 1954, was contemplating writing a book about his clandestine life and wanted some advice about problems he might encounter.[6] During one of several conversations held while he was visiting London, I asked about GARBO, and Bristow confirmed that he had some knowledge of the case because he had been instructed to perform some small task for him when he had been assigned to MI6's Madrid station between November 1947 and April 1953. He also remembered, slightly mysteriously, that GARBO's personal affairs had been 'very complicated'. He did not elaborate but, most significantly, he claimed that one of the minor jobs he had undertaken relating to GARBO had occurred *after* Philby had been dismissed from the Secret Intelligence Service, an event that occurred in June 1951. This clue suggested that GARBO had probably not died in Angola in the 1940s. As regards his true name, Bristow was hesitant, but when I said vaguely that I already knew it to be 'Juan or José García', he corrected me by asserting 'Juan Pujol García'. Finally, I knew GARBO's true identity.

Recognising that Pujol was a common Catalan name, shared with the then president of Catalonia, I hired an acquaintance, José Escoriza, as my researcher in Barcelona. His first challenge was to check the local telephone directory and find out how many entries it contained with the right initials. His depressing answer was more than two hundred, but, undaunted, I asked him to call every number and ask three simple elimination questions concerning their age and their whereabouts during the war years: are you old enough to remember the war, were you in England between 1942 and 1945 and does the name GARBO mean anything to you, apart from a cinematic context? A negative to the first two questions ruled out the candidate, and in the event of an affirmative, I had a longer list of supplementary questions. Among them: had he known Tommy and Hilda Harris and had he received a decoration from the British government?

Several months later, Escoriza broke the news to me that he had not achieved a single positive response from any of his calls. I was almost ready to abandon the project when, on a hunch, I asked if any of the calls had been unusual. He told me that one person, a youth much too young to have been GARBO, had become quite aggressive and had demanded to know who was so interested in Juan Pujol García. Escoriza had offered the explanation that we had prepared, that friends from the 1940s were anxious to be reunited with Pujol, and this had seemed to satisfy him. I asked Escoriza to re-establish contact with the young man who, after a few longer conversations, admitted that he was called Juan Pujol and shared the name with his uncle. Furthermore, he had received a postcard from his uncle postmarked Venezuela some years earlier, and he knew that he was now in his early seventies and that he had been in London during the war.

This seemed to be a potentially strong lead, and I was determined, in this pre-internet era, to find Juan Pujol García in South America. I began by looking for freelance researchers and was recommended Cesar Dias, a sharp young television trainee in Caracas who agreed to trawl through the local Catalan community to find anyone that fitted GARBO's profile. An added problem, which I had not considered in the early years of my search, was the possibility that even if I found GARBO, he might deny his role or maybe go into hiding. After all, why had he not revealed himself years ago? Did he fear retribution from former Nazis? I urged Dias to exercise great discretion and tact but had to accept that GARBO might well vanish if he thought some unknown European was trying to find him.

Early in May 1984, Dias called with the news that he had found, but not yet spoken to, a man named Juan Pujol and had been given the telephone number 941 1945 to reach Juan Pujol's son in Caracas. He explained that if I called at a particular time, I could speak to the person I was starting to believe was GARBO. Before I made the call, I considered the likely outcomes and sketched out some possible scenarios. I needed to convey immediately that I did not pose any threat and that it was in his best interests to hear what I had to say. Although I was far from sure Dias had found the right person, I was strangely comforted by the idea that he could be reached on a telephone number ending '1945'.

At this time, the fortieth anniversary of the D-Day landings was fast approaching, and the media had given considerable coverage to the plans that had been made to celebrate the occasion on the Normandy beaches. Margaret Thatcher, François Mitterrand and Ronald Reagan were scheduled to take part, and I thought this might be a very appropriate moment for GARBO to make a reappearance. The challenge was how to persuade someone as shy as him, who had deliberately shunned the limelight for so many years, to emerge to the gratitude he was due. The coincidence that after all these years GARBO might emerge on the eve of a major anniversary was really too good to overlook, but could it be leveraged to gain Pujol's cooperation?

There was nothing I could do if Pujol simply refused to take the call or even slammed down the receiver. If he did so, did I give up or instruct Dias to pursue the matter further? The solution was to tempt GARBO into the open by offering him a prize so attractive, even he would not be able to resist it. What I had in mind, no amount of money could buy. I telephoned the Duke of Edinburgh's private office at Buckingham Palace and spoke to an equerry, Commander Wynn, to whom I gave a rather abbreviated account of how the celebrated wartime double agent codenamed GARBO was to visit London for the fortieth anniversary of the D-Day landings and would greatly appreciate the chance to attend a formal investiture at the palace to receive the decoration he had been awarded in conditions of great secrecy in December 1944. Apparently, GARBO had received the medal from Sir David Petrie at a private ceremony held in a London club, without the usual appearance in the *London Gazette*, because of the secrecy that had necessarily surrounded him. The duke, whom I knew to be a committed reader of espionage non-fiction, responded with typical enthusiasm. After initially protesting that 'everyone knows GARBO is dead', he agreed to hold an investiture for him. This set the scene for our first conversation. When I telephoned Caracas, I identified myself as calling on behalf of Buckingham Palace with instructions to invite Juan Pujol García to an investiture to commemorate his contribution to the Allied victory. Who would decline such an invitation?

When the call was answered, I found myself talking to an elderly man who gave the right answers to all my questions. He went much further than I had anticipated and began to reminisce about London, almost as though he was under an obligation to prove who he was. Indeed, he told me that he had lived in Hendon during the war, and when he mentioned Crespigny Road, I remembered that MI5 had accommodated a pair of Norwegian double agents, MUTT and JEFF, in the same street. I had actually taken both men, John Moe and Tor Glad, to the same address. He even recalled the number 45, which was the same house, and I became increasingly convinced I had the right man. He had known Tommy and Hilda Harris and Harris's three sisters, Violetta, Conchita and Enriqueta. And yes, he still possessed the medal the British had given him in 1944. Finally, and to my growing excitement and relief, he confirmed his willingness to meet but demanded that this should happen in New Orleans the following week.

Initially baffled by the insistence on New Orleans, I would later learn about another extraordinary coincidence that, just a week earlier, had made Pujol decide that he should tell his two sons about GARBO. It turned out that Pujol's youngest son Juan Carlos was studying medicine at Tulane University and he and his American girlfriend Patty had suffered some racial abuse from local women in a supermarket. Juan Carlos had quite a dark complexion and the women had commented on what they perceived to be a mixed-race relationship. Pujol had been outraged when his son had told him of his disagreeable experience and had wanted to tell him, for the first time, about his contribution to the Second World War and about the number of American lives he had helped save. Pujol had started to explain about GARBO, but he could see that his son disbelieved him, and it was only when I had telephoned unexpectedly that he had realised that I might be able to describe his extraordinary exploits to the family he had raised after the war. Thus, far from resenting my unexpected appearance, Pujol had regarded it as particularly fortuitous.

I flew into New Orleans on 19 May and, having checked into the Windsor Court Hotel, walked over to the Hilton where Pujol had requested we meet at midday the following afternoon. My reconnaissance was intended to reduce the risk of a last-minute mishap, and when I saw the venue, I was horrified. We had agreed to meet in the lobby but the Hilton was an enormous building, covering an entire city block, with probably a dozen street entrances. The hotel was also busier than most major railway stations.

It was with some trepidation that I tried to find Pujol the next day, and when I failed, I returned to the Windsor Court crestfallen. I then persuaded myself that I should make a second attempt, and this proved successful. Pujol was bald, short and stout, accompanied by his two sons, Carlos Miguel and Juan Carlos and his wife, Carmen Cilia Alvarez. Greetings were exchanged and photographs taken, and then I was asked by Pujol to tell his story, as I knew it, to his sons. Both men listened, wide-eyed with disbelief, as I recounted how their father had originally acted as a fabricator by inventing reports from his network of agents in England, while in reality he had travelled no further then Lisbon and his spy-ring existed only in his imagination. To say both young men were stunned would be an understatement.

Having gained Pujol's confidence, he agreed to fly to London with his wife, and a reunion was arranged for him at the Special Forces Club in Knightsbridge. I had invited several MI5 and MI6 veterans to meet GARBO again, and a few of their number were doubtful that I really had been successful in my quest. Tommy Robertson and Cyril Mills were particularly dubious. However, it was a very moving occasion when GARBO walked into the club's drawing room and fell into their arms. These hardened intelligence professionals burst into tears and were soon absorbed by their memories. I was also able to reunite GARBO with two of Harris's surviving sisters and with his secretary, Sarah Bishop. On the afternoon of Thursday 31 May, we took a cab to Buckingham Palace where Pujol received his decoration and was formally thanked for his remarkable contribution to the Allied cause.

GARBO's visit to the Normandy beaches on 4 June 1984, accompanied by his old MI6 contact Desmond Bristow, was also a resounding success. The elderly double agent grew rather misty-eyed when he saw the acres of war graves in the Allied cemeteries above the most contentious battlefields. What particularly pleased him was an advertising campaign run by the *Mail on Sunday*, which announced its intention to reveal the identity of 'D-Day's Greatest Hero' on the anniversary.

Pujol's full story was subsequently published in *Operation GARBO* the following year, and he was delighted by the collaboration. He wrote half the book, dealing with his early life and his experiences in the Spanish Civil War, while I concentrated on what I could reconstruct of his wartime activities from the texts of the radio messages he had transmitted to the Abwehr. I knew from a deleted source note in Fleetwood-Hesketh's magnificent *Fortitude* that MI5's own record of the GARBO case ran to fifty volumes, but when asked to lend Pujol a copy, the Security Service's legal adviser, Bernard Sheldon, refused. This was a bitter blow to Pujol, who insisted that Tommy Harris had always promised him a complete copy of his own account, *A Summary of the GARBO Case*, which he had completed in 1945 and which had been drawn upon by Masterman. Nevertheless, with the generous help of Fleetwood-Hesketh, who contributed a foreword to *Operation GARBO*, the book was completed and contained dozens of GARBO's original messages.

Official acknowledgement that Pujol was indeed GARBO materialised in the most indirect way five years later. Volume 4 of the official history, *British Intelligence in the Second World War*, was written by Professor Sir Harry Hinsley and Anthony Simkins and entitled *Security and Counter-Intelligence*. Although the GARBO case took up a great deal of space in the book, there was a single footnote referring the reader to *Operation GARBO* by J. Pujol.[7] Further confirmation was contained in Volume 5, published the following year, which also devoted much space to GARBO's extraordinary story.

• • •

Undoubtedly, Pujol had been responsible for saving many thousands of Allied lives, but even after Paris had been liberated, the Germans continued to have full confidence in their star agent. At the end of the war, Pujol had undertaken a further mission to find his controller in Madrid and learn of any plans for a Nazi revival or resistance. MI5 was also anxious to learn the whereabouts of certain Abwehr personnel and discover their plans before they were deported by the Spanish authorities. Pujol's route back to Madrid was necessarily complicated and roundabout because he had claimed in a message to the Germans to have been a fugitive in England and was therefore obliged to go through the motions of executing a clandestine exfiltration. This was achieved by Pujol masquerading as one of Anthony Blunt's art students at the Courtauld Institute, ready to travel across Latin America to study architecture. Armed with the appropriate credentials provided by Blunt in his capacity as an MI5 officer, Pujol had flown to New York and then travelled to Cuba and Caracas, where he obtained a new Spanish passport, before embarking on a liner bound for Barcelona in August 1945.

He need not have worried about his reception by the remnants of the defeated Abwehr because his principal contact, Karl-Erich Kühlenthal, had never suspected ALARIC of being a double agent and gave him a hero's welcome, admitting that the defeat had been total and there was no hope for the Nazis. He himself was under house arrest in the ancient walled town of Avila and feared his deportation back to Germany, where he expected a hostile interrogation by the victorious Allies. Having completed his assignment, Pujol reported to London that the Abwehr had disbanded, even though plenty of its personnel had chosen to stay in Spain or take refuge in South America. Neither Kühlenthal nor his dispirited subordinate Fritz Knappe-Ratey represented any threat, and their main concern, so GARBO reported, was simply self-preservation in an increasingly hostile country that previously had treated them as honoured guests. Now Kühlenthal was in isolation and under police surveillance at his home in Avila, while Knappe-Ratey was under house arrest in Caldas, apparently as a result of pressure exerted on the Spanish authorities by the Allies.

In the book written by us, the story trails off at the end of the war. Pujol had always been rather vague about his post-war experiences, and I sensed that enquiries into this latter part of his life would be unwelcome so I did not pursue the matter, although when I learned what had really happened, I acknowledged I ought to have been rather more inquisitive. The true story that emerged only years later was truly astonishing, and revealed the role played by his first wife, Araceli González Carballo, whom he had married in Madrid in April 1940. They subsequently had two sons: Juan, born in Madrid and Jorge, born in London in September 1942. When we first met, Pujol had said nothing about Araceli, nor their children – who were then in Spain, under the impression that their father had died in Venezuela in 1949. To complicate matters further, Juan's second wife, Carmen, and their two sons, to whom he had introduced me in New Orleans, were unaware that Pujol had been married before and had three children currently living in Spain.

Upon his return to Spain in 1945, Pujol prepared a new life for himself and his family in Venezuela where Shell Oil had been persuaded to give him a job as an interpreter at its refinery at Maracaibo. There the Pujols had a third child, Maria, but Araceli grew increasingly homesick and thought she had persuaded her husband to move back to Spain. Convinced he would follow her as soon as he had sold their house and car, Araceli took her three children to Spain in 1948, only to have the news broken to her by a diplomat from the British embassy in Madrid that Pujol had died before he could leave. In fact, he had simply faked his own death and persuaded MI6's local station commander to help him cover his tracks. Informed that she had been widowed, Araceli married an American diplomat, Ed Kreisler, in 1958, who adopted her children as his own. She believed herself to be a widow and evidently never suspected that Pujol was alive and well in Venezuela where he had started a second family with Carmen.

This extraordinary state of affairs would have continued uninterrupted and undiscovered if Pujol had not been persuaded to participate in the celebration of the D-Day landings. The resulting publicity instantly spread to Madrid, and there was also considerable media interest in the shy Spaniard. Flanked by Bristow, who acted as an interpreter and minder, pictures of Pujol and news of his unique wartime adventure were splashed across Europe. When the publicity reached Madrid, a shocked Araceli learned for the first time that, far from having been widowed, she was an unwitting bigamist and her first husband was at that very moment being feted in London by royalty. The impact of this development on Araceli and her children can only be guessed at, but Pujol himself was devastated by his reunion with his daughter Maria, whom he had not seen since she was a baby. To compound the matter further, his first three children discovered they had acquired two half-brothers living in Caracas.

Pujol's account of his wartime work as a double agent, *Operation GARBO*, drew a discreet veil over both his families and made no reference whatsoever to Araceli or their children, doubtless to protect them from further distress and unwanted publicity. All that was to change in 1999 when GARBO's official MI5 file was released to the Public Record Office in London, which revealed the turbulent nature of Araceli's relationship with her husband during the war. On one occasion, angered by his frequent, unexplained absences, Araceli had threatened to visit the Spanish embassy in Belgrave Square and denounce Pujol as a British spy, a catastrophe which would have imperilled MI5's entire Double-Cross System and had a disastrous effect on the Allied deception campaign at a critical moment in the war. A police cordon had been hastily thrown around the building to prevent Araceli, whom MI5 described as 'a hysterical, spoilt and selfish woman', from reaching the entrance and the situation was saved.[8] Nevertheless, Araceli and Pujol continued to have tempestuous fights, although according to MI5's dossier, none were to match the dangerous incident involving the embassy. Doubtless this went some way to explain Pujol's later decision to abandon her.

GARBO's story remains one of the most extraordinary of the Second World War and is, as M. R. D. Foot observed, 'a classic of espionage'.[9] The long-term impact on GARBO's family, of course, is harder to assess, but there was at least one agreeable consequence. Desmond Bristow, the MI6 head of station in Madrid after the war, was prompted to write his memoirs, and in *A Game of Moles* he recorded his MI6 career and his friendship with Kim Philby. It proved a success with the public and proved that books could be written about secret intelligence operations without compromising sensitive information. Pujol died in October 1988 and is buried in Choroni, beside the grave of his daughter Maria Elena, who died in 1975 in childbirth aged twenty-two.

CHAPTER VI

CABINET WAR ROOM 2

One of the mysteries that emerged from Winston Churchill's history of the Second World War was the site of a secret structure known officially as 'CWR2' and codenamed PADDOCK. The intrigue and speculation had begun when Churchill mentioned in his second volume, *Their Finest Hour*, that a citadel had been constructed 'near Hampstead' to provide alternative secure, bomb-proof accommodation for the war Cabinet and the chiefs of staff as a contingency in case the offices under Whitehall had to be evacuated.[1]

The plan to build a series of indestructible fortresses in London from which the government could conduct its business was a direct reaction to the large-scale bombing of cities by the Luftwaffe's Condor Legion during the Spanish Civil War. The idea of targeting the civilian population for aerial bombardment was a new, ruthless concept but had been adopted by the Germans as a potentially effective method of modernising warfare and adapting military strategy to take advantage of new technology. The introduction of purpose-built aircraft designed to carry large payloads of munitions deep into enemy territory, rather than concentrating on ground support in the area off the front lines, was both novel and frightening. Could a terrorised civilian population influence the conduct of a war? Would the Nationalists subjugate Republican-held territory by bombing them into submission? These were the issues that preoccupied some of Whitehall's planners, who had become aware of London's vulnerability. The sheer size of the capital made it impossible to defend from air attack, and recent studies had demonstrated that conventional anti-aircraft artillery, in an era before the development of proximity fuses, was only effective one in a thousand rounds.

A ruthless policy of subjecting a population living far from a combat zone to a bombing campaign had added the concept of mass civilian casualties to the horrors of modern warfare, but the Whitehall planners thought wholesale evacuation was impractical and likely to be bad for morale. The issue would become extremely relevant when, in 1940, German blitzkrieg tactics were shown to include the infiltration of specially trained commandos behind the lines to seize bridges and other strategic strong points long before the main assault troops had arrived on the scene. This novel strategy would prove highly effective during the Nazi invasions of France, Belgium, Denmark and the Netherlands, and the lessons were learned by the various British departmental sub-committees set up to make recommendations. The issue of population protection would become highly politicised when leftists began to campaign for a shelter programme, which eventually led to the deep stations of the Northern line being made available to the public. In particular, the CPGB saw an opportunity to apply pressure on the government by circulating assessments made by Professor J. B. S. Haldane who had made a special study of the impact of German air-raids on Madrid.

One solution adopted by the war Cabinet was the construction of protected accommodation for five key ministries with, most notably, the Admiralty transferring its operational offices into a huge, purpose-built citadel on the Mall, close to Admiralty Arch. The other sites included the Ministry of Education to Curzon Street; the War Office to the Royal Military School of Music at Kneller Hall in Whitton; the Admiralty to Cricklewood; the Air Ministry to the Stationery Office annex in Hounslow; and the Ministry of Home Security to Cornwall House in Stamford Street. Rather than build entirely new structures, the decision was taken at some of those sites to enhance the sub-basement protection and add reinforced concrete overhangs to reduce the risk from deep-penetration bombs.

MI5 was also preoccupied with the implications of German espionage and exploiting what was then termed a 'fifth column' of traitors and saboteurs. A very secret contingency plan codenamed HEGIRA was devised by Cyril Mills to accommodate key personnel and selected double agents in the Welsh resort town of Colwyn Bay, under the guise of protecting his family's famous circus. In reality, a list of vulnerable double agents – among them TATE, STORK and SNOW – was drawn up and plans were made to whisk them away to Llandudno in the worst-case scenario.[2] The local regional security liaison officer was indoctrinated into the project, and he made reservations at various hotels and boarding houses to accommodate the fugitives. The codename HEGIRA, of course, was the Arabic word for Muhammad's enforced departure from Mecca in AD 622.

The main Cabinet War Rooms, deep under Great George Street and protected by six feet of steel and concrete, had not been considered sufficiently safe, being considerably below the level of the

Thames which was just two hundred yards away. Therefore, PADDOCK, which Churchill described only as 'far from the light of day', had been prepared in the event of an emergency. According to Churchill's account, PADDOCK had been used only twice. First, on Sunday 29 September 1940 when a 'dress rehearsal' had been held and then for a full meeting of the Cabinet two days later, on 1 October. So where was PADDOCK? The issue fascinated historians, especially when Sir Jock Colville, Churchill's wartime private secretary, recalled in his memoirs that he had accompanied the Prime Minister to the secret site but the need for secrecy precluded him from disclosing any further details. The speculation increased in 1970, when Peter Laurie released *Beneath the City Streets*, an impressive survey of Britain's secret underground bunkers.[3] Laurie revealed that the country had been covered by a network of structures designed to protect the government in the event of a nuclear attack, and although he correctly identified dozens of citadels, 'sub-regional controls' and 'regional seats of government', he had been unable to positively identify PADDOCK. His best guess, which seemed to be consistent with Churchill's clues of 'far from the light of day' and 'near Hampstead', was the old Bull & Bush underground station, located on the Northern line halfway between Hampstead and Golders Green. This was the deepest stretch of underground track in Britain, and the old station, accessible only through a lift shaft, had been abandoned before the war. As Laurie pointed out, the government had taken advantage of the capital's underground system before, and the old Down Street station in Mayfair had been used as the bomb-proof headquarters of the Railway Executive Committee during the war. But was Laurie right?

I had shared Laurie's fascination and was put onto the trail of the real PADDOCK accidentally when I was researching the wartime Cabinet records at the Public Record Office in Chancery Lane. This proved to be a very time-consuming project, as their files were in the process of being moved to a new home, a purpose-built modern complex overlooking the Thames at Kew. As it turned out, the Cabinet archive was among the first of the Whitehall collections to be scheduled for transfer to Kew. I obtained permission to access the material in its new home and thus became one of the first holders of a reader's ticket at Kew. It was while I was trawling through these Cabinet papers that I came across a very obscure memorandum written to the Prime Minister on 21 September 1940 from the Royal Marines officer who was responsible for administering his personal security and for supplying the guards to the Cabinet War Rooms. What caught my attention was the fact that the document was headed 'CWR2' but there was nothing else in the text, which concerned very minor bomb damage from a Luftwaffe air-raid the previous evening on Brook Road in Dollis Hill, a week after his visit to PADDOCK.

Now why would the officer in charge of Churchill's personal security be anxious to inform the Prime Minister about an inconsequential air-raid in an obscure district of north London with a reference to CWR2? The answer, I concluded, must be in Brook Road, but as I drove the length of the road, I was struck by the name of one of the adjoining streets: Paddock Road. Was it really likely that the codename PADDOCK was nothing more than a very transparent address? Standing on the corner of Paddock Road, I looked across into the grounds of what had, up until very recently, been the Post Office Research Station, and I realised that I was staring at a large, windowless one-storey structure built of reinforced concrete, bearing all the hallmarks of a surface access to a much bigger underground bunker. Money passed hands with the security guard on the gate, who confirmed that the abandoned building had been used by the government. A guided tour followed, and although the very lowest level was partially flooded, it was clear that the mystery of CWR2 had been solved. The bunker was huge, and apart from a large operations room was partitioned off into fifty smaller rooms and dormitories, many of them bearing the names of various services – a feature shared with many emergency nuclear bunkers.

Further research in the Public Record Office showed that of all the key civil servants scheduled for emergency evacuation to secret, strengthened sub-basements beyond Whitehall, in a dispersal known as the BLACK MOVE, only 184 people knew the actual location of PADDOCK.[4] I recorded this in *MI5: British Security Service Operations 1909–45*, and gave the site a central role in my first novel, *The Blue List*.

Although the main Cabinet War Rooms in Whitehall would become one of London's most successful tourist attractions and would eventually be managed by the Imperial War Museum and accommodate the Churchill Museum, CWR2 never achieved anything like the same status, although the site would gain recognition as a key component in the signals intelligence dimension of the Second World War. The Post Office Research Station had opened in 1921, although construction of the main building would not be completed until 1933. Precisely what kind of work was undertaken at Dollis Hill seemed difficult to pin down, and it would be some years before it emerged that much of the most important wartime engineering research had been done here and had resulted in the development by the legendary Tommy Flowers of Colossus, the very first programmable analogue computer. Colossus had been designed to race through the complex permutations of the Lorenz ten-rotor high-speed radio teletype *Geheimschreiber* (secret writer) cipher machine on which the German High Command relied for the encryption of its strategic and long-distance communications.

Flowers had established his reputation by supporting the Bletchley Park cryptanalysts dedicated to solving Enigma. He had then turned his attention to the TUNNY – the British codename for the Lorenz machine – non-Morse traffic intercepted at Ivy Farm in Kent. The British used the generic term FISH for the traffic generated by the German cipher machines, so this term also covered the communications generated by a Siemens device known as STURGEON, which transmitted at a speed of sixty-two words a minute. The capture of two *Geheimschreiber* in North Africa greatly accelerated Allied understanding of how FISH was generated, and in June 1942, Flowers's team delivered the first apparatus to Bletchley where it was designated 'Robinson' because of its ramshackle appearance with wheels, pulleys and perforated tape. Despite its unprepossessing appearance, the Robinson worked, giving access initially to the Vienna-Athens TUNNY channel. A further twenty-four were ordered. Colossus, the next generation, was so-called because of its size, each employing some 1,500 valves.

Thus, while disclosures about Bletchley Park influenced a revision of the history of the Second World War from 1974, enhanced by a ministerial statement in January 1978 by Dr David Owen which freed retirees from their duty of secrecy, little attention was paid to Dollis Hill where Post Office technicians, normally preoccupied with improving telephone switching gear, had made a truly historic contribution to the Allied victory and beyond. At the beginning of the Cold War, Ivy Farm would focus on the interception of Soviet traffic and then would move its antenna field to Culmhead in Somerset. As for Dollis Hill, it remained operational until 1968, when its staff were moved to Martlesham Heath in Suffolk and the Brook Road estate was sold off for residential housing. However, the indestructible nature of CWR2 made it impossibly expensive to demolish, so the bunker's surface entrance remains intact even if the lower levels are largely flooded. Just like the Admiralty citadel in the Mall, the walls proved so thick that the contractors advised that it was uneconomic to even attempt their destruction.

CHAPTER VII

ADMIRAL CANARIS'S MISTRESS

It was during a conversation with Nicholas Elliott that the truth emerged behind one of the strangest stories of the Second World War. I had asked him if, after the disclosures about ULTRA and MI5's double agents, there were any really significant secrets left to be revealed. Elliott was the ideal person to ask because his experience had been wide and although he had made his career in MI6, his professional interest had begun with a brief employment by the Security Service. Even better, he had initially served, albeit briefly, under Tommy Robertson in B1(a) in the very early stages of the development of the Double-Cross System, when SNOW had been virtually the only Abwehr agent under MI5's control. Only after his apprenticeship under Robertson had he switched to MI6's Section V and been posted to Istanbul.

Elliott's intelligence experience had actually predated his recruitment into MI5, for early in 1938, as a holiday job, he had worked at the British embassy in The Hague as what was then called an honorary attaché. The appointment has long since disappeared, but before the war it was not unusual for the children of the well connected to be given unpaid posts in the colonial and diplomatic services, in order to gain a knowledge that might help them after they left university. As Elliott's father had been one of Eton's most famous headmasters, he was nothing if not replete with contacts in every walk of life, especially Whitehall and Westminster, and it was Elliott's luck to have been in the Dutch capital in November 1939 during the entire Venlo fiasco when the frontier incident became the absolute centre of attention, at least for those who knew the ramifications and were aware of just what this ostensibly insignificant episode really meant. Elliott had been on the scene and had known many of the key players, among them Rodney Dennys and Lionel Lowe, and naturally had been drawn into the embassy's desperate attempts to find out exactly what had happened to the two Britons and had to respond to the increasingly frantic calls and telegrams from London. This was Elliott's first taste of the clandestine world, and his friendship with Dennys, who was later to be one of the first MI6 officers to be assigned to Section V, was an enduring one.

A great raconteur with an impish sense of humour, Elliott may have seemed an unlikely spy, but he had the sharpest of minds and had scored an impressive coup in Turkey during the war. Afterwards, he served as head of station in Berne and much later succeeded Peter Lunn in Beirut. It was at this point, in January 1963, that he had been given the task of confronting his old friend Philby with the evidence of his treachery and offering him immunity from prosecution. This had been the encounter reconstructed for *Spy!*, at a time when Elliott's role as an MI6 officer was regarded as an official secret.

Elliott's great wartime triumph in Istanbul had been the cultivation, recruitment and finally the defection of senior Abwehr officer Erich Vermehren and his wife. Both, like Elliott's wife Elizabeth, were devout Roman Catholics and were targeted as potential recruits when Vermehren's covert role as an Eins Heer (foreign military intelligence) attached to the local *Kriegsorganisation* was revealed to Section V by ISOS intercepts. The two couples, both active on the diplomatic circuit in neutral Turkey, became friends and Elliott skilfully played on the Vehmehrens' instinctive distaste for the Nazis to the degree that the two Germans decided they could no longer stomach defending the indefensible or, as Elliott put it, live with their Christian consciences when they knew of the atrocities committed by Hitler and his henchmen.

Born in Lubeck in December 1919, Vermehren was the son of a well-connected Hamburg lawyer whose wife was a correspondent for *Das Reich*. He had been prevented from taking up the offer of a Rhodes Scholarship at Oxford University because he would not join the Hitler Youth. Vermehren had converted to Roman Catholicism when he met Elisabeth von Plettenberg, an anti-Nazi activist who was known to the Gestapo as a distributor of subversive pamphlets.

After qualifying as a lawyer, Vermehren's military service was deferred on medical grounds. In 1942, his cousin Adam von Trott zu Solz intervened to arrange a posting to the Abwehr. Vehmehren would work for the intelligence agency as an interpreter at Oflag V-IB, a PoW camp near Dössel.

Another exercise in family influence resulted in one of his father's colleagues, Paul Leverkuehn, arranging for a transfer in December 1942 to Turkey to supervise the infiltration of local agents into Iran and Iraq. His cover story there was that he had been assigned the task of acquiring fifty Société Française de Navigation Danubienne tugs, which had been constructed in France for deployment on the Danube but had been interned by the neutral Turks.

In August 1943, Vermehren made a formal request to Berlin for his wife to join him, and some of the correspondence was spotted in the Abwehr's intercepted ISOS traffic. From a message dated 22 September 1943, it seemed as if the matter had been referred to Admiral Canaris, who had been unsympathetic: 'Ref letter KONO No 4/9/43 Secret of 1/9/43, Amtschef [Canaris] has rejected Vermehren's application for his wife to enter the country, bearing in mind the state of leave on the front.'[1]

While on home leave, Vermehren tried again – only this time he acquired a Vatican passport for her through Monsignor Angelo Roncalli, the papal nuncio in Istanbul. Armed with this travel document, Elisabeth had persuaded family friend Marshal von Bieberstein to authorise her travel to Bulgaria, where she somehow talked her way onto a flight to Istanbul on Christmas Day 1943.

Soon after being reunited with his wife, Vermehren made contact with the British assistant military attaché who passed a message to Elliott, and a meeting was arranged for Monday 18 January. Neither man ever revealed what was agreed when they came to terms, but three days later on Thursday, 21 January, Vermehren informed his office that he was unwell and would be absent on the following Monday. No suspicions were aroused, and the Vermehrens attended a rendezvous with Elliott and arranged their travel by train to Palestine and onward journey by air to Cairo, where he underwent a lengthy interrogation. The first MI6 assessment based on Vermehren's information was circulated as 'The German Secret Service in Turkey':

> A well placed and reliable source whose previous information has been substantiated by our records, has produced the following information on the organization and personalities of the Abwehr station known as Kriegsorganisation Nahe Osten, the headquarters of which are situated in the German Embassy building in Istanbul. This organisation is usually known in Abwehr circles by the short title 'KO NO'.[2]

In addition, Vermehren provided four pages of wiring diagrams to illustrate the KONO's organisation and its role within the Abwehr. Although the Allied intelligence community had built up an understanding of the enemy's order-of-battle, based on double agent reports and ISOS intercepts, Vermehren's contribution ran to numerous appendices and indices detailing some forty cover names. Most of these had been 'carded' by MI6 analysts but Vermehren was able to provide additional details and personality profiles of each individual. According to Vermehren, there were five Abwehr officers in KONO responsible for conducting external agent operations, working a special section headed by Willi Hamburger whom he predicted (correctly) would also defect to the Allies. The Vermehrens were accommodated in Cairo until mid-April 1944, when they were flown to London via Algiers. Here, Elisabeth developed pneumonia, leaving her husband to continue his journey via Gibraltar.

Implied in MI6's offer was a promise of confidentiality, but once the operation had been completed successfully and the Vermehrens had undergone a detailed interrogation to reveal the Abwehr's organisation across the region, a press statement was released in Egypt announcing the defection of the Vermehrens, who were aghast. The impact of the Vermehrens' defection has been debated since the end of the war because it appeared to act as a catalyst for the *Sicherheitsdienst*'s absorption of the entire Abwehr. Canaris, its chief, had lost his independence, his organisation had been emasculated, and the Turkish debacle had been used as an excuse by the Nazis to portray the Abwehr as an incompetent nest of anti-regime dissent. Following the 20 July 1944 plot to assassinate Hitler, in which the Abwehr's senior management was heavily implicated, a bloodbath had ensued. Had the Vermehrens any moral responsibility for what had happened? Certainly, Vermehren did not admit to any when I interviewed him, but I later learned that he had been consumed by guilt when he learned that his family had suffered terribly as a consequence of his desertion and his mother had been incarcerated at Oranienburg concentration camp.

Elliott revealed that after the war, the Vermehrens had been resettled in Switzerland and had become active in the Opus Dei movement. Naturally, he would not confide their new identities, but this information was enough for me to start researching Opus Dei to find a couple that I calculated to be quite elderly and somewhat reticent about their background. There was indeed just such a couple living near Clarens, in a villa overlooking the lake, who were described as among the leading Opus Dei activists in Switzerland. When I contacted them, explaining I was working on the wartime history of the Secret Intelligence Service, Erich, now calling himself Erich de Saventhem, seemed willing to meet, especially when Nicholas Elliott's name was casually dropped into the conversation.

When I met Vermehren in April 1982 at his home, he readily acknowledged his true background but only on the condition that his new identity should be protected. Having given this undertaking,

I heard the extraordinary story of how he and his wife became increasingly disenchanted with the Nazis and eventually decided they could bear the pretence no longer. They were persuaded to join the Allies by Elliott but only realised the gravity of what they had done when the British made propaganda broadcasts exploiting the defections. By that time, of course, there was no question of a change of mind, and they were sucked dry of their knowledge of the Abwehr. Surprisingly, Vermehren claimed that he had not read any of the post-war literature about the demise of Canaris and the Abwehr and seemed genuinely surprised that their defection could have had any wider impact on the organisation. He was of no great seniority, knew relatively little about the Abwehr's operations beyond Turkey, which had been thoroughly penetrated by the British and the Americans anyway, and had devoted the remainder of his life to supporting Catholic charities. Unlike other Abwehr defectors such as Otto John – who played an active part in the reconstruction of Germany and had been the British nominee to head the Federal Republic's security service, the BfV – the Vermehrens had deliberately maintained a very low profile. His contact with MI6 had lapsed after Elliott had been posted away from Berne in 1947, but he remained indebted to his old friend for facilitating his escape from the Nazis. He revealed that they had been recalled to Berlin and initially had procrastinated, seeking help from von Papen to get the order rescinded. When the recall had been confirmed, they had feared the worst and opted to seek refuge with MI6 who, naturally, had wanted to take maximum advantage of the situation.

Vermehren adopted an air of scepticism when I pressed him on the impact of his defection, but it did not appear to be contrived. I imagined he must still stir strong feelings among his fellow countrymen, so in order to protect him I deliberately did not ask about what had happened after his arrival in England. I later learned that he had worked as a schoolmaster at the Benedictine's Worth Abbey before finding a job in the Lloyd's insurance market. Evidently, he had prospered and suffered no significant adverse consequences of his decision to switch sides in 1944.

The Vermehrens' version of events was included in *MI6: British Secret Intelligence Service Operations 1909–45*, but another major disclosure, also from Elliott, was much more significant, especially as it directly concerned Canaris, the enigmatic figure at the heart of the anti-Hitler conspiracy. To what extent had Canaris sided with the plotters? How much had he known about the extent to which his deputy, Hans Oster, had been implicated in the 20 July plot? Had Canaris played a central role in the drama, as many believed, or had he merely turned a blind eye to their subversion? Two post-war biographies had failed to get to the bottom of this remarkable character who was hanged on a meat hook in Flossenbürg concentration camp in April 1945. When asked whether he believed there were any further wartime secrets to be revealed, Elliott remarked that the fact that Canaris had actively collaborated with a woman he knew to be a British agent, who was also his mistress, was probably the last great secret of the war. Instantly pressed for more information, Elliott revealed only that one of his first tasks upon taking up his appointment in Berne had been to arrange for Canaris's mistress to travel to the UK with her two daughters where they were given a convent education at MI6's expense. Elliott refused to name this remarkable woman but described her only as the widow of the pre-war Polish military attaché in Berlin. With that clue, it did not take long to identify the attaché as Colonel Antoni Szymański, a senior Polish officer who had been presumed lost when, after his internment in September 1939, he was dispatched to Moscow and then not heard of for quite some time. Enquiries about his wife proved fruitless. Certainly, she had three daughters but my Polish sources knew nothing about her apart from confirming that Halina Szymańska had been allowed to return to Warsaw after her husband's arrest.

My efforts to trace Szymańska were extraordinarily simple. Working on the basis that either she or her daughters had retained their surname and were still in the UK, I wrote an identical letter to every person of that name in the London telephone directory. There were only half a dozen, but the response was unexpected, for it was a telephone call from the editor of the *Mail on Sunday*, Stewart Steven. He explained that his Polish wife Inka was a close friend of Szymańska's daughter Ewa, who was nervous about replying to my unsolicited letter. When I explained that I had good reason to believe that Szymańska had been a British agent and had also been Canaris's mistress, Steven, who was himself a German Jew from Hamburg originally named Stefan Cohen, immediately recognised the news value of the story and gave me his support, urging Ewa to cooperate. Having played a significant role in publicising *Operation GARBO*, Steven – who had come to the UK as a refugee at the age of six – and his unexpected intervention proved very helpful. With a lifelong fascination for Second World War espionage stories, he sensed this was a front-page item.

It turned out that Ewa lived in a flat in South Kensington, not more than a mile away from my home in Fulham Road, and when we met, she agreed to put me in touch with her mother who was then living in Mobile, Alabama. She confirmed that her father had indeed been the Polish military attaché in Berlin before the war and recalled that as a small child she had been taken with her sisters to Switzerland, where they had lived until the end of the war and then moved to England. She knew nothing of her father's fate but presumed he had been one of Stalin's Polish victims. She was confident that her mother would be able to explain if she had acted at any time as a British agent.

Halina Szymańska's story, as she told it to me in her son's small bungalow in a suburb of the dismal southern oil city of Mobile, was not only astonishing but was backed up by two crucial pieces of evidence: her old wartime passport, complete with entry and exit stamps for Italy in 1941, and a forged French identity card which gave her name as 'Marie Clenat'. She explained that after her husband had been interned along with the rest of the Polish embassy staff when the Nazis invaded in September 1939, she had returned to Warsaw and, quite by chance, soon afterwards had encountered Canaris whom she had known in Berlin before the war. Taking pity on her, Canaris had arranged for her to travel back to Berlin and then had given her and her three girls an escort to Berne, where he established her in an apartment. She claimed that over the following two years, he had made occasional visits to her, and on his instructions, she had made contact with one of her husband's colleagues. At the time, the Polish government-in-exile was in close collaboration with MI6, and the officer assigned to be her contact was Andrew King. According to Szymańska, talking late in the afternoon on a spring day in Mobile about events that had occurred more than forty years earlier, Canaris knew she was in touch with the British and dictated messages that she was to pass on to MI6, among them a warning in

May 1941, delivered in Italy, that Hitler was planning to attack the Soviet Union. The proof that she had undertaken the visits to Italy was in her old passport, clearly showing her exit and entry stamps, and confirmation that she had indeed been in constant touch with the Abwehr's leader was to come from King, who acknowledged, once he was satisfied that Szymańska had disclosed her historic role, that he had acted as her case officer throughout the war until Elliott had taken over the MI6 station in Berne. Elliott arranged for her to travel to London accompanied by her two surviving daughters Ewa and Marysia – Hanka having died in Switzerland.

The revelation that Szymańska had been the link between the Abwehr and MI6 was sensational and settled, once and for all, the issue of Canaris's true loyalties. However, in 1985, Christopher Andrew asserted in *Her Majesty's Secret Service* that 'the story is at best unproven and is unsupported by any evidence in SIS or other closed files' – the implication being that he had been granted access to MI6's files to check the claim.[3] Furthermore, he cited his source as Volume 1 of Sir Harry Hinsley's official history, *British Intelligence in the Second World War*, where the relevant footnote stated:

> As there will be speculation on this subject we may say that insofar as the British records are any guide A-54 was the sole Abwehr officer who collaborated with the Allied intelligence organisations. As will be mentioned later in the text General Oster, the second in command of the Abwehr, who was also a member of the German resistance, confined himself to giving last-minute warnings to various authorities on the continent of impending German attacks.[4]

This footnote concerned a spy codenamed 'A-54', now known to have been an Abwehr officer based in Prague who had adopted the alias Paul Thümmel. Evidently, Andrew had misinterpreted Hinsley's unequivocal statement, in relation to Abwehr officers cooperating with Allied intelligence agencies upon the outbreak of hostilities, as a comment that could be applied to Szymańska and Canaris. However, all further doubt was squashed when King agreed to verify his role, and any controversy was eliminated when Hinsley footnoted that Canaris had used a Polish intermediary to convey information to MI6 in Switzerland.

Szymańska kindly lent me her forged French *carte d'identité* and her genuine Polish diplomatic passport, which were reproduced in *MI6: British Secret Intelligence Service Operations 1909–45*, thus proving beyond doubt that she had acted as an MI6 agent in Switzerland during the war. According to MI6's official historian, Keith Jeffery, who addressed the issue in 2010, Szymańska was an intermediary for former Gestapo officer Hans Bernd Gisevius, who regularly travelled from Berlin to pass secrets to her for onward transmission to London. Jeffery stated that 'between August 1939 and December 1942 Geneva sent London twenty-five reports' with information supplied by Gisevius.[5] Jeffery also recorded that on 19 October 1941, Halina dined with Canaris, and this event was 'the only recorded face-to-face meeting between Canaris and anyone reporting directly to SIS'.

CHAPTER VIII

SPYCATCHER

Of all the political controversies that were to engulf Thatcher's administration, a substantial proportion were related to security and intelligence issues, and of those, the one with the most lasting consequences proved to be the British government's futile attempt to ban the publication of *Spycatcher*, the memoirs of retired MI5 officer Peter Wright.[1] While the book became a worldwide bestseller, in spite of or probably because of the efforts to prevent it, and the lengthy litigation received global publicity, very little was ever disclosed about precisely how the book came to be written.

The origins of the *Spycatcher* saga can be traced to the legendary molehunter Arthur Martin, who had sought my help in extracting a deathbed confession from his principal candidate for the Soviet spy he was sure had penetrated the post-war Security Service. His connection with my publisher Barney Blackley was through Stephen de Mowbray, a retired Secret Intelligence Service officer with whom he had collaborated to edit the memoirs of the controversial KGB defector Anatoliy Golitsyn. When Golitsyn had defected unexpectedly in Helsinki in December 1961, he had delivered a disturbing picture of the KGB's Machiavellian plots to destabilise the west. Having established his credentials by compromising several spies, among them John Vassall, Golitsyn warmed to his theories of labyrinthine schemes hatched by Directorate S, a secret unit set up in Dzerzhinsky Square to exploit Soviet skills at *dezinformatione*, the Kremlin's policy of concealing its true intentions. Golitsyn claimed that the security and intelligence apparatus in the UK, the US, France and Germany had been hopelessly compromised and held a series of meetings with western counter-intelligence personnel to sell his message of widespread Soviet mischief, manipulation and penetration. His charges sparked off numerous molehunts as his adherents searched the files for clues to treachery and espionage, and among his many supporters were Martin, who had supervised the defector's abbreviated visit to London in 1963, and Stephen de Mowbray, then the MI6 station commander in Washington DC. Entranced by Golitsyn's interpretation of both trivial events and momentous political developments, Martin and de Mowbray had edited his book *New Lies For Old* and had persuaded de Mowbray's old schoolfriend, Barney Blackley of The Bodley Head, to publish it.[2] Thus, when Martin had expressed an interest in meeting me, Blackley had been able to put the two of us in touch with each other instantly.

Martin had dedicated his life to the unpopular cause of sniffing out the clues to treason. Among those he investigated were two former directors general, Sir Michael Hanley and even the revered Sir Dick White. Martin had been a terrier, not driven by instinct or prejudice but by the evidence.

During one conversation, I had asked Martin whether in his twenty-year career in the Security Service any of his activities had made any significant impact, and after a few moments he said, 'I suppose bringing down the Macmillan government would be counted as significant.' His explanation was that in July 1961, when he had been the D1 in charge of the main Soviet counter-espionage section in D Division, he had been told by one of his subordinates, Keith Wagstaffe, that he had just met 'the most beautiful girl in the world'. Wagstaffe had been lunching with his new agent, Stephen Ward, and afterwards they had gone back to his flat, where they had been served tea by a girl who turned out to be Christine Keeler.

Martin had authorised an operation to entrap the Soviet assistant naval attaché Eugene Ivanov, a suspected intelligence officer who had been positively identified as a GRU professional by Oleg Penkovsky, the GRU colonel and spy for MI6 and the CIA. Better still, Penkovsky had mentioned that Ivanov had a reputation as a womaniser, and as he was married to the daughter of a member of the Supreme Court of the Soviet Union, Martin calculated that he might be a good candidate for blackmail or defection if he could be compromised. Unfortunately, Martin never knew that Keeler was in a relationship with Jack Profumo MP, the Secretary of State for War, but he did know that Ward was friendly with him, and as a precaution, he had arranged for the Cabinet Secretary to approach Profumo discreetly for his help in ensnaring Ivanov. This fateful encounter had taken place soon after a Cabinet sub-committee meeting in the Cabinet Office and had been completely misinterpreted by Profumo, who instantly turned down Sir Norman Brook's relayed request for assistance from MI5. Brook had broached the subject so obliquely that Profumo had thought he was being warned off his affair with Keeler and promptly wrote to her breaking off the affair. Thus, Profumo was left with the mistaken impression that MI5 knew all about the Ward–Keeler–Ivanov triangle, whereas all

Martin had wanted was to satisfy protocol and avoid embarrassing a senior minister. The consequence of this chronic misunderstanding was a hideous scandal that led to Profumo's resignation and the death of Ward. A clumsy, misconceived police investigation into Ward's pimping activities resulted in his prosecution, and although Wagstaffe had pleaded with Sir Roger Hollis for permission to intervene, the director general feared an even greater debacle and ordered Wagstaffe to remain silent and disconnect his contact telephone number. As Ward only knew Wagstaffe by his alias, Keith Woods, and could obtain no reply, his claims that all his activities had been directed by his MI5 case officer were disbelieved. The fact that Wagstaffe had recruited Ward would haunt Wagstaffe and MI5 for many years.

Martin retired before he could conclude his investigation of a Soviet spy whom he was convinced had burrowed deep into the Security Service, but he became my mentor and used me as a surrogate to follow up the clues he had been unable to pursue himself. Martin knew I had interviewed Blunt at length, as he had been the officer who had finally confronted Blunt in his flat above the Courtauld Institute in April 1964 and had extracted his confession in exchange for the controversial immunity from prosecution. It had been Wright who had continued the interrogations, and I found myself in a strange shuttle, comparing Blunt's replies to answers given to Wright and Martin years earlier. This analysis required constant contact with Wright, who had retired to breed Arabian horses in Cygnet, Tasmania.

Wright has often been portrayed as either a zealot with a mission, determined at any cost to prove that Hollis had been a traitor, or a disgruntled former employee, bilked out of his pension and hell-bent on revenge on MI5, but he was neither of those things. His initial disclosures had been made through the veteran Fleet Street journalist Chapman Pincher, with whom he collaborated to produce *Their Trade is Treachery* in 1981.[3] This in turn had prompted a statement by Thatcher to the Commons on 26 March 1981 concerning Hollis, which contained the one sentence that so alarmed Wright. The Prime Minister, reading from a paper drafted by the Security Service, asserted that all the evidence of hostile penetration could be attributed to Anthony Blunt, but this simply was not true. Wright and Martin, and indeed every other counter-intelligence expert who had studied the problem, knew that Blunt had returned to academic life in 1945, and apart from intermittent contact with his colleagues and any gossip he might have picked up from his occasional interrogators until his confession in 1964, he could not have been responsible for compromising so many operations.

Wright interpreted Thatcher's apparently carefully chosen words as conclusive proof that MI5 had not just been penetrated but now preferred to suppress the truth. His solution was to resurrect a project he had worked on before Victor Rothschild had introduced him to Pincher, which consisted of a scrappy manuscript locked in his bank's strongroom, but he faced several obstacles before it could be published. First, the document itself required a great deal of editorial work before any publisher would even contemplate investing in it. Second, Wright was becoming increasingly frail and possessed neither the physical strength nor the research facilities to undertake the necessary work. Third, Wright had been disadvantaged by his covert association with Pincher, to whom he had given large quantities of information in the expectation of sharing the rewards. Much to his surprise and irritation, these benefits had never materialised, but he had not been in a position to challenge Pincher's bland insistence that *Their Trade is Treachery* had incurred unexpected expenses, which had eliminated the financial benefits he had anticipated. Pincher and Wright had sealed their partnership by channelling the income from the book and lucrative sale of the newspaper serialisation rights to the *Daily Mail* through a company registered in the British Virgin Islands. Outmanoeuvred by the shrewd Pincher, Wright was robbed of his royalties but was powerless to bring any pressure on the veteran journalist.

This was Wright's dilemma when he was approached by two Granada Television journalists, John Ware and Paul Greengrass, who had bought the rights to my book *A Matter of Trust: MI5 1945–72*. A condition of my deal with Granada was that I should use my best efforts to persuade a list of eight potential interviewees to participate in the making of a documentary based on the book. I helped compile the list and provided contact numbers for each, including Wright's telephone number in Tasmania. It had been this introduction that had brought the two journalists and Wright together. Ware conducted a lengthy interview with Wright, taking him through the evidence of hostile penetration and touching on several other sensitive topics including WORTHINGTON, the investigation conducted by MI5 into the astonishing possibility that Harold Wilson might have been a KGB asset. Had a clique of right-wingers in MI5 invented the allegation to destabilise an unpopular, left-wing government, or had the Security Service been duty-bound to pursue any evidence of espionage, wherever it led? Wright subsequently recanted, but, initially at least, he appeared to have admitted that he had participated in a highly irregular, unauthorised operation that had been intended to rid the country of its democratically elected leader.

Whatever the merits of Ware's memorable, filmed encounter with Wright, his colleague Greengrass won Wright's trust and agreed to ghost a joint venture, *Spycatcher*. When news reached London of Wright's plan to give his version of events, ostensibly in reply to Thatcher's inaccurate statement on the inconclusive Hollis inquiry, the Attorney General Sir Michael Havers advised that, while there could be no Official Secrets Act extradition or prosecution in Australia, there was a civil remedy available, which was to injunct Wright on the basis that he was in breach of his contractual obligations to his former employer. This was judge-made law, established over many years, in which courts had held that servants owed their employers a duty of confidentiality. It subsequently emerged that there were two flaws to this solution.

One was that, like Wright's other MI5 colleagues, none had ever signed a formal employment contract and thus were held to have acquiesced in an 'implied contract', a concept that went unrecognised in the US and so would fail to prevent an American edition. The second flaw was that it would be up to the plaintiff, in this case the Crown, to prove that the information disclosed by Wright was entirely new and had not been published elsewhere. The problem with this position was that Thatcher's government had failed to act against both *Their Trade is Treachery* and *A Matter of Trust*, and there was even evidence in both examples to suggest a degree of collusion. When the British application to ban *Spycatcher* reached the High Court in Sydney, defended by a sharp, ambitious Australian lawyer, Malcolm Turnbull, the issues had become the focus of intense media interest, and the charge of double standards was aggravated by the embarrassing testimony, given under cross-examination, by the Cabinet Secretary, Sir Robert Armstrong.

Famously, he admitted to having been 'economical with the truth' and conceded that no action had been taken against Pincher, even though he personally had read an advance draft of the book, which had been obtained by clandestine means. Pincher's publisher, Sidgwick & Jackson, was partly owned by Sir Charles Forte, a hugely patriotic immigrant from Italy who was so concerned about the explosive content of *Their Trade is Treachery* that he had quietly passed a copy of the proofs to an MI6 acquaintance, who in turn copied them to MI5 and finally to Armstrong, who had to play along in a charade designed to protect Forte's transaction. With considerable reservations, Armstrong agreed to ask Sidgwick & Jackson for an advance copy of the book and pretend he was not already in possession of it. The deception had been intended to protect Forte but severely weakened the Crown's case in Sydney where Forte's identity was concealed, leaving the impression that the hapless Armstrong had dishonestly stage-managed the entire debacle.

Wright won the court's approval to publish in Australia, and the British government was powerless to prevent an American edition. The only crumb of comfort to the government was a landmark decision in the House of Lords upholding the principle of a 'lifelong duty of confidentiality' in an action brought against the *Sunday Times*, which had serialised extracts from *Spycatcher*. Henceforth, all security and intelligence personnel were obliged to sign the most restrictive contracts of employment, which could be enforced in virtually any jurisdiction.

The fiasco caused Thatcher much discomfort, but doubtless she would have endured rather more if my unseen role in the affair had become public knowledge. In the end, *Spycatcher* sold millions of copies across the globe and was translated into dozens of languages, while the Thatcher administration suffered a bitter, expensive humiliation at immense cost to the taxpayer. Unresolved was the extent to which *Spycatcher* made entirely new revelations, and it was not until the former director general Dame Stella Rimington, another MI5 retiree, exercised her rights under the new Human Rights Act 2000 to publish her memoirs that the public learned that the technical information and the operational codewords disclosed by Wright had all been entirely authentic, an endorsement that could not have been made safely in open court during the Cold War.

Wright never returned to Britain but Greengrass certainly did, and pursued a hugely successful career as the director of such blockbuster movies as *United 93*, *Captain Phillips* and the Jason Bourne film franchise. Turnbull later turned his attentions to leading the republican movement during the Australian referendum on retaining the monarchy and was elected Prime Minister in 2015, while Armstrong was ennobled and retired to the House of Lords. But the *Spycatcher* case was not to be the last example of MI5 attempting to suppress the publication of revelations by insiders. Indeed, there were two further cases in which I had played yet another unseen hand. The first was *One Girl's War*, written by Joanna Phipps using her maiden name Joan Miller, which was released in Ireland in November 1986 in the teeth of threats from the Security Service and an injunction to prevent distribution in the UK.[4] We had met in Malta where she was one of Ronnie Seth's closest friends, and she had given me a detailed version of her role in the investigation and prosecution of Anna Wolkoff in 1940, which had been included in *MI5*. Phipps, who died in June 1985, had worked for B1(b), the wartime counter-espionage section headed by the legendary agent handler Maxwell Knight. An Ulster journalist, Pat Craig, had edited the memoir, and when the injunction was lifted in March 1992, *One Girl's War* became the first inside story to describe B1(b)'s operations against suspected fifth columnists in London. Joanna had acted as an agent provocatrice and had entrapped several Nazi sympathisers based at Wolkoff's tea room in South Kensington.

The other book with which I was closely associated and encountered significant legal problems was *Inside Intelligence*, a candid memoir written by a former MI6 officer, Anthony Cavendish.[5] A delightful raconteur and generous *bon vivant*, often hosting long lunches at the Cavalry & Guards Club, Cavendish told me that his MI6 career had been terminated by a late-night motor accident in post-war Vienna, which coincided with a complaint from the American ambassador who had objected to Cavendish's relationship with his daughter. Cavendish's family background was wrapped in mystery. Reportedly, his father had been a physician in St Moritz where Cavendish was brought up under another name. The fact that he later adopted the name 'Castle' prompted speculation among his colleagues that his true name was 'Schloss'. He certainly spoke *Schweizerdeutsch* fluently and in the war had worked for Security Intelligence Middle East in Cairo, where he had encountered the future MI6 chief Maurice Oldfield. It was in defence of Oldfield that Cavendish, who had become a highly successful merchant banker, emerged from the shadows in 1986 through the letters page of *The Times* to defend his old friend's reputation when Pincher claimed that Oldfield had confessed to having a secret life as an active homosexual.

Outraged by MI6's apparent lukewarm support for its late chief, who died following a misdiagnosis in March 1981, Cavendish announced that he intended to release his memoirs, which resulted in an injunction. Undeterred, the mischievous Cavendish privately printed the book and distributed it to his very wide circle of friends as a Christmas card. The government's legal action had been to deter the author by seizing royalties but Cavendish was never motivated by the prospect of book sales. This expedient circumvented the injunction, which would eventually be lifted in Scotland, allowing another legal loophole to be exploited and the book to be published in Scotland. Cavendish had a highly developed sense of fun and counted Jonathan Aitken and Marcia Falkender as trusted friends. His good nature was only challenged once, when I described him in *The Faber Book of Espionage* as 'the Bulgarian who changed his name to Cavendish'. However, he soon forgave me and invited me to attend Julian Amery's group, Le Cercle. He died in January 2013, convinced to the end that Oldfield had been the victim of a monstrous plot to discredit him.

In retrospect, the *Spycatcher* affair can be seen to have been a colossal misjudgement that stemmed from a sequence of events triggered by MI5's disastrous advice to Thatcher in November 1979. It is reasonable to speculate that if, at that stage, the Security Service had acknowledged there had been a suspicion of hostile penetration up until at least September 1963, or simply omitted the offending sentence in her statement, the organisation would not have endured the consequent controversies. Arguably, Wright would not have been motivated to scheme with Rothschild and engage Pincher as his ghostwriter. Pincher turned out to be a less than optimum choice as collaborator and this had motivated Martin to take up the challenge. Even worse, with Wright aggrieved by Pincher, he had taken on Greengrass as his new co-author, and thereby detonated *Spycatcher*, the book which can be said to have had a greater impact than any other on the history of modern intelligence...

CHAPTER IX

GREVILLE WYNNE

There are many problems associated with writing intelligence histories, not least of which is the challenge of acquiring accurate information from reliable sources that can be verified. While today we live in an internet era with a bonanza of declassified official records, this apparent commitment to openness is a relatively recent phenomenon. Previously, an approach to a current or past intelligence professional carried considerable risks, only the CIA and FBI employed media spokespersons and declassification was a word with no relevance in a British context. While it is true that the 1960s saw the publication of dozens of personal memoirs relating to SOE activities in wartime France, Yugoslavia and Crete, and in the 1970s attention shifted to accounts of service at Bletchley Park, there remained great challenges in researching espionage in the post-war decades. In the US, the records of the Office of Strategic Services, which existed from June 1942 to September 1945, were passed into the safekeeping of the CIA, and in Britain, Whitehall clung to the convenient fiction that MI6 only had a wartime existence. In such circumstances, it is hardly surprising that a search of the open sources usually amounted to a heavy reliance on newspaper clippings, and this in turn often meant the compilation of news articles about operations that had gone wrong – a really successful intelligence operation should remain *sub rosa* in the hope of an opportunity to repeat it.

In consequence, some of the early books written about security and intelligence agencies on both sides of the Atlantic tended to focus on failures rather than successes. For example, when, in April 1956, British naval diver Lionel Crabb died while undertaking an inspection of the Soviet cruiser *Ordzhonikidze*'s hull in Portsmouth Harbour, the event sparked considerable political scandal. There was little mention that MI6 and the Admiralty had pulled off several similar missions against Soviet warships without anything going wrong. While in Britain there was a tendency to catalogue perceived failures and embarrassments, successive American administrations found themselves targets of self-styled whistle-blowers – disaffected former employees who were opposed to government policy in Angola, Chile, Mexico or Vietnam. The resulting literature lacked balance, and this in turn delivered the impression of a moral flexibility. In an environment dominated by the disclosure of the Pentagon Papers, the Profumo affair, Watergate and the Church and Pike Committee congressional investigations, the public's diet of misconduct, political corruption and security lapses reflected poorly on the west's intelligence communities, a situation exacerbated by Hollywood, which was anxious to portray British perfidy and CIA abuses.

These were the somewhat fetid conditions in 1986 when I embarked on a history of the post-war Secret Intelligence Service entitled *The Friends: Britain's Post-War Secret Intelligence Operations*, which tackled some controversies from the era dominated by colonial conflicts. For example, during the Palestine Emergency, MI6 attached limpet mines to the hulls of five (empty) ships intended to carry Jewish refugees, all survivors of the Holocaust, to Palestine while they were docked in port. This was an operation codenamed EMBARRASS, headed by past editor of *The Spectator* Derek Verschoyle and former SOE officer Harold Perkins. Incidentally, this was no example of off-the-books freelancing by one of the 'robber barons' but a fully sanctioned project approved by Foreign Secretary Ernest Bevin and known to a small group with the Foreign Office who, once indoctrinated and placed on the appropriate BIGOT list, were said to have been 'embarrassed'.

The facts were so startling that the accuracy of my account was challenged – but then obligingly supported by one of the saboteurs. David Smiley, who had led the attack on the SS *Pan Crescent* in Venice to try and prevent it from reaching Palestine, confirmed to *The Observer* his role in the mission and that there were no casualties. Smiley's EMBARRASS team was disbanded in April 1948 in anticipation of the British withdrawal from Palestine planned for the following month. Clearly, MI6 was not too concerned about EMBARRASS as the authorised history *MI6*, published for the centenary in 2009, contained a lengthy, unapologetic account of the episode, albeit without identifying the participants.[1]

A revelation that did cause some irritation was an account of MI6's plan, ordered by Prime Minister Anthony Eden, to assassinate EOKA leader Georgios Grivas. The operation, codenamed SUNSHINE, was of some significance because it was one of only two post-war cases which had raised the issue of a 007-style 'licence to kill'. The plan was cancelled at the last moment when a settlement of the Cyprus crisis was about to be reached through negotiations in London, but not before an MI6 volunteer, Stephen Hastings, had been briefed on where Grivas was believed to be hiding. Hastings had fought with the SAS in Libya during the war and later with SOE in Italy and had acquired a ruthless and blood-thirsty reputation, which in later years he often boasted about.

Hastings, who had been elected to the Commons in March 1960, gave me a detailed description of his participation in SUNSHINE, but I took care only to say in the relevant passage that Hastings had been 'transferred from the Paris station to be in at the kill'. Hastings gave his approval to the draft, but he did not mention that he still owned a villa in Cyprus. After publication, MI6 advised him not to visit the island for the rest of the year. Suitably enraged, he complained that he should not have been named, but he dropped the matter when he was reminded of his approval.

The other item in *The Friends* that stirred Whitehall was the background to the Suez crisis of October 1956, when Eden had been persuaded by MI6 that the Egyptian leader Colonel Gamal Abdel Nasser was being cultivated by Moscow and likely to become a Soviet satellite. MI6's source for this political intelligence was John Farmer of the Rome station, a seasoned SOE veteran who thought he had recruited Nasser's chief of air intelligence, Squadron Leader Mahmud Khalil, codenamed LUCKY BREAK. In December 1957, Nasser announced that he had foiled what he termed a 'restoration plot' and decorated Khalil who was credited with having penetrated the conspirators' organisation and betrayed them. The sequence of events strongly suggested that MI6's reliance on Khalil had been misplaced from the outset, but the episode was important in historical terms because it explained the missing dimension in all the previously published accounts of the Suez affair. In retrospect, the

Suez crisis – encompassing the secret deal in Paris with the Israelis, the opposition of the Eisenhower administration, the threat of intervention by the Kremlin and the Soviet invasion of Hungary – was one of the great milestones of modern history and especially of the then-fragile Anglo-American relationship. It had been MI6 reporting from LUCKY BREAK that had convinced Eden that Egypt was about to become a Soviet client state and had motivated him to authorise Nasser's assassination. It had been this directive that had led the Foreign Secretary's deputy, Sir Anthony Nutting, to resign not just from his ministerial post but leave Parliament altogether. Thereafter he maintained a silence on the subject for eleven years until the publication of his book *No End of a Lesson* in 1967.[2]

As it turned out, MI6 researched the possibility of killing Nasser and abandoned the project. Ultimately, the president, who was a heavy smoker, succumbed in September 1970 to his third heart attack.

One of the principal items on the credit side of MI6's balance sheet during the period covered by *The Friends* was the release from Moscow in April 1964 of a courier, Greville Wynne. Wynne had been arrested in Budapest in November 1962 and released in April 1964 when he was exchanged in a spy swap for the former KGB illegal *rezident* in London, Gordon Lonsdale. Superficially, Wynne's story was one of the Cold War's more remarkable clandestine operations. Wynne's role as an intermediary and courier between MI6 and Moscow had enabled a spy in Moscow, high-ranking GRU officer Oleg Penkovsky, to pass important secrets to the west over a period of eighteen months from April 1961 to his arrest in October 1962.

However, during my research, I learned that nothing was quite what it seemed about the story that had been told originally in *The*

Penkovsky Papers.[3] The book had been published posthumously in 1965, ghostwritten by KGB defector Peter Deriabin, who collaborated with *Newsweek* journalist Frank Gibney, who had served in US naval intelligence. Subsidised and promoted by the CIA, *The Penkovsky Papers* were supposedly based on Penkovsky's own notes of his covert life. In reality, it was based on Penkovsky's reporting, circulated by the CIA and MI6 as IRONBARK, which consisted of copies of the limited circulation Soviet periodical *Military Thought* in which officers discussed current military doctrine. A second codename, CHICKADEE, was used for the recordings made of Penkovsky's conversations with his MI6 handlers, Michael Stokes and Harry Shergold, and his CIA case officers, George Kisevalter and Joe Bulik. The transcripts covered a total of 140 hours, and the reporting from these two sources was distributed under the codenames ARNIKA and RUPEE, giving the impression that two independent assets had been recruited. The sheer quantity of the material was astonishing. Penkovsky had met his debriefers on forty-two occasions, and the transcripts ran to 1,200 pages.

Publication of *The Penkovsky Papers* therefore proved a propaganda triumph for the CIA. However, Wynne was disappointed to have been sidelined in the text and in 1967 produced his own memoir, *The Man from Moscow*, which was greeted with horror by MI6.[4] The main issue, which Wynne had declined to take advice about, was his insistence on an entirely imaginary account of his intelligence professionalism and his background in wartime counter-espionage. Worse, he contradicted ministers who, during the period of his imprisonment, had insisted that he was an innocent businessman seeking trade opportunities in eastern Europe and emphatically not a spy.

The Americans, by contrast, were rather less concerned about embarrassing British ministers. However, Bulik had been aghast at Wynne's drinking and his unexpected reappearances in Moscow to re-establish himself with Penkovsky after he had been warned off further participation in the operation because the CIA believed he would endanger it.

Wynne's second marriage to a Dutch student named Herma Van Buren in 1970 ended because of the 'drunken rages' caused by his abuse of alcohol which, she told the *Daily Express*, had 'changed his personality'.[5] He moved from Malta to the Canary Islands, Marbella and finally to Majorca, where he became a well-known figure in the bars frequented by the expatriate community in Palma. 'Wynne's drink problem started in Lanzarote where whisky was cheaper than a glass of mineral water,' recalled Van Buren.[6] Wynne had been employed on commission to sell villas at a development in the grounds of the San Antonio Hotel, but his efforts ended in failure.

In 1981, Wynne, having undergone a severe breakdown, teamed up with his ex-brother-in-law Robert Latona to produce another memoir, *The Man from Odessa*, in which he claimed to have been involved in the exfiltration in 1959 of a GRU defector, Sergei Kuznov.[7] Ironically, because Wynne's second book was demonstrably untrue, there was rather less official objection to its publication, but whenever any doubts were raised, Wynne rehearsed his role as a national hero and threatened to issue libel writs. Among his victims were the BBC, the *Sunday Telegraph* and Sir Fitzroy Maclean.

As my research began to focus on *The Man from Odessa*, several problems emerged. Firstly, there was no record of any Soviet defector, KGB or GRU, named Major Sergei Kuznov. Admittedly, not all defectors are publicly declared, but most are or at least are known to their colleagues. However, no other former Soviet GRU or KGB officer had even *heard* of such an individual. All undergo resettlement in their new countries, and many write their autobiographies, but Kuznov is not among them.

Secondly, the *Uzbekistan*, the ship on which Kuznov was allegedly smuggled out of the country, had not yet been built in 1959. It was also not launched until two years later, in 1961. Thirdly, Wynne's claim to have accompanied Penkovsky on a secret visit to the White House in July 1961 to be thanked personally by President John F. Kennedy was a logistical impossibility. Accordingly, in *The Friends*, I concluded that Wynne had 'succumbed to what might be described as "post-usefulness syndrome", a craving for attention, especially from the media'. Wynne promptly issued a libel writ.

When it was pointed out to Wynne during the 1988 litigation that it would have been a physical impossibility to have undertaken the transatlantic flight in 1961 in the time claimed, Wynne conceded having made a slight error and provided further details of the trip, which he suggested proved the authenticity of his claims. His revised itinerary included a car journey to Manchester, a further ride to an RAF airfield and then a transatlantic flight. Significantly, he failed to alter the other details, such as the 'military jet liner' he had claimed he had travelled on. In fact, in 1961, the US Air Force possessed only one such aircraft and that was President Kennedy's personal Boeing 707, which was deployed elsewhere at the critical time. Furthermore, the additional details supplied by Wynne actually lengthened the journey's duration and made it even more improbable than ever. Nevertheless, many accepted his version. According to Professor Christopher Andrew, 'So valuable did the CIA consider Penkovsky's intelligence that during one of his visits to London with a Soviet trade delegation he was flown on a day trip to the White House to receive the personal thanks of President Kennedy.'[8]

Further research in Washington and the JFK Library and Museum in Boston confirmed that neither Wynne nor Penkovsky ever visited the president. The recently declassified visitors' log for the period Wynne said he had been in Washington showed that Kennedy had constantly been in the company of others and that his time had been fully accounted for on a minute-by-minute basis. This was further confirmed by his personal secretary, Evelyn Lincoln, who swore an affidavit insisting that Wynne was mistaken. Indeed, she was supported in this view by the then deputy director of Central Intelligence for Plans, Dick Helms, with whom I lunched at his Georgetown home. A great Anglophile, married to an English wife, Helms volunteered his evidence: Wynne had been useful at the outset, but had become a fantasist and a liability.

Penkovsky's CIA case officer Kisevalter and the CIA's distinguished counsel, Walter Pforzheimer, who had briefed Congress on the case, also swore that Penkovsky never came to America in July 1961… or at any other time. Their recollection was supported by nine other CIA officers who had a knowledge of the case. All agreed that Wynne had exaggerated his own role and made numerous claims that were completely unsustainable.

The last straw would be a matter of trifling simplicity concerning his claim to the military rank of either major or lieutenant-colonel. On the very first line of his statement of claim, which initiated the defamation action, he asserted that he 'had finished up at the end of World War II a major'. This was a claim easily shown to be untrue by reference to the Army List, the official War Office catalogue of commissioned personnel, in which Wynne's name never appeared. Wynne then withdrew the libel action and died two years later on 28 February 1990.

Apparently in an effort to make his second book relevant to contemporaneous events, Wynne had somewhat gratuitously made an ill-conceived contribution to the controversy concerning hostile penetration of MI5 by describing the former MI5 director general Sir Roger Hollis as an 'MI6 mole' when Hollis had never worked for MI6 and suggesting that in 1961, Hollis had been 'the acting director' of that organisation. In reality, Hollis was director general in 1961, a post he had held since 1956. At the time of *The Man from Odessa*'s publication, there had been considerable media coverage of Chapman Pincher's *Their Trade is Treachery*, and this may have encouraged Wynne to make a contribution to the debate.

Wynne's unwelcome intervention, denouncing Hollis as having been a long-term Soviet spy, served to muddy the waters further. MI6 had tolerated Wynne's antics in part because Wynne had been recruited by Dickie Franks, who in 1978 had been appointed MI6's chief. He had been a popular appointment and had always felt a sense of personal responsibility for Wynne. A graduate of Queen's College, Oxford, Franks was also the last MI6 chief to have fought in the war, having been parachuted into Serbia from Cairo for SOE to lead sabotage operations against Axis shipping on the Danube in 1944. He was due to retire later in the year, at the height of the controversy surrounding the penetration of Britain's intelligence services. This controversy was perceived to have undermined the exalted status of the Penkovsky case, which previously had been widely regarded as having been a timely coup, even if Penkovsky and Wynne had been tried on espionage charges in Moscow.

Franks would have been aware (although Wynne was not) that a few people had questioned MI6's celebration of the Penkovsky affair. Aspects of the case had been reassessed by (among others) Anatoliy Golitsyn, the KGB defector codenamed SAWDUST who, following his escape from the Helsinki *rezidentura* in December 1961, had reinterpreted the entire operation as a likely deception manipulated by the KGB. Plenty of MI6 careers had benefitted from Penkovsky, who had rejected offers of defection and who, in Joe Bulik's opinion, was set on a path of self-destruction. Certainly, there were loose ends in the affair that required answers, such as why Wynne had travelled to Budapest ten days *after* Penkovksy had already been taken into custody in Moscow.

Wynne's mischief-making did not end there. In another passage in *The Man from Odessa*, Wynne turned his attention to the Tupolev-144 supersonic aircraft that had crashed at the Paris airshow in June 1973 and claimed the incident had been sabotage and an elaborate scheme to plant false information on the Soviet designers. Once again, Wynne had unwittingly touched on a potentially sensitive issue. A decade later, KGB archivist Vasili Mitrokhin defected to the UK and identified a long-term Line X (a section of the KGB assigned to acquire western science and technology) asset codenamed ACE who had been recruited in London in 1967. An MI5 investigation identified the spy as an aeronautical engineer named Ivor Gregory who had access to the blueprints of the Rolls-Royce Olympus engines, which powered Concorde. Gregory, born in Hong Kong in 1909, had been credited with selling some 90,000 technical documents to the KGB before his death in Northwood in March 1982, aged seventy-three. However, the French security service (DST) had already detected considerable KGB interest in

Concorde, the Anglo–French plane which the Tupolev-144 appeared to so closely resemble. Whether Gregory had acted as a double agent remains to be seen, but probably the only occasion Wynne spoke the truth was when he admitted in a radio interview with the distinguished psychiatrist Dr Anthony Clare that he had great difficulty in telling truth from fiction.

CHAPTER X

BILL CASEY

My relationship with the CIA began on the morning of Prince Charles's wedding to Diana Spencer, although I was oblivious to that at the time. I had been invited by a friend, the NBC TV bureau chief in London, to appear on the morning breakfast show from a studio opposite the Victoria Memorial in the Mall on 29 July 1981. My brief was not to talk about the royal couple but to explain why Bill Casey was such a good choice as director of central intelligence (DCI).

I had known Bill Casey for some years, as he had asked me to visit him in New York to discuss editing the part of his draft memoirs that covered his wartime role in London for the Office of Strategic Services (OSS).[1] I had been recommended to him by Roger Fleetwood-Hesketh, the author of the official history of Operation FORTITUDE, whom I had been helping obtain permission to publish.[2] We met in his office at Rogers & Wells on Park Avenue, and as soon as I saw the manuscript, I knew the task would largely consist of correcting his misspelling of virtually every English name mentioned. Prior to our meeting, I had only the vaguest knowledge of Casey as having been the chairman of the US Securities and

Exchange Commission in the Nixon administration. He was clearly a busy man, but he was passionate about the two years he had spent in London and wanted to be reminded of how his old friends had fared in the post-war intelligence community.

This was a subject I had some knowledge of. While researching *MI5*, I had learned that the Security Service management, led by Guy Liddell, had decided to leave liaison with the Irish G-2 (Irish Intelligence Service) largely to the OSS contingent attached to MI5. Although Liddell's brother Cecil headed B Division's Irish section, it was realised that the Americans, among whom were several Irish Americans, would be more acceptable to Dublin than even the Liddell brothers. Accordingly, four officers were appointed to act as intermediaries, and they had developed a first-rate relationship with G-2, to everybody's advantage. I was confident that Casey's stock was high among his circle in London, and I explained some of this background when I was interviewed live on Casey's suitability for the post of director, to which he had been nominated in January 1981 and confirmed in April.

Later that same day, I received an unexpected call from an American businessman, Geoffrey Jones, who headed Veterans of OSS, a non-profit group of retirees who had served in the same organisation. He explained that Casey had watched my interview and had been delighted by my remarks because later that same day he was to face cross-examination by a Congressional committee, most of whose members had also watched the interview. They had been impressed to know that Casey was well respected in London and had quite the best contacts. According to Jones, Casey wanted to express his gratitude, and wanted to see me when I was next in Washington DC. A couple of hours later, I received another call from John Shaheen, an oil company executive based on Long Island, who explained that he was acting as my link to Casey, and he gave me the direct telephone lines to Casey's three private secretaries, Betty Murphy, Debbie Byrer and Doris Gibbons.

Evidently, Casey had mobilised Veterans of OSS into a lobby group of his supporters. A week later, I lunched with Jones in London to confirm that I intended to be in Washington at the end of August.

When I reached Washington, I put in a call to the director's office and was told to be ready to be collected by a limousine on the afternoon of Sunday 30 August. Sure enough, a car pulled up at my hotel at the appointed time and I was whisked to Langley. I was waved through security, escorted to the seventh floor and ushered into the director's office, where Casey greeted me like an old friend. It seemed to me that he didn't have much to occupy him as the afternoon rolled on and we continued to talk about intelligence issues. I was served coffee and the conversation continued until an officer interrupted us to inform Casey that a huge bomb had detonated inside the Iranian Prime Minister's office, killing Prime Minister Mohammad-Javad Bahonar and President Mohammad Ali Rajai. I got up to slip away, but Casey insisted I remain, so I did and witnessed the proceedings. This was a spell-binding episode, with the director's suite alive with senior CIA officers discussing the atrocity, speculating on who might be responsible and wondering about the number of casualties and the implications for the regime. Finally, I slipped away, amazed at having sat through the crisis as a spectator.

The following day, I lunched with *Newsweek* correspondent David C. Martin, who was also the author of *Wilderness of Mirrors*, one of the best books written about the CIA's counter-intelligence challenge.[3] His father had been a career CIA officer, so David had a good grounding in the community and thought he enjoyed good access. However, when I described my experience, he feigned outrage: 'Casey hasn't granted a single interview to any American journalist!' I protested that my visit had not been an interview.

Subsequently, Casey invited me to his very modest apartment in Virginia to meet his wife Sophia and daughter Bernadette. I learned of his bibliographic interest, which we shared. He told me that on every overseas trip he always found time to celebrate early morning mass and to drop by at a local second-hand bookstore, usually on the way to the airport where he used a transport aircraft fitted with a shipping container that had been converted into an office and bedroom.

My connection with Casey led to another invitation, which I gladly accepted. During the Church and Pike Committee hearings, when the then director Bill Colby thought the CIA might be dismantled by Congressional critics, a group of its retirees created the Association of Former Intelligence Officers (AFIO) to defend the organisation and, where necessary, respond publicly to ignorant comments circulating in the media. One example was Jim Angleton's remarks about the necessity of misleading Congress to protect vital secrets, and another was the silenced dart gun offered in evidence to members who thought it was an instrument of assassination. In fact, it was a non-lethal weapon designed at Fort Detrick to anaesthetise guard dogs so as to facilitate covert entries into sensitive foreign diplomatic premises to access material such as codebooks. The CIA could hardly correct the impression gained in the open hearings, so it was left to AFIO to provide the real explanation.

Henry Coombe-Tennant was a Benedictine monk who took holy orders in 1961 after resigning from MI6. His influence led several of his pupils to choose a career in intelligence. A successful escapee from a German PoW camp, 'Dom Joseph' made an epic journey across Europe to Gibraltar. In this post-war photograph, Coombe-Tennant is pictured with his regiment, the Welsh Guards.

Source: Mark Coombe-Tennant

Codenamed SONNY by the KGB, this photograph was in Kim Philby's KGB file in Moscow and recovered by the author in April 1996. Having defected to the Soviet Union in January 1963, Philby did not tell his Soviet controllers that he had been offered and had pretended to accept an offer from MI6 of immunity from prosecution in return for his cooperation and confession.

Source: KGB Archive

The wife of the former Polish military attaché in Berlin, Halina Szymańska was established in Berne by the Abwehr's chief, Wilhelm Canaris, to act as an intermediary with MI6. The author tracked her down to Mobile, Alabama, where she revealed her wartime role.
Author's collection

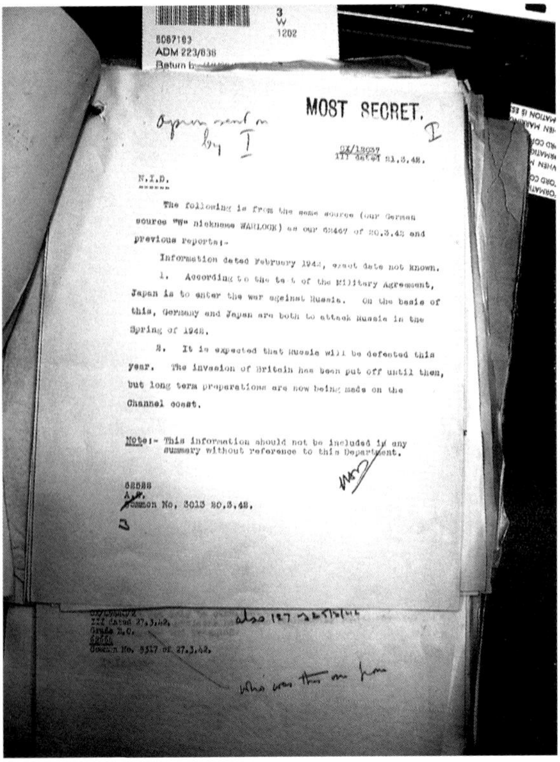

ADM 223/838

MOST SECRET.

III dated 21.3.42.

N.I.D.

The following is from the same source (our German source "W" nickname WARLOCK) as our 62467 of 20.3.42 and previous reports:-

Information dated February 1942, exact date not known.

1. According to the text of the Military Agreement, Japan is to enter the war against Russia. On the basis of this, Germany and Japan are both to attack Russia in the Spring of 1942.

2. It is expected that Russia will be defeated this year. The invasion of Britain has been put off until then, but long term preparations are now being made on the Channel coast.

Note:- This information should not be included in any summary without reference to this Department.

62528
A.F.
Common No. 3013 20.3.42.

MI6 circulated Halina Szymańska's reporting under the codename WARLOCK, often abbreviated to simply 'W'. This file reveals the reasons for the dismissal in 1942 of Field Marshal Walther von Brauchitsch, information that could only have come from the highest level in Berlin.
Source: UK National Archives

OBERKOMMANDO DES HEERES
Gen St d H / Abt. Fremde Heere West
Nr. 3000/42 geh.

H. Qu. OKH, den 10. 4. 1942

GEHEIM

DAS BRITISCHE KRIEGSHEER

Stand Anfang April 1942

A 457-page German analysis of the British order-of-battle, dated April 1942, named *The British Army* and marked 'secret'. Captured during the Allied raid on Dieppe in August 1942, it was one of the most important intelligence documents to survive the war as it provided the first proof that bogus military units, created as part of the Allied strategic deception to mislead the Axis powers, had been accepted as genuine by the enemy.
Author's collection

One of two MI6 officers abducted at Venlo in 1939, Sigismund Payne Best was found by the author in Calne, Wiltshire, in June 1976. In his interview, Best admitted that he had fabricated many of his pre-war intelligence reports and invented non-existent sources codenamed TABLE and ARMCHAIR. The attribution of household items reminded Best that the source was bogus.
Source: Wikimedia Commons, Oseveno

In May 1984, the author learned the true identity of the celebrated wartime double agent Juan Pujol García, codenamed GARBO. Having traced him to Caracas, he arranged for him to attend a private investiture at Buckingham Palace to receive the medal he had been awarded in secret in 1944, in recognition of his vital role in supporting the D-Day deception campaign.

Exposed by Prime Minister Margaret Thatcher in November 1979 as having been the 'fourth man' in the Cambridge spy-ring, Anthony Blunt had confessed in April 1964 to having spied for the Soviets throughout the five years he had worked at MI5 during the war. At the time, it was not revealed that Blunt had enjoyed unrestricted access to MI5's most sensitive operations because of the monthly reports he drafted for Winston Churchill. This is the photograph from Blunt's KGB file in Moscow.

Source: KGB Archive

ABOVE Shortly before his death in October 1992, the MI5 double agent Wulf Schmidt, codenamed TATE and later known as Harry Williamson, accompanied his former wireless operator Russell Lee and his MI5 controller Tommy Robertson to the field in Cambridgeshire where he had landed by parachute in September 1940. Pictured here is TATE and the author as they search for the exact spot where he landed. Author's collection

LEFT The only person to have headed both MI5 and MI6, Dick White was preoccupied with hostile penetration of the Security Service. White leaked information to the BBC journalist Andrew Boyle and then in May 1978 to the author. Source: Wikimedia Commons, Pigsonthewing

NEWS DIGEST

1 NOVEMBER 1981

1 NOVEMBER 1981 No 8209 Price 35p

THE SUNDAY TIMES

COLOUR MAGAZINE 160 PAGES | REVIEW | BUSINESS NEWS | FOCUS

The Victorian way of love

Save to beat inflation 57

IRELAND: is the South ready for unity? 15-17

Brezhnev's arms carrot

Swedes pursue another sub

Unwanted words

Bombing threat

Kidnap killers

Strikes go on

Ice-cream blast

Welsh marxist loses

Ocean-beater

Korchnoi draws

EXPOSED: Ex-officer who spied for Blunt

EXCLUSIVE

Leo Long: "I feel deep remorse. I got caught up"

BL men strike but will vote on peace terms

Britain's EEC bill falls to just £1m a week

Ministers split over rate curbs

Dressing-the way you like it

SHEILA FOLLISS

Harrods-for more than money can buy

Harrods

When the *Sunday Times* confronted Leo Long at his home in north London in October 1981, he admitted that he had been recruited to work for the Soviets by his friend Anthony Blunt. At the time, in 1941, Long had been an MI14 expert engaged in the analysis of the German order-of-battle. This information was considered extremely important in Moscow. After the war, he had been appointed deputy head of the British Control Commission's intelligence division.

When visited unexpectedly at his home, Long answered the door with the author's new book *MI5* in his hand. He had read the passage referring to him and had understood it meant that his true identity was known to Nigel West.

ABOVE To celebrate the publication of the author's *MI5* in September 1981, a reception was held at Hyde Park Hotel, the venue that had hosted the pre-war IP Club – gatherings restricted to 'Intelligence Persons' who had cooperated with the Security Service. This event was the largest post-war gathering of double agents and their handlers. The Polish double agent BRUTUS is in the centre holding a copy of the book, surrounded by the guests who ignored MI5's advice not to be photographed. Author's collection

LEFT Identified in the VENONA traffic as the Soviet spy codenamed HOMER, Donald Maclean proved a challenging surveillance target for MI5 because his home in rural Surrey was so isolated and his sister Nancy, who had worked for MI5, might have compromised their covert techniques. Source: KGB Archive

ABOVE Guy Burgess was never an espionage suspect until after his defection on 25 May 1951. The false narrative surrounding Burgess and Maclean in the September 1955 White Paper would burden the Security Service with the fear of hostile penetration for decades. Source: KGB Archive

LEFT A brilliant scientist and lifelong CPGB member, J. B. S. Haldane (codenamed INTELLIGENTSIA) was a member of a London spy-ring active in 1940, mentioned in the VENONA traffic as the X GROUP. Two decades later, MI5 analysts wrongly identified INTELLIGENTSIA as Haldane's friend, Ivor Montagu. Haldane died in December 1964, just as the VENONA decrypts became available, so he was never confronted with his crimes. Source: Esther M. Zimmer Lederberg, http://www.estherlederberg.com/home.html

Within AFIO was the New England chapter, which had been headed by David Atlee Phillips, a former CIA chief of Latin American Operations. He had been targeted by the KGB, which had sought to discredit him by circulating forged photographs of him accompanied by Lee Harvey Oswald, as part of a highly successful KGB campaign to blame the CIA for the assassination of President Kennedy. The KGB had manufactured dozens of fake documents that supposedly incriminated Phillips, and they were distributed by an East German historian, Julius Mader. Many authors fell for this disinformation, including Irish journalist Anthony Summers, whose book *The Kennedy Conspiracy* was serialised in the UK by *The Observer* and contained some of the offending allegations about Phillips, who planned to sue the newspaper for libel.[4] However, Phillips had been advised by his solicitor that *The Observer* would try and defeat his case by obtaining an order for security of costs, a procedure that required foreign-based plaintiffs to lodge large sums of cash with the court to cover any future liability for costs in the event of an adverse finding. One way to avoid this hefty obstacle was a personal guarantee provided by a British resident, and I agreed to undertake that role. As predicted, *The Observer* obtained the order but withdrew and apologised to Phillips as soon as a British resident guarantor was declared.

Phillips was an immensely decent man and was very popular within AFIO. He enthusiastically sponsored my honorary membership of the New England chapter, which I attended quite regularly as I had been invited by a State Department retiree, Michael Speers, to help edit *Intelligence Quarterly*, a periodical dedicated to publishing articles about the intelligence community. Speers lived in Vermont where he and his wife ran a very rural mail-order book business, and we became firm friends. Over the years, as *Intelligence Quarterly* gained circulation, I became acquainted with a group of bibliophiles, the Foreign Excellent Raincoat Company, which was named after a wartime GRU network based in Brussels. This shared interest would encompass the remarkable Walter Pforzheimer, formerly the CIA's general counsel who drafted much of the 1947 National Security Act, and Hugh Montgomery, one of the last OSS veterans to be employed by the CIA, where he worked until his death in April 2017.

Soon after my dinner at Casey's home, Jones and Shaheen were in touch asking if I needed anything, and I reeled off a list of CIA officers I would like to meet. All made themselves available, and I embarked on a project that would eventually become *The Third Secret: The CIA, Solidarity and the KGB's Plot to Kill the Pope*, the inside story of a series of linked events that resulted in a democratic government elected freely in Poland, the introduction of Stinger missiles in Afghanistan and ultimately the collapse of the Soviet Union. One aspect of this chronology was the abduction of Bill Buckley in Beirut, which would have a seismic impact on the CIA and would involve the incarceration of the Archbishop of Canterbury's envoy, Terry Waite.

Buckley was something of a legend in the CIA's Clandestine Service and had agreed to go to Beirut as station chief after Casey asked him personally to replace the previous station chief, Ken Haas, who had been killed in a car bomb attack on the embassy in April. Buckley was unmarried, but really, he was too well known to be on such a frontline assignment. Of course, Casey should never have chosen Buckley but the fact that he did so had a significant impact on the director, who felt personally responsible for ensuring he was brought back from Beirut alive. Alas, that never happened and served to create an even greater burden for Casey. The other contributing factor was Buckley himself, a decorated war hero from the Korean War, where he had won the Silver Star for wiping out an enemy machine-gun nest.

In an organisation staffed by some very exceptional men and women, Buckley was liked and respected as a highly professional officer who had established his reputation in Vietnam. He spent seven years in Vietnam, much of which as Tucker Gougelmann's deputy running the Provincial Reconnaissance Units (PRU). In counter-intelligence terms, the PRU was a rare success in an otherwise hopeless counter-insurgency conflict that did huge damage to the CIA. Although directed and sponsored by the CIA, the PRU was a Vietnamese project. It was made notorious by the PHOENIX campaign, managed by the Vietnamese National Police's Special Branch, which employed Vietcong defectors to identify the Communist cadres in South Vietnam's rural districts. The results were impressive, although some of the tactics adopted became increasingly hard to justify. The membership of the local Vietcong infrastructure was well known to their neighbours, and when individuals were denounced, often by paid informants, they were not inclined to surrender peacefully, hence the difficult statistics which led critics to describe PHOENIX as an assassination programme organised by death squads. In the year ending June 1969, the PRU had been involved in the capture of 12,000 Vietcong guerrillas and the deaths of 6,000 cadres. Furthermore, it was estimated that the capture of each administrative cadre provided sufficient intelligence to take out an average of seventy-six Vietcong insurgents.

The Vietnam War was unpopular, and the CIA shouldered

much of the condemnation associated with the conduct of the war, but Gougelmann and Buckley were among the few to emerge as having made a really positive contribution to the CIA's participation. Almost as a portent, Gougelmann, who married a Vietnamese woman, would remain in the region after his retirement from the Agency in 1972 but was arrested, imprisoned and murdered in 1975 after he had returned to Saigon to rescue his family.

Meanwhile, Buckley's career took him to Kinshasa, Phnom Penh, Cairo and Islamabad. His six years in Egypt covered the period when the CIA exercised considerable influence on President Anwar Sadat to negotiate peace terms with Israel. Among Buckley's duties was to train Sadat's personal security staff.

Two other significant events had an impact on Buckley's future. The first was the disclosure by the CIA renegade Philip Agee in the radical magazine *CounterSpy* of Buckley's true role. Agree had tried to supply information to the KGB in 1973 but, having been turned down by the suspicious *rezidentura* in Mexico City, was taken on as an agent by the Cuban Dirección General de Inteligencia and encouraged to compromise dozens of CIA personnel operating abroad under diplomatic cover. Buckley was one of them, and in November 1979 he almost suffered the consequences in Islamabad when Islamist rioters besieged and then occupied the US embassy, forcing Buckley to seek refuge in the British High Commission. Four American embassy staff were killed, and several diplomats were taken hostage during the occupation, although another CIA legend Gary Schroen and some of the other members of the CIA station survived undetected in the secure communications vault.

Buckley fully understood the dangers of another posting to the Middle East, especially when a colleague, Richard Welch, had been shot dead in Athens in December 1975 after being named by Agee in *CounterSpy* as the local CIA station chief. Nevertheless, Buckley accepted the assignment, and the major political scandal known as the Iran–Contra affair, which rocked the Reagan administration, was in large measure a direct result of Casey's determination, with the president's approval, to do whatever was necessary to find and free Buckley.

On the evening of Thursday 15 March 1984, Buckley had been driven to his apartment block in the Christian enclave of west Beirut and had dismissed his protection, saying he intended to meet a contact. The next morning, at around 7.30 a.m., as Buckley left his second-floor apartment and drove himself out of the underground garage, his path was blocked by a white Renault. Three masked men bundled him into their car and drove off at high speed. It was last seen in the southern suburb of Khalde, heading for Syrian-controlled territory. Buckley was the second American kidnap victim in just over a month and just one of four to be seized in the spring of 1984. Having represented the CIA on the Inter-Agency Group on Terrorism and having been a frequent visitor to Delta Force at Fort Bragg, he would have completely understood the gravity of his situation.

The organisation that was the principal suspect for the abduction was Lebanon's Islamic Jihad Organization, a particularly militant cell led by Imad Mughniyeh, a young, well-educated Shi'ite from southern Lebanon. A known religious fanatic, he had commanded the bodyguard of the Shi'ite religious leader Sheik Mohammed Hussein Fadlallah, and his brother-in-law had been convicted of bombing the French and American embassies in Kuwait with other members of a group called al-Dawa ('the call') just three months earlier in December 1983. The CIA believed it significant that the first American to be kidnapped in Beirut that year, Professor Frank Regier, had been seized the day before the al-Dawa trial had opened in Kuwait. However, in spite of offers of assistance from Mossad and the mobilisation of every relevant contact the federal authorities could muster, there was no trace of Buckley or his captors.

The kidnappers struck again on 3 December 1984 when Peter Kilburn, a librarian at the American University of Beirut, was taken. A month later, on 8 January 1985, Catholic priest Father Lawrence Jenco was also grabbed. Jenco shared his captivity with Benjamin Weir, the Presbyterian minister abducted eight months earlier, and Jeremy Levin, the CNN reporter taken hostage around the same time as Buckley.

The first firm information about the captives emerged on 28 January 1985. They appeared in a video released by their captors, in which Buckley, obviously under duress, confirmed that he was well and was being held with Weir and Levin, who were also still in good health. A fortnight later, Levin escaped and made his way to a Syrian Army checkpoint in the Beqaa Valley. Released into American custody in Damascus, Levin pinpointed correctly the house where he, Kilburn, Buckley, Weir and Jenco had been held, which was a villa next to the heavily fortified Sheik Abdullah barracks in the Iranian-controlled Beqaa Valley. Intense surveillance was focused on the site but the other hostages had been moved to another location as soon as Levin had escaped. Buckley is thought to have died in early June 1985, but the kidnappers did not announce his death until October of that year.

During the months of Buckley's incarceration, Casey did everything possible to arrange his release, and some of the schemes he participated in were either borderline or outright illegal. However, he and his supporters regarded their cause as a noble one and were undeterred by the niceties of UN sanctions and arms embargoes. If Hezbollah was holding Buckley and the Iranians were behind Hezbollah, it made sense to deal directly with the paymasters in Tehran.

Essentially, there were three aspects to Casey's strategy. The first was to evade the restrictions imposed by Congress regarding oversight. He had experience of this, having authorised the deployment of anti-shipping sea mines outside the Nicaraguan ports of Corinto, Puerto Sandino and El Bluff over three months in early 1984. The intention was not to sink any shipping, although eight vessels suffered some damage during the campaign, but to create the circumstances in which the international marine insurance market would designate Nicaraguan waters a war zone and thereby hike premiums to uneconomic levels. This was the modern-day equivalent of a blockade of the Sandinista regime, with the mines were sewn clandestinely at night so there would be no proof of who was responsible. Any attempt to undermine the local economy would obviously benefit anti-Sandinista CIA-backed rebels, known as Contras.

This issue became controversial when, in April 1984, Congress complained that the oversight committees had not been informed of – let alone approved of – the operation. Casey insisted he had briefed the House and Senate committees, but their members asserted that they had not understood Casey's famously mumbled diction. Based on a hostility towards and distrust of congressional oversight, Casey avoided the need to consult Congress by employing National Security Council (NSC) personnel, rather than CIA staff, to undertake the tasks that otherwise would have to be reported for oversight approval. Thus Casey, having been less than transparent over CIA involvement with the Contras, outmanoeuvred Congress by appointing the NSC's staff officer for counterterrorism, Colonel Oliver North, to manage his hostage release project. As neither congressional committee enjoyed powers over the NSC, Casey's gambit effectively circumvented the troublesome mechanism which mandated notifying Congress 'in a timely fashion', though not necessarily *before* the action had been initiated.

The second unique aspect to Casey's strategy was his personal relationship with the president. Having headed Reagan's election campaign and having been the first director to be made a member of the Cabinet, he was very close to the commander-in-chief and this was understood by other White House policymakers. As a shrewd lawyer, Casey understood the need for political cover, and Reagan was apparently prepared to provide this, in both the Contra imbroglio and the measures relating to Buckley, through the novelty of retrospective decision directives or 'findings'. These undeclared presidential orders, known as Memorandums of Notification, were the legal foundation of covert action taken on behalf of the administration. Previously, presidents had signed off such documents on new and *future* policies, and they had not been issued to provide political sanction for *past* actions. However, there was no legislation covering the point, so Casey took the view that retrospective decision directives were entirely valid. Accordingly, Reagan had issued a secret presidential finding back in 1981, relating to the interdiction of arms shipments from Nicaragua to leftist guerillas in El Salvador.

Casey's third tactic was to conceal the negotiations with the

Iranian regime with a plausible cover plan supervised by North, intended to explain how Buckley's release had been achieved through the humanitarian intervention of an intermediary. In this case, Terry Waite, the representative of the Archbishop of Canterbury, would appear as the front man to explain how his skilled negotiations had resulted in the CIA officer's release, thereby deflecting any unwanted questions about what potentially embarrassing quid pro quo had been agreed to secure the release.

By the end of June 1985, seven American hostages had been seized in Beirut: Jenco, Kilburn, Weir, Levin, along with David Jacobsen, an American University of Beirut hospital administrator, Terry Anderson, chief Middle East correspondent for Associated Press, and Thomas Sutherland, an academic also working at the American University of Beirut. The impression was given in Washington DC that all the captives were valued equally in terms of efforts to achieve their freedom, whereas in reality the CIA's efforts were concentrated on Buckley and an Israeli-sponsored scheme to exchange the CIA officer for a consignment of embargoed weapons. The weapons were desperately needed by the Iranians, who had been fighting a war with Iraq since Saddam Hussein's invasion in September 1980. They required replacements and spare parts for their depleted stocks of US-manufactured equipment. One covert conduit had been established by a pair of Mossad retirees, the London-born David Kimche and his business partner Yaakov Nimrodi, who had invested in Israeli-designed solar desalination plants in Iran. The pair had also used their commercial and political connections to sell Copperhead laser-guided anti-tank weapons and Hawk anti-aircraft missiles to the Iranians.

According to Ted Shackley, who had retired from the CIA in

1979, Kimche's Iranian contacts would release Buckley and three other American hostages in December 1984 as part of a purchase of TOW anti-tank guided missiles. Also included in the deal was a quantity of Soviet weapons captured from the Iraqis and a T-72 tank. Shackley's proposal was rejected by the CIA and the State Department, with the chief of the CIA's Near East and South Asia Division Tom Twetten remarking, 'We have in the DDO probably 30 to 40 requests per year from Iranians and Iranian exiles to provide us with fancy intelligence, very important internal political insights, if we in return can arrange the sale of a dozen Bell helicopter gunships or 1,000 TOW missiles or something else that is on the contraband list.'[5]

Apparently undeterred by the CIA's scepticism, Nimrodi came up with a second plan in May 1985. A well-known Saudi businessman, Adnan Khashoggi, would act as an intermediary and buy 508 TOW missiles from the Israelis and then sell them to Tehran for $10,000 each, with a 20 per cent commission for Khashoggi. This transaction appeared to avoid any direct American involvement, although the Israelis would look to the US government to replenish their missile stocks.

The first consignment of ninety-six TOW missiles were flown to Tabriz on 20 August 1985, followed by a second delivery in September. Having taken delivery of the missiles, at the last minute the Iranians declared that Buckley was 'too ill' to be moved and instead released the Presbyterian cleric Benjamin Weir outside the British embassy in Beirut into the hands of Terry Waite. Neither Weir nor Waite had any knowledge of the missile sale, an item that North had neglected to mention to the archbishop's envoy. Weir, an outspoken critic of American policy and very pro-Shi'ite, prompted one NSC staffer to wonder if Hezbollah might be persuaded to take him back.

When debriefed, Weir expressed the view that Buckley had died in June, but nevertheless Casey continued his efforts to trace him. A third deal was negotiated, coordinated by North, for the purchase of eighty Hawk anti-aircraft missiles, which were to be delivered to Tabriz in November by an El Al cargo-configured Boeing 747. However, at the last moment, the aircraft became unavailable, and North requested the CIA's Dewey Clarridge to authorise the participation of a CIA proprietary Boeing 707. Clarridge, then chief of the CIA's European Division, got consent from his superior, acting deputy director of operations Ed Juchniewicz, and later testified under oath that he was unaware of the nature of the cargo.

The first consignment of eighteen Hawks eventually reached Tabriz, having been routed through Cyprus, which involved yet another CIA officer, the station chief in Nicosia. A final attempt to make a delivery to secure the release of the hostages collapsed when Casey's deputy, John McMahon, asked for the president's personal approval. The extent to which the CIA had been directly involved in North's efforts to sell embargoed weapons to the Khamenei regime would cast a long shadow over the remainder of Reagan's administration. Casey himself was never called before Senator John Tower's commission because he was diagnosed with brain cancer on 15 December 1986 and died nearly five months later on 6 May 1987.

Another unexploded bomb waiting to detonate, thought by many to have been defused, was the issue of how much Vice-President George H. W. Bush really knew of the illicit transactions. The evidence to the Tower Commission of Robert Gates, the then deputy director Clair George and his successor Tom Twetten seemed to lay the matter to rest. However, in April 1991, CIA director Judge Webster announced his retirement and Gates was once again nominated for the post of director. This was an unexpected development – Gates had withdrawn his original nomination following Casey's death because he had then been considered too controversial a figure to obtain the necessary congressional confirmation. Gates's decision to make a second bid for the CIA's top job imperilled the president by granting his political opponents in the Senate another opportunity to examine the Iran–Contra scandal. In July 1991, Alan Fiers pleaded guilty to two misdemeanours in return for testimony contradicting Clair George's previous evidence that he had known nothing about the arms-for-hostages scandal. After a mistrial, George was found guilty on two counts of making false statements to congressional committees but was then pardoned by Bush. He died in August 2011.

The Iran–Contra affair would have a lasting impact on the CIA, but external commentators never seemed to grasp that the underlying imperative for trading embargoed weapons to Tehran was the overriding necessity to free Bill Buckley from incarceration and torture. Casey fully understood the depth of feeling on this subject within the CIA, and in retrospect, given the close relationship between Casey and Reagan, it is inconceivable that he did not act with the confidence that he had the president's support. As for Terry Waite, who had provided North with a plausible cover for the anticipated release of the American hostages, he was abducted in January 1987, and would not be freed until November 1991. He would describe his ordeal in his book *Taken on Trust* and receive a knighthood in June 2023.[6]

CHAPTER XI

FARZAD BAZOFT

In September 1989, 31-year-old *Observer* journalist Farzad Bazoft checked in at Baghdad Airport for his flight back to London. While waiting for his flight, he was detained by the police and placed in solitary confinement at Abu Ghraib prison where he was questioned by a team of Mukhabarat interrogators led by Colonel Kadem Askar. A few weeks later, on 1 November, Iraqi television broadcast an interview with Bazoft, smartly dressed in a blazer and tie, in which he appeared to confess that he had been recruited by Mossad to undertake a secret mission while in Baghdad. Thirty-four allegedly incriminating photographs of military sites were found on his camera. On 15 March 1990, he was hanged.

Bazoft was originally from Iran but travelling on temporary British travel documents. He had been brought to London by his parents in 1975 at the age of sixteen and had become a freelance journalist. The original, stated purpose of his sixth visit to Iraq had been to cover elections in Kurdistan, but he had persuaded British nurse Daphne Parish to drive him to the Al-Hillah military complex at Iskandaria, half an hour south of the capital, where he had collected soil samples as part of his investigation into reports of a massive explosion at the site, in which several hundred people were alleged to have been killed.

According to the Mukhabarat, a search of Bazoft's contact book had revealed the London telephone number of Yaakov Nimrodi, a very well-known figure in the Middle East's intelligence community who had spent a lifetime in Mossad and then, in his retirement, had become a newspaper proprietor in 1992 by buying *Maariv*. In many ways, Nimrodi was the quintessential Israeli intelligence professional, having served in the Haganah against the British and having joined the Palmach before independence. In July 1956, he was credited with the assassination of the head of Egyptian Military Intelligence on Israel, Colonel Mustafa Hafez, who had been engaged in supervising a bombing campaign in Israel. Nimrodi had then been posted to Tehran under diplomatic cover, where he remained for nine years, fostering close links with SAVAK, Iran's feared security apparatus. Reportedly, he was credited in August 1966 with having masterminded DIAMOND, an operation conducted to persuade Iraqi pilot Munir Redfa to defect and fly his MiG-21 to Israel. Designated *Fishbed* by NATO, the supersonic aircraft was of consummate interest to western intelligence analysts and aeronautical engineers – this was the most advanced Soviet fighter plane at the time and the first complete specimen made available to the US Defense Intelligence Agency for inspection and assessment.

When Nimrodi retired in 1967, he maintained his intelligence connections and went into business with David Kimche, a former deputy director of Mossad, and spent much of his time in London where he owned a flat in Exhibition Road, South Kensington. The nature of Bazoft's relationship with Nimrodi is a secret Nimrodi took to his grave in August 2023, when he died at the age of ninety-seven. However, to have possessed Nimrodi's contact details while visiting a frontline Arab country must be seen as an act of great folly.

The issue of Bazoft's intelligence links were further complicated when Home Secretary Douglas Hurd disclosed in a parliamentary statement that Bazoft had maintained contact with the Metropolitan Police Special Branch, reporting on Iranian refugees and political activists. It is perfectly possible that Bazoft's Special Branch role had nothing to do with foreign espionage, but according to Simon Henderson of the *Financial Times* in his book *Instant Empire*, Bazoft had been recruited as an agent by MI6 and shortly before he had set out to catch his flight at Baghdad Airport, he had passed the Al-Hillah soil sample to 'Michael', his case officer at the British embassy, who had promptly sent it to London for analysis.[1]

Others were convinced that Bazoft was working for Mossad. He was expelled from Tunisia, accused by the authorities of having taken covert photographs of the Palestine Liberation Organisation (PLO)'s headquarters south-east of the capital, only days before it was attacked by eight Israeli F-15 fighter bombers on the morning of 1 October 1985. The aircraft flew nearly 4,000 kilometres, conducted several complex mid-air refuelling operations, jammed air defence radars and dropped their bombs with pinpoint accuracy, without a single loss. The damage inflicted on the PLO was considerable, with sixty dead and fifty injured, and the prevailing view among the cognoscenti was that such an undertaking could not have been contemplated – let alone executed with such flawless precision – without the most comprehensive preparations, which would have required the kind of detailed reconnaissance that can only be conducted on the ground.

According to Henderson, Bazoft had been 'trained in the arts of espionage' and was 'already on the books of British intelligence', the latter being a reference to Detective Chief Superintendent Drummond Marvin, his Special Branch handler since 1984, to whom he reported about the activities of politically active Iranian émigré groups in London.[2]* According to an official statement, Bazoft had been in touch with Special Branch four times between 1987 and 1988.

Bazoft's background was certainly unusual. In 1981, when he was a student living in Banbury, he had been convicted of robbing the Heart of England Building Society in Brackley by threatening the counter staff with what he claimed was a bomb – something he neglected to mention to *The Observer*'s editor, Donald Trelford. He was sentenced to eighteen months' imprisonment, of which he served a year, but the judge's recommendation that he be deported was overturned on the grounds that Bazoft was at risk of persecution in Tehran if he returned home.

On the day before he was arrested, Bazoft had met another journalist, Liesl Graz, and she was so disturbed by what he told her that she immediately sent a memo to Trelford. During their conversation, Bazoft claimed that he had travelled the previous day to the Al-Hillah site, driven by a friend in a hospital car, and he had posed as an Indian doctor. Although he did not name his driver, it had been Daphne Parish, an English nurse working for an Irish-run private hospital, who was later to be sentenced to fifteen years' imprisonment for her role but released in July 1990. Bazoft said he had made a sketch map of the site, taken photographs, recovered

* Drummond Marvin subsequently retired to Spain and wrote *Prelude to Skullduggery*.

a damaged shoe and collected a soil sample, which he had delivered to a contact at the British embassy for immediate dispatch via the diplomatic bag to a Ministry of Defence laboratory for analysis. He had asked Graz to send his story to London from Cyprus, knowing that she was intending to fly there the following day for the weekend. Reluctantly, the journalist agreed, although she recorded her strong reservations in her note to Trelford and advised Bazoft to leave the country quickly. Bazoft confided that he was in touch with James Tansley, a British diplomat with second secretary rank at the embassy, who had given him the same advice. Graz and Bazoft shared a car to the airport the next morning, but while her Swiss passport proved no obstacle, he was detained by Mukhabarat agents and later charged with espionage. Tansley, who had been named by Bazoft as his embassy contact, was subsequently expelled from Baghdad in November 1990, having been accused of using 'inappropriate language' to demonstrators.

When Bazoft was hanged in Abu Ghraib prison there was widespread condemnation and protest from around the world, the loudest being from the editor and staff of *The Observer*. Curiously, Trelford, who strenuously denounced those who speculated about Bazoft's intelligence connections, never publicly admitted having received the memorandum from Graz, accepting only that he had urged Bazoft's former landlady in Banbury to remain silent about her ex-tenant's criminal conviction in case the news prejudiced his chances of release. After his execution, I was among those that had been interviewed about the journalist's past and was accused by the radical Australian journalist John Pilger of circulating a smear inspired by British intelligence and of actively working for some ill-intentioned security agency. When Pilger made these false accusations, I sought an explanation and in the absence of a response, sued him for defamation. Pilger eventually acknowledged his accusations were untrue and was obliged to apologise and pay substantial damages. He died in December 2023.

Although I was often pressed to express an opinion about the potential for overlap between intelligence collection and journalism, I took care to avoid the subject during the period of Bazoft's incarceration and made no public comment on his predicament. However, following his execution, I expressed the commonplace view that the issue of intelligence agencies adopting journalistic covers was fraught with danger, although the problem had been solved in the US by the CIA's much publicised ban on employing American (as opposed to foreign) journalists, clerics and current members of the Peace Corps. The prohibition followed the Church Committee's revelation that the CIA had about fifty journalists on its payroll, among them my good friend David Doyle who had posed as a magazine journalist in the Far East before, very unusually for an officer under non-official cover, returning to headquarters.

The author Frederick Forsyth mentioned in his 2015 memoirs *The Outsider* that he had worked for MI6 throughout his long career as a foreign correspondent for Reuters and then the BBC.[3] As a former RAF pilot, it might have been expected that Forsyth would have been on nodding terms with some old MI6 pals but his remarks went rather further, and he described how in 1968 he had been approached by a case officer whom he named 'Ronnie'. Ronnie had good knowledge of South East Asia and spoke good Mandarin, but to his bewilderment, he had been made head of the Africa desk. He knew little about Africa and less about what was going on inside Biafra.

Forsyth also described his role as a courier for MI6 when he drove to Dresden to collect a package from a Soviet colonel in 1973. His cover story, under instructions from 'Phillip', was an assignment to write about the local museum, where he would rendezvous with the Russian officer. All went well, and Forsyth returned to the Federal Republic to be greeted by Phillip. An innocuous enough tale, but the response was fury at Vauxhall Cross, where MI6's senior management protested that such disclosures jeopardised 'legitimate' journalists – apparently unaware that Reuters had been funded by MI6 since 1916. The covert arrangement had only ended in 1984 when the company had been privatised, and MI6 had rarely demonstrated any qualms about any ethical problems arising from it. Indeed, President Jimmy Carter's inexperienced DCI, Admiral Stansfield Turner, attended a private dinner with MI6 chief Sir Maurice Oldfield, who caused him dismay by describing how helpful the media was to his organisation. Evidently, Oldfield showed not the slightest concern about cultivating correspondents working abroad, academics and sympathetic businessmen. 'International journalists keep in touch with key thinkers and politicians in countries where they've served,' remarked Oldfield, whose organisation, Turner alleged, had been 'stymied by not being able to keep pace with the technical revolution ... and by spiralling costs'. Oldfield continued, 'Although contacts of these kinds aren't likely to have access to the inner secrets of the local Politburo or Cabinet, they will have an excellent feel for the state of the economy, the degree of societal unrest, or the prospects for incipient political movements.'[4]

I began to ponder the advantages and disadvantages of collecting information from our own citizens, though I was amused that the old spymaster's primary lesson was not how to recruit a secret agent or to effect some other esoteric technique of espionage but how to make use of resources openly available, at no risk to anyone.

Although Turner claimed to be appalled by Oldfield's attitude, he accepted the reality that the CIA had in the past tapped into the local expatriate community for advice and help when the occasion had demanded it. This was a more economic expedient than incurring the immense cost of setting up commercial enterprises purely to provide cover for intelligence professionals. That practice had been compromised by the Watergate burglar E. Howard Hunt, who had worked in Spain as non-official cover (NOC). Similarly, my colleague Ken Crosby had spent much of his CIA career pretending to be a Merrill Lynch stockbroker, a role he had adopted in Buenos Aires in 1942 where he had been sent by the FBI to study Nazi espionage in Argentina.

For all his faults, Turner understood how the relationship between the media and intelligence collectors had worked but acknowledged that the trust had gone, as had the era when a station chief found it useful to exchange ideas with a journalist who had access to different sources of information from his – for the journalist, there was always the hope the station chief would let slip a good lead. The station chief often found that the reporter had a circle of acquaintances, which the station chief hoped to tap indirectly. Since both parties were basically trying to learn as much about the country where they were posted as possible, they had much in common. Almost all the relationships between the CIA and journalists were informal. Most were no more than informed conversations on subjects of mutual interest, a comparing of notes. Some few developed to the point where the reporter agreed to seek specific information needed by the CIA. In even fewer cases, the CIA paid the newsperson to work actively for it.[5]

The symbiotic relationship ended with the congressional investigations post-Watergate, leaving the CIA's Clandestine Service to cultivate already-established commercial entities who might be willing to secrete an officer within its staff. This was, and is, an expensive undertaking, and the risks are so high that discussion of NOCs is discouraged. For MI6, operating on a vastly smaller scale, there is also a taboo on what is sometimes termed 'unofficial assistance'. However, the contamination of the media brought a double jeopardy, as demonstrated when the British Army in Northern Ireland issued press accreditation to some undercover personnel, thereby sparking a major protest from the National Union of Journalists.

The war correspondents understandably protest that their lives are dangerous enough without the added threat of involvement in espionage, and they cite examples where it is presumed that the legitimate activities of a journalist have been mistaken for spying. The distinguished CBS reporter George Polk was shot by Greek communist guerrillas in Salonika in May 1948; David Holden of the *Sunday Times* was executed with a bullet in the back of the head in Cairo in December 1977; ABC's Bill Stewart was murdered in June 1979 by a Nicaraguan government militia; and David Blundy, then working for the *Sunday Correspondent*, was killed by a sniper in November 1989 during the civil war in El Salvador.

Some in the media, especially those who must have been embarrassed by Bazoft's true background, were quick to condemn the British government for failing to apply sanctions or some other pressure on Saddam Hussein after Bazoft was arrested. However, the real negligence was manifested by his colleagues, who had done nothing to dissuade him from his recklessness.

CHAPTER XII

THE FIFTH MAN

Soon after my lunch with John Cairncross at the Hotel Hassler in April 1981, he moved to the Var in the south of France where he rented a run-down farmhouse and lived with American opera singer Gayle Brinkerhoff. We kept in touch, and over lunch at La Bonne Auberge in Antibes on 30 September 1994, Cairncross explained that he had started on a draft of his memoirs, to be entitled *Agent for the Duration: Memoirs of the Fifth Man*, in which he wished to set the record straight concerning his involvement in Soviet espionage during the war, insisting that his participation had been strictly limited to the war years and had never touched on atomic secrets, to which he had never had access. When I pointed out that the *Spycatcher* judgment in the House of Lords meant that he would be bound by a lifelong duty of confidentiality by virtue of his past employment by GCHQ and MI6, he seemed crestfallen. Unless the agencies gave their consent, he would not be able to publish. Furthermore, by his own admission he could not risk returning to the UK and those same organisations might require him to travel to engage in negotiations in person in London.

By the end of a very pleasant afternoon, we thought we might have found a way to satisfy all parties. The proposed strategy was that the St Ermin's Press would issue a contract for the book, which I would ghost, in the expectation that I could persuade MI5 that we would comply with any reasonable requests for excisions from the final manuscript. Since this was a well-trodden path, I was confident of success.

As soon as I returned to London, I contacted MI5's legal adviser David Bickford to test the waters, and he indicated that so long as the final draft complied with the agencies' requirements, the book could be released. However, he would not express an opinion on how vulnerable Cairncross would be if he returned to the country. While these discussions continued at a relaxed pace, Brinkerhoff mailed me the material taken from Cairncross's notes and drafts, which she had transcribed onto computer diskettes.

At that stage, I was unaware of two significant matters. One was that Cairncross had already approached several publishers in London and New York who had declined his synopsis on the grounds that he was subject to the *Spycatcher* judgment. Nor did I know that he was in failing health, having experienced two strokes, and had moved to a rented house near Pembridge in deepest Herefordshire. Here I visited them and learned that Cairncross had returned to the UK for medical treatment and had so informed MI5. The good news I conveyed to him was that MI5 had put in writing confirmation that Cairncross would receive permission to publish, on condition that St Ermin's Press would undertake to submit the manuscript for clearance.

Cairncross died a few months later in October 1995, just ten days after I had delivered the final draft. Brinkerhoff unexpectedly announced that the book's title was to be changed to *The Enigma Spy* and that as Cairncross had not been the 'fifth man', there would be no mention of that role. There followed a meeting at the Oxford home of John's brother, the distinguished economist Sir Alec Cairncross, who was anxious to distance the family from any suggestion there had been a 'fifth man'. Furthermore, Brinkerhoff had engaged a literary agent who wished to renegotiate the terms of our agreement. We had reached an impasse and, upon the repayment of the St Ermin's advance, we quietly slipped away.

Soon afterwards, as I trawled through the KGB file on MOLIERE or LISZT – both codenames given to Cairncross – in Moscow, I realised by how much Cairncross's wartime and post-war espionage – for which he had received a coveted decoration, the Order of the Red Banner – had been underestimated. He most certainly had been the fifth man and had been a highly productive agent over a very long period. What made Cairncross different to the rest of the Cambridge Five, who allegedly knew each other to be spies, was that the mildly homophobic Cairncross had not liked Blunt and had been recruited by James Klugmann, a British communist and fellow spy for the Soviets. Although Cairncross had worked in the same room in the Foreign Office as Donald Maclean, he had never realised he was also a Soviet agent. He had worked with Kim Philby at MI6's Section V in 1943, but he never knew him to be a spy either. He had no hint from any of them that they knew him to be a fellow conspirator.

In his book *KGB: The Inside Story*, co-authored with Oleg Gordievsky, Christopher Andrew remarked:

> The most important agent talent-spotted by Anthony Blunt was the 'Fifth Man', the Trinity undergraduate John Cairncross.

> Together with Philby, Burgess, Blunt and Maclean, he is remembered by the Centre as one of the 'Magnificent Five', the ablest group of foreign agents in KGB history. But for the conspiracy theories surrounding the career of Sir Roger Hollis, and the other false trails which confused the media molehunt in the 1980s, Cairncross might well have been unmasked as the Fifth Man even before Gordievsky provided the clinching evidence. Though Cairncross is the last of the five to be publicly identified, he successfully penetrated a greater variety of the corridors of power and intelligence than any of the earlier four.[1]

So, what was Gordievsky's 'clinching evidence'? The defector claimed that in anticipation of his posting to London in 1982, he had been allowed into the 'memory room' at the First Chief Directorate (FCD) headquarters in Yasenevo and given access to their internal history, which supposedly had identified Cairncross by name. The problem with this version of events is that it ignores all the previous evidence of Cairncross's espionage, such as Cairncross's confession to MI5's Arthur Martin in 1964, Blunt's subsequent confession, Cairncross's public admission to espionage in 1979 when he was living in Rome, and the passage I had written in *MI5: British Security Service Operations 1909–45* in 1981.

Whatever Gordievsky said amounted to nothing more than hearsay, and Gordievsky and Andrew really had nothing new to reveal about Cairncross except perhaps the assertion that in Moscow the Cambridge Five were better known as the 'Magnificent Five', although this term is not mentioned in any of the KGB files declassified to date. Indeed, on 11 June 1988, Andrew announced at an intelligence conference in Windsor, Ontario that he was about to release *KGB: The Inside Story* with his co-author Oleg Gordievsky, in which the identity of the fifth man would be revealed for the first time. Much to everyone's embarrassment, John Costello was in the audience and asked if Andrew's candidate for the fifth man was John Cairncross, who had been exposed some eight years earlier. Looking distinctly flustered, Andrew declined to answer.

The background to Cairncross's public exposure as a spy was remarkable. First there had been the *Sunday Times* article by Barrie Penrose in 1981. Then there was my own contribution later the same year in *MI5*, which sketched his background as a Cambridge modern languages graduate who had joined the Treasury and been transferred to GCHQ at Bletchley for wartime service, dealing with German Air Force intercepts:

> Cairncross underwent a further interview in the United States where he … made a full statement on his role as a Soviet agent. Although he was able to fill in a number of gaps about Burgess, he was unaware of Blunt's talent-spotting and thus failed to name Blunt as a suspect. Cairncross wisely decided not to return to England and went to live in Rome when the American Department of Immigration declined to review his visa.[2]

As Cairncross was still demonstrably at liberty and had not been charged with any crime, let alone convicted, this paragraph carried a considerable risk, but I had relied upon Penrose, Blunt, Blunt's interrogator Peter Wright and of course, Cairncross himself.

When *KGB: The Inside Story* was published in October 1990 with no new or compelling proof of Cairncross's guilt, Cairncross sought to capitalise on this by changing two specific parts of his chronology. Firstly, Cairncross denied he had ever been in a position to pass atomic secrets to the Soviets during the war, even though his name appeared on the minutes of the Cabinet's Scientific Advisory Committee dated 30 June 1941 as the secretary. Cairncross insisted that 'theoretical discussions about the atomic bomb would have been of little interest to the Soviets' and maintained that he had 'never enjoyed access to atomic material'.

This assertion is contradicted by the MOLIERE/LISZT file in Moscow, which recorded that during 1941 Cairncross had delivered 3,449 documents to the Soviets. Among them was a seventeen-page report from the Uranium Committee, delivered by Cairncross on 3 October 1941, on the subject of problems with the industrial separation of U-235 in preparation for a bomb.

In another report, signed by NKVD intelligence chief Pavel Fitin in August 1945, Cairncross was singled out as having been a vital source of atomic information – designated ENORMOZ – during the war:

> Extremely valuable information on the scientific developments of ENORMOZ reaches us from the London *rezidentura*. The first material on ENORMOZ was received at the end of 1941 from LISZT. This material contained valuable and highly secret documentation, both on the essence of the ENORMOZ problem and on the measures taken by the British government to organize and develop the work on atomic energy. This material formed the point of departure for building the basis of and organising the work on the problem of atomic energy in our country.
>
> In connection with the reception in Britain of American and Canadian material on ENORMOZ, in accordance with the exchange

> program of technical information, we are receiving material from the London *rezidentura* which throws light on the state and course of the work on ENORMOZ in three countries: Britain, the USA and Canada.[3]

Secondly, Cairncross asserted that his Soviet espionage had ceased at the end of the war when he had been posted to the Treasury, where he 'now almost regretted my earlier association with the KGB which still seemed determined to keep me on as a kind of sleeping partner … Files marked "secret" were practically non-existent and even when one occasionally passed through my hands, I felt no obligation to transmit it to the KGB'.[4]

Cairncross explained that he had effectively ceased his espionage and no longer dealt with information that might be of interest to the Soviets:

> My contact with the KGB during this time remained merely formal. No doubt they hoped that I would in time obtain access to more important information, although I was now busy organising my departure from the Civil Service. The kind of information I passed in those post-war years was relatively innocuous and only consisted, for example, of telling my controller how the Air Ministry was able to make deductions about a Russian aeroplane on the basis of the size of its wheels. The moment for me actually to sever my KGB connection never came, but sometimes one is forced into a move which one should have had the energy or the initiative to make of one's own accord. In short, my problem was solved by events.[5]

The reality, of course, is very different, as the MOLIERE/LISZT file, marked with his third codename, KAREL, documented. It had been the defection of Igor Gouzenko in Ottawa in September 1945 that had caused the NKVD to suspend contact with Cairncross, and contact was not resumed until March 1947. In December that year, Burgess reported that Cairncross's position had improved because Sir Stafford Cripps had been appointed minister, and this had prompted the *rezidentura* to suggest a renewal of the contact. Moscow eventually agreed, although contact was not re-established until 11 June 1948 because Cairncross, as he later admitted, had forgotten the arrangements and responded only to an emergency call. However, at the next meeting, held in July 1948, he started to pass documents again. At the time, Cairncross worked in the Treasury department dealing with War Office personnel and he had access to the army, navy and air force lists, which were considered especially valuable by Moscow. He also enjoyed access to War Office papers on military requirements, civil defence personnel and on pre-mobilisation measures, as well as the *Technical Intelligence* bulletin.

Although Cairncross did not have direct access to material relating to atomic weapons development, he reported that his good friend George Oram headed the section dealing with defence supplies and he did have access to this kind of information. Moscow had promptly dampened Cairncross's zeal by banning such a risky venture.

At a meeting on 21 February 1950, Cairncross delivered a large quantity of valuable files accompanied by a personal note in which he boasted of a new appointment, which would give him more access to material likely to be of interest to Moscow:

> I have been appointed Treasury representative to the Western European Union which means that all military documents of the Union will be or should be sent to me. Most of them are of considerable interest. I am already transmitting the old documents. I shall be working under Humphrey Davis (from my old section), but will do a lot of work for E.G. Compton. At present I am sitting in the same room and sharing the same drawer as Oram who is dealing with atomic energy, military research and development. Finally I have part access, which, in time, I hope, will be full, to all documents and minutes of the Defence Committee.[6]

The *rezidentura*'s report of this rendezvous was attached to the file, expressing satisfaction with Cairncross's performance:

> One can judge from the documents passed by KAREL at the meeting on 21 February 1950 that documents of the highest secrecy pass through his hands. KAREL's new appointment opens to us great possibilities for acquiring interesting material. Among the papers passed by KAREL are a few files related to the atomic problem. In as far as can be judged from the remarks in the margins of these documents, they belong to Cairncross's friend Oram with whom he evidently shares a safe. Among this same lot of papers were also documents on bacteriology.[7]

In July 1950, upon the outbreak of war in Korea, Cairncross's importance as a source increased, and he supplied various papers dealing with the influence of events in Korea on British interests, foreign policy in the Far East and an assessment of the war. However, in

August 1950, another batch of documents was accompanied by a note from Cairncross that caused consternation: 'I regret that I have to report that my relations with Compton are becoming so strained that I am not at all sure that I can keep this job if the appointment which I now hold will be given a higher grade.'[8]

Sure enough, in September 1950, he was transferred to the foreign currency control section: 'As I feared, the appointment which I held has been upgraded and has been given to one of my colleagues. I hope, however, to get a job in the Ministry of Supply where I shall be dealing with re-armament questions.'[9]

Subsequently, Cairncross was transferred from the Treasury to the Ministry of Supply, where he started work on 1 May 1951. The idea of a transfer had been mooted by the personnel department and not by Cairncross, and at a meeting on 4 June 1951, he told his handler he was working in the planning section where he was dealing with questions related to the land forces.

The KAREL file showed that in June 1951, within a month of the Burgess and Maclean defection, Cairncross had resumed his regular schedule of attending meetings held in person with a contact from the London *rezidentura*. Typically, these encounters took place close to a suburban tube station after elaborate precautions, usually taking several hours, had been taken to detect any hostile surveillance. If both parties were satisfied they were not under observation, they would stroll to a nearby pub and enjoy a drink together. Apparently, Cairncross liked and respected Yuri Modin, who was the fifth of his Soviet handlers, having taken over from Ivan Milovzorov in 1947. The respect was not mutual, for Modin found his agent to be absent-minded and incapable of working a camera.

Despite Cairncross's poor tradecraft, his position in the Ministry of Supply as assistant to high-flying senior civil servant Elizabeth Ackroyd gave him access to important papers relating to armaments circulated by the War Office, the Joint War Production Committee, the Committee on Production Capacity and other Whitehall departments, including the Chiefs of Staff Committee and the Cabinet. In June and July 1951, KAREL passed no fewer than 1,339 pages of classified documents to Modin.

The *rezidentura* seemed strikingly confident that it could respond to Moscow's appetite for information at the height of the Korean War without putting its agents 'on ice'. Considering that the NKVD usually exercised tremendous caution when it came to the safety of its assets, the crisis over the exposure of Burgess and Maclean was managed as if it were a minor challenge rather than an existential threat. Quite apart from KAREL, who had easily discoverable links to Burgess and past membership of the CPGB, there was Philby, who was then in a state of limbo after being dismissed from MI6 in June 1951, and Blunt – to name but three of the conspirators. In addition, there were several vulnerable individuals on the fringes who could incriminate the spies.

Modin coached Cairncross at their monthly rendezvous on 20 August 1951 so he was well prepared for the inevitable interview with MI5, which was conducted by Arthur Martin in September. Cairncross intended to concede that he had met Maclean a few times in 1937 and 1938 at the Travellers Club, but they had not dined together. He would not admit having seen Burgess since 1943 but would acknowledge a single lunch together. If MI5 had unearthed his past CPGB membership it would be dismissed as a passing student flirtation, the consequences of which would probably be a transfer to non-secret work. From Moscow's standpoint, this would be a disappointing outcome, but the *rezidentura*'s measured reaction was far from panicked, exuding confidence that gave Cairncross sufficient backbone to face down Martin and his colleague Jock Whyte.

When that encounter happened, Cairncross was taken by surprise when Martin produced a pre-war letter addressed to Cairncross, which contained communist jargon. Martin interpreted this item as evidence of a stronger and longer political commitment than Cairncross had admitted. Cairncross was clearly rattled by this bruising experience, which had been exacerbated by a further, shorter interview with Whyte alone in December.

Cairncross intended to report the problem to Modin at their next rendezvous, which was fixed for January 1952, but because Cairncross made a mistake in the time, it did not take place until 3 March. On that occasion, Cairncross attended empty-handed and explained that MI5 had connected him with Burgess, mainly through some new evidence. A quantity of his pre-war correspondence with Burgess had been found in a suitcase left in Burgess's Mayfair flat during a search conducted after his defection. The handwritten material was in Cairncross's distinctive, spidery style, and showed that Cairncross had shared classified information with Burgess. His lame excuse was that he had considered Burgess to be cleared for such material.

Modin agreed the date for their next rendezvous, but MI5's in-house interrogator Jim Skardon visited Cairncross in his office on 31 March and again on 2 April, an event that led Cairncross to send an emergency signal to the *rezidentura* on 6 April. Consequently, the *rezidentura* received Moscow's permission to suspend all further contact and thereafter, the Soviets had no idea of his fate until 11 January 1957, when the *Times Literary Supplement* published a review of his new book.

One of the last entries in the KAREL file was a report from Philby dated 4 August 1959 in which he said that:

> When Guy's flat was searched MI5 found among other things a handwritten memorandum containing intelligence information. Investigation of the handwriting led to Cairncross and he came under serious suspicion. He was able, however, to show that this was merely a memorandum from one civil servant to another and that it had no connection with any foreign power. I doubt whether this explanation fully satisfied the authorities, but, apart from dismissing him from the Treasury, no further steps were taken.[10]

In the light of the MOLIERE/LISZT dossier, it is evident that Cairncross lied about his involvement in atomic espionage and lied about the nature of his post-war relationship with the Soviets, which lasted until March 1953. The fact that Cairncross was never prosecuted caused much embarrassment to the government law officers familiar with his case. To compound the embarrassment, Cairncross outlived the other members of the Cambridge Five and even returned to the UK and published a self-serving web of lies, *The Enigma Spy*.

CHAPTER XIII

THE FALKLANDS CONFLICT

While on the after-dinner lecture circuit, I was often in demand, speaking at venues ranging from large audiences at the US Air Force's Office of Special Investigations headquarters at Boulder, Colorado to tiny groups gathered in small village halls. It was one such engagement, in a community centre in south Devon in June 1995, that led to my writing *The Secret War for the Falklands*. My topic had been intelligence failures, and the talk covered the reasons why the US had been taken by surprise at Pearl Harbor in December 1941, the Tet Offensive in Vietnam in January 1968, the invasion of South Korea in June 1950 and the Yom Kippur War in October 1973. These were the classic examples of lapses in either the collection or analysis of intelligence.

At the time of my speech there was considerable interest in how Saddam Hussein had occupied Kuwait at a time when satellite imagery, overhead reconnaissance aircraft and signal intelligence (SIGINT) were supposedly available to alert countries to imminent aggression. I explained how the Iraqis had concealed their intentions and seized Kuwait before the UN could respond, but I balanced my remarks by referring to some successes, often unpublicised, where a timely warning had resulted in a swift intervention to prevent bloodshed. Specifically, I cited the arrival of HMS *Victorious* and *Bulwark* in Kuwait City in July 1961 to land the 42 Commando Royal Marines and deter a predicted Iraqi invasion and the deployment of British carrier-borne Buccaneers off HMS *Ark Royal* to Belize to protect the former British colony from an invasion by Guatemala in January 1972.

At the end of this particular dinner, several members of the audience came forward to ask the speaker more questions. As usual most of those who engaged me in conversation were far from hostile, but on this occasion, a man took quite an aggressive attitude and demanded to know why I had failed to give any details of what he insisted was the greatest intelligence failure within recent years – the Argentine invasion of the Falklands in April 1982. I attempted to explain that the conflict had been too recent for any of the official documents to be released and the circumstances of the war were probably still too sensitive for any of the key participants to speak out. Citing my books on MI5 and MI6, I insisted that even when the relevant files could be seen in the Public Record Office, it was absolutely essential to have an insider who could join all the dots together, interpret Whitehall double-speak and guide me in the right direction. The man was clearly unimpressed by this feeble excuse, but then introduced himself as Colonel Stephen Love, formerly the British defence attaché in Buenos Aires who had been expelled when General Leopoldo Galtieri's troops had taken the islands.

Love insisted that the British government had been given clear and unmistakable warnings of imminent aggression, and that nobody – including Lord Franks, who had conducted the official inquiry into the background to the disaster – had really got to the bottom of what had actually happened.[1] Love knew, he said, because he had been called to give evidence to Franks and had kept all the relevant papers, including his own classified report, written in January 1982, in which he had predicted a sudden *coup de main* that would leave the Falklands under a foreign occupation…

This was a sensational disclosure, and over the next few weeks I made several visits to Love's farm near Brixham, where the retired soldier raised sheep, to examine the documents and sketch out the basis for a possible book. Love's own role turned out to have been pivotal but his motivation was not one of self-aggrandisement. He had fallen out with the embassy's naval attaché, had no time for the ambassador and took a dim view of the Falklands governor Rex Hunt, but he was on good terms with Nick Barker, the captain of HMS *Endurance* and Mark Heathcote, formerly the MI6 station commander. According to Love, almost everything in the public domain regarding the invasion was untrue and what had really happened had been quite breathtaking.

Heathcote, he claimed, had been declared to the Argentines and therefore was really present in Buenos Aires in a purely liaison role, certainly unable to collect intelligence from clandestine sources. Previously, some of Heathcote's predecessors had declared the Secret Intelligence Service station to the host government and then had inserted an undeclared officer into the embassy staff, a practice that was unpopular with the Foreign Office and was considered by MI6's management as 'deep cover'. Nor was there any opportunity for MI6 to run sources from a neighbouring country as Heathcote was the only MI6 officer on the entire continent, the next nearest being a money-laundering expert based in Barbados.

The best information on Argentine intentions came from GCHQ, which read much of the diplomatic wireless traffic and monitored the signals of the only military unit capable of launching a major amphibious operation. According to GCHQ, this particular unit had been trained at the Special Forces school at Fort Bragg, North Carolina and was permanently posted in the Andes, overlooking the Chilean frontier. Although the SIGINT analysts had advised the Joint Intelligence Committee (JIC) that they could give three weeks' warning of any significant threat to the Falklands, it turned out that the invasion fleet had assembled virtually unnoticed and that the unit identified by GCHQ had remained in the same position throughout the conflict.

Having unintentionally lulled the complacent JIC machinery into a false sense of security, the Argentines had devised a cover plan for the invasion, which purported to be a joint naval exercise conducted with Uruguay. This may have been a somewhat primitive measure, but it turned out to be highly effective because naval analysts would be less suspicious about manoeuvres conducted with another country's navy.

Love's other claims were equally trenchant and bound to be controversial. He stated that HMS *Endurance* was actually a SIGINT platform manned by GCHQ linguists and intercept operators. Although this was top secret in the UK, the Argentines were perfectly aware of the ship's true role, and whenever the Antarctic patrol vessel had put into an Argentine port, the local naval intelligence staff had been alerted to take the crew drinking in an effort to find out their home addresses. Any from the Cheltenham area were considered to be GCHQ personnel.

The regime in Buenos Aires had also measured the priority given to the Falklands by Whitehall. Love claimed that the publication of John Nott's Defence White Paper, which had led to the resignation of navy minister Keith Speed, had been greeted with disbelief and delight by Galtieri's junta in response to the announcement that HMS *Endurance* would be scrapped without a replacement. The only possible explanation for getting rid of one's main intelligence asset was that there was no longer any interest in protecting any possession in the region. In other words, Thatcher's government had simply given up on the intransigent islanders and was no longer willing to pay for their defence. Short of an open invitation, this was the next best thing – a fact that Eddie Shackleton ruefully confirmed to me when asked whether Love's interpretation of events was justified. A Labour peer, Shackleton had conducted an economic survey of the Falklands for the government and had been baffled by Nott's decision to eliminate the only SIGINT platform in the area. Perhaps, he had speculated, Nott's civil servants had failed to tell him of *Endurance*'s very secret function. Shackleton told me that when the White Paper had been released, he had received a call from the Argentine ambassador in London who had been bewildered and had sought the peer's advice about the implications. Shackleton had admitted that he too was completely baffled by the cuts.

Love's other observations were equally electric. For example, he knew the real reason why Nick Barker's many warnings about an imminent attack had been ignored in Whitehall. The conventional wisdom was that the captain's predictions had been discounted because he had wanted a future role for *Endurance* or its replacement, but the truth was that Barker had fallen for an extremely attractive Argentine journalist and had taken every opportunity to break his voyages and slip into an Argentine port where he would meet her for a tryst. Unfortunately, word of this illicit romance had leaked to Whitehall, so the Foreign Office and the Ministry of Defence had simply ignored the captain's reports, assuming that they were nothing more than excuses for further unscheduled visits to his girlfriend.

But how did Love come to know so much about the Falklands conflict? By his own account, he had been expelled to Montevideo as soon as the invasion had happened, and although he had been attached to the Ministry of Defence, advising the JIC during the remainder of the hostilities, he had hardly enjoyed a grandstand view. Love's answer to this was incredible but turned out to be true. When the government had announced that Lord Franks would lead an inquiry into the background to the war, Love had been invited to give evidence and he had insisted that his memorandum on a likely *coup de main* be traced. With the greatest of reluctance, a copy had been found by the Foreign Office and this had been forwarded by Franks to Love for verification. Unfortunately, this version had been annotated dismissively by an unknown hand and contained some very unflattering comments about the ambassador. Franks had also sent Love a large quantity of other material but by some oversight had never asked for its return. When Love retired, he assumed that as a civilian he was entitled to keep the documents and these were the papers he had shown to me. All the Franks documents were, claimed Love, de facto declassified, although I was not quite so confident.

Nevertheless, they amounted to proof that over a time, the JIC had been presented with masses of clues to a renewed military threat to the Falklands and no appropriate countermeasures had been taken. Love was especially annoyed because although he had completed and submitted his very prescient report, every obstacle had been placed in his path and he suspected that the document had subsequently been buried out of political expediency – not least because it directly contradicted the Prime Minister's insistence in her memoirs that 'the invasion was a surprise … it could not have been predicted'.[2] In fact, Love *had* predicted the invasion and had even provided a detailed blueprint explaining precisely how the islands could be seized, what military units would be deployed and the tactics they would adopt. The result had been a plan to capture the islands which proved almost identical to the strategy adopted by the Argentines, right down to his suggestion of a preliminary reconnaissance by an aircraft feigning engine trouble. In the event, the local station manager for the Argentine domestic airline (who was an air force regular) played a key role in guiding the invading troops into Stanley, precisely as predicted, and a Hercules transport obtained permission to make an emergency landing in preparation for the main assault. No wonder Love had been actively discouraged by his former MoD colleagues from appearing before Franks.

The obstacles Love had overcome to complete his survey had been considerable but his determination had been evident throughout. The Foreign Office had raised the strongest objections to his request to visit the Falklands in 1981, claiming it might be interpreted as a deliberate provocation by the easily offended Argentines, and he had fought a lengthy bureaucratic battle to negotiate the terms under which he would be allowed to make a tour of inspection. In the end, Love agreed to fly into Stanley during his vacation, accompanied by his wife, and agreed not to take his uniform. Such a trip could not possibly antagonise the junta. Yet, after his trip, Love had been irritated by the refusal of the Foreign Office to follow any of his recommendations regarding countermeasures and, unsurprisingly, had been outraged when his report was 'lost' by both the Foreign Office and the MoD.

One aspect of Love's narrative was particularly troubling and concerned the JIC, which was a very secretive body that had existed since 1936 with almost zero public scrutiny. I learned that the only Prime Minister ever to be invited to attend a meeting, held traditionally on Thursday mornings while ministers were in Cabinet, had been Thatcher. Supposedly, the composition of the JIC was a mystery and Whitehall was anxious to avoid any public acknowledgement that the CIA station chief in the UK was an *ex officio* member. There was no routine public identification of the JIC chairman (always a Foreign Office deputy secretary) and there was secrecy about the assessment staff and the individual Current Intelligence Groups (CIG). Even I was surprised to learn that the Latin American CIG, which had been responsible for monitoring developments in the South Atlantic, had consisted of just four people: two diplomats, an army officer and a naval pilot, all on temporary secondments. Incredibly, its chairman was also responsible for four other CIGs.

After listening to Love's catalogue of complaints, I began to suspect there might have been a problem with the JIC, which may not have been keeping its eye on the ball.

Love's perspective on the 1982 conflict had been dominated by a particular episode codenamed Operation JOURNEYMAN that had gone unreported anywhere. In 1977, MI6 had received a credible report that Argentina intended to invade the Falklands, so a task force led by the nuclear submarine HMS *Dreadnought* had been deployed down to the South Atlantic to deter the aggression. *Dreadnought*'s unexpected presence in the area had been made known to the Argentines, who (wisely) had changed their minds about the wisdom of dispatching a surface fleet to the islands while one of the world's most modern atomic-powered submarines was ready to sink every ship. This, Love claimed, had been a classic example of how a naval deterrent should be used, and it was to the credit of both Prime Minister James Callaghan and his Foreign Secretary David Owen that neither had attempted to claim any political capital from the deployment, which had been kept completely secret.

Love had been hazy about precisely how the Argentines had been allowed to learn that *Dreadnought* was operating in the area, and there were a couple of explanations. One had it that MI6's chief Sir Maurice Oldfield had been authorised to arrange a deliberate leak in Buenos Aires, whereas another version suggested that the submarine had surfaced close to an Argentine merchant ship and had even raised the white ensign to aid recognition and ensure a report of the sighting was signalled straight to Buenos Aires. Either way, I obtained confirmation about JOURNEYMAN and realised that it would be a key component to Love's account of the conflict. He also explained that the many 'goodwill visits' made in the area by the Royal Navy, and in particular by nuclear submarines to Rio de Janeiro, were all part of a carefully planned strategy of deterrence. The Argentine naval attaché in Brazil would always receive an invitation to go aboard so he would report Britain's continuing presence in the region. Far from demonstrating goodwill, these visits were intended as – and were understood to be – very firm reminders of the Royal Navy's powerful reach and a classic example of the effectiveness of 'soft power'.

With Love's encouragement, I researched the almost completely overlooked role of Britain's submarines during the conflict and learned about the extraordinary mission undertaken by HMS *Valiant* as a part of an enemy aircraft early warning system, keeping watch in very shallow water off the Argentine coast on certain airfields from which bombers had been flying against the Task Force.

Before continuing further on the project, I read every book written about the conflict and noted that none had given much consideration to the intelligence scenario and few mentioned the role of the submarines, apart from HMS *Conqueror*'s successful attack on the *General Belgrano*. No book covered the work of the JIC, nor the JIC's advice to Cabinet, and there were three other glaring omissions which deserved some study. One was Operation MIKADO, the SAS's abortive raid on the airfield at Rio Grande. The second was the deployment of an RAF radar unit to Chile and the third was MI6's efforts to prevent Argentina from acquiring reloads for its stock of the lethal French-built Exocet missile. In short, two narratives had developed since the conflict. One was a remarkable war story which had resulted in the liberation of the British dependency. The other was a tale of clandestine operations, which had snatched victory from the jaws of Whitehall incompetence.

• • •

It was common knowledge that the attack on HMS *Sheffield* had changed the course of the war dramatically, but almost nothing was known about what the British had done to prevent a repetition. I learned from friends in the SAS that the regiment harboured a dark secret about B Squadron, which directly related to the measures taken to eliminate the Exocet threat. Codenamed Operation MIKADO, the SAS had been tasked by its director General Sir Peter de la Billière to attack the Rio Grande airbase, blow up the Super Étendard aircraft, kill their pilots and destroy the remaining stock of Exocet missiles. While DLB, as he was known, had been enthusiastic about the project and had committed the regiment to it, the men of B Squadron had been rather less keen to participate in what they had perceived as a suicide mission. Due to the extreme range from the nearest British airfield at Wideawake on Ascension Island, DLB's plan had required two Hercules C-47s to crash-land on the runway, disembark the troops to complete their assignment and then withdraw to the safety of neutral Chile. When informed of DLB's scheme, the soldiers, who had stormed the Iranian embassy in London in 1980, had baulked at the prospect of such a risky undertaking.

In the event, no such operation had happened but there had been a mysterious, hitherto unexplained incident in which a Sea King helicopter had been found abandoned outside Punta Arenas in Tierra del Fuego. According to my sources, the helicopter had been an attempt, codenamed PLUM DUFF, to insert a reconnaissance party into Argentina within sight of the Rio Grande airbase, as a preliminary reconnaissance mission before MIKADO, but at the last moment the operation had been compromised and aborted. More significantly, B Squadron had refused to participate in MIKADO and DLB had sacked the squadron's commander, Major John Moss. Nobody had talked openly about this, but DLB's memoirs *Looking for Trouble*, ghosted by Duff Hart-Davis, had made an oblique reference to some undefined, embarrassing incident in which his troops had not shown much enthusiasm for a particular task and DLB had been obliged to discipline the senior officer involved.[3]

It did not take long to establish what had happened. When DLB had unveiled MIKADO, the most senior NCO in B Squadron had asked Moss to be excluded as he regarded the plan as sheer folly, and when Moss had reported the remark to DLB, he added that he agreed with his verdict. DLB had reacted with fury and had sacked Moss on the spot, which had created some considerable dissention among his men. Ugly words like mutiny had been mentioned, and although DLB had been reticent when challenged on the subject, Moss had confirmed much of the detail. He had been willing to lead an attack from Chile but had become persuaded by the RAF that the frontal approach on Rio Grande by air was an invitation to disaster. As for the exfiltration, either by hijacked vehicles or on foot to Chile, too much had been left to chance. The last straw had been the loss of the advance party, sent to reconnoiter the airfield, which meant that the operation would have to be executed blind, entirely contrary to the SAS's principle of planning for every last contingency.

I was now confident that my book would have to reveal not just the intelligence background to the war but would have to cover MIKADO, the role of the submarines and MI6's operation in Paris to stop the Argentines from purchasing more Exocets. The latter had been completed largely by veteran MI6 agent Tony Divall, who for years had reported from Hamburg on the 'grey market' in arms. Information from Divall had enabled MI6 to intercept at least two consignments of weapons destined for the Provisional IRA and he had been in an excellent position to dupe the Argentine naval intelligence officer who supervised his country's procurement programme. A visit to Divall in Hamburg on 20 July 1995 satisfied me that this was an important dimension to the story, but I was also sure that there were other aspects that required coverage: the CIA's role during the war, the donation of newly introduced US satellite communications equipment, the RAF's SIGINT flights, the covert radar station in Chile, and the Argentine standpoint.

My contacts in the CIA put me in touch with Vinkler 'Vinks' Blocker, the station chief in Buenos Aires at the time of the invasion. He was also able to talk to others in Washington DC who had witnessed the war at close quarters, among them the legendary General Vernon Walters who had flown down to persuade Galtieri that a swift withdrawal from the Falklands would be the only way to avoid humiliation at the hands of the Iron Lady.

Equally important had been the Argentine perspective, and I researched this in September 1995 with the help of Carlos Doglioli, the most senior Argentine intelligence officer to have been taken prisoner by the British during the conflict. However, his experience had been rather different from the rest of the Argentine troops who were shipped back to the mainland after the surrender. Doglioli and some of the other senior officers were detained on the *St Edmund*, a chartered Harwich car ferry which was moored in Port Stanley. They were to be kept in custody for a month until the end of June when the junta in Buenos Aires formally acknowledged the surrender – almost as hostages to force the junta to concede defeat. To their surprise, the prisoners were treated with great courtesy and were saluted by their British captors. Meanwhile, with considerable tact, the Argentine troops were shipped back to Puerto Madryn on the *Norland* and the *Canberra*, acquiescing with a confidential request that the disembarkation should take place at night without the British escorts wearing sidearms.

Far from being embittered by his experience, Doglioli had become a convinced Anglophile, determined that both sides of the war should be told fairly. Satisfied that I would show the fairness displayed by the military historian Martin Middlebrook, Doglioli introduced me to his many friends who had fought in the conflict.[4] After his release from captivity, Doglioli had been appointed Argentina's chief of counter-intelligence and in that role he had found that several of the senior posts in the army and air force had gone to veterans of the war, all equally willing to collaborate with a writer keen to distinguish between fact and myth. Thus, it was Doglioli who introduced me to the naval pilot who had led his squadron's Exocet attack on the *Sheffield* and to the ingenious technician who had improvised a surface-launched version of the missile that had crippled HMS *Glasgow*.

One of Doglioli's friends was the marines officer who had been in charge of ground security at the Puerto Deseado airbase. He described to me how he had sewn a fake minefield near the perimeter fence on the coastal approaches, with the intention that the earthworks should be visible to satellite surveillance and thus deter an expected attack from British Special Forces. When I asked him why he was so confident that the enemy would land on the beach and attack the airfield, he replied, 'This wasn't guesswork. I've attended the clandestine infiltration course at Fort Monckton!'

As it turned out, he was not far wrong. It was only the Argentine surrender that cancelled a Special Boat Service mission codenamed KETTLEDRUM to the mainland, aboard HMS *Onyx*. The diesel electric submarine was recalled while en route to its target.

Finally, having visited Rio de Janeiro and Buenos Aires, I flew to Santiago where General Augusto Pinochet granted me an interview and disclosed details of Chile's covert cooperation with the British during the war, including the deployment of RAF SIGINT aircraft in Chilean colours. The clandestine radar and SIGINT dimension to the conflict turned out to be very sensitive, not least because the supposedly neutral Chileans were deliberately coy about the extent of the facilities they had extended to the British, for fear of provoking the Argentines. Nevertheless, the cooperation had been crucial and had involved three RAF Nimrod aircraft and a Marconi radar apparatus uprooted from the Shetland Islands. They had been flown to San Félix, the largest island of the four in the Desventuradas, arguably one of the most remote and secret sites in the world. At just two square kilometres, it was not much more than a tiny barren volcanic outcrop with a runway dominating the landscape. Located 850 kilometres north-west of Santiago, it was far from almost anywhere in the Pacific Ocean and manned by a rotating group of Chilean naval personnel who maintained the airfield and operated a SIGINT facility aimed at Peruvian communications. The island had been visited by RAF officer Wing Commander Sidney Edwards, formerly the air attaché in Madrid and recently posted to the embassy in Santiago, accompanied by General Vincente Rodriguez, the head of D-2, Chile's air intelligence branch.[5] This initial reconnaissance was undertaken in anticipation of the deployment of the aircraft, an operation codenamed ACME.

The Chileans had wanted to buy Hawker Hunter jets, an aircraft they had bought in the past, and had expressed an interest in a couple of photographic reconnaissance Canberras. They had also bought the guided missile destroyer HMS *Norfolk* and had offered not to take delivery, but the suggestion had been politely declined. However, it was agreed to delay the handover of the RFA *Tidepool* and the tanker had filled up at Curaçao and joined the Task Force. These were all very positive gestures of goodwill – the junta was acutely aware that there were two brigades of Argentine marine infantry positioned along the border, posing a serious threat, and had expressed the view privately that if the Falklands fell, Chile's territory on Tierra del Fuego would be invaded 'within three weeks'. On the other hand, if things went badly on the islands, there was a view that Buenos Aires might launch a distraction attack anyway. Accordingly, Santiago had a big investment in a British victory.

After his visit to San Félix, Edwards had reported that although the runway was in excellent condition, there was insufficient fuel stored at the airfield to support even one Nimrod and at 2,000 meters, the strip was not long enough for a fully laden Nimrod to take off safely. Accordingly, it had been suggested that the aircraft should fly from San Félix with only limited fuel and then land to refuel at night at Concepción, 500 kilometres south of Santiago. With a range of 9,000 kilometres, the R-1 could comfortably fly through Chilean and international airspace at 40,000 feet, peer over the Andes, venture into the south Atlantic for an operational patrol and return to San Félix.

The Chileans had agreed to allow an R-1 to fly from San Félix and thus far it had completed two missions, the first on 9 May and the second the following afternoon. A third was scheduled for Monday, the very next day, with take-off just a few hours away. The trick would be to coordinate the Nimrod flight with the night that PLUM DUFF was infiltrated into the mainland, thereby allowing any Argentine reaction to be monitored in real time. There was also a hope that the aircraft, painted in Chilean livery and operating from the inhospitable dormant volcano midway between the mainland and Easter Island in the Pacific, would be able to locate British-designed Type 42 destroyers *Hércules* and *Santísima Trinidad* and help *Conqueror* to keep them under observation.

The R-1, with discreet Chilean support, was a crucial part of the intelligence dimension, which even the Cabinet was unaware of. Only members of Thatcher's smaller war Cabinet knew that maritime patrol Nimrods had been deployed to Ascension within three days of the invasion and had been briefed about a long-range reconnaissance flight completed the previous day that, supported by Victor tankers, had lasted just over nineteen hours and had taken the aircraft within sixty miles of the Argentine coast. The R-1 had the potential to find elusive targets such as the *San Luis*, lurking underwater somewhere near West Falkland, which would be unlikely to be found by any other means. However, it had been recognised that due to the delicacy of the situation, Pinochet might easily terminate the clandestine cooperation if there was a major diplomatic incident that compromised Chile's supposed neutrality. PLUM DUFF had just that potential.

Operation PLUM DUFF had been assigned to B Squadron's Boat Troop, which had not got off to a good start when it had departed Hereford at 5.00 a.m. and been driven in a four-ton Bedford army truck to Brize Norton for the flight, scheduled for take-off at 10.00 a.m. They had finally landed at Wideawake on Ascension to be accommodated at the makeshift barracks in the settlement known as Two Boats. Then there had been an interminable wait, checking equipment, test-firing their high-velocity M16 Armalites, cleaning moving metal parts and removing condensation by reloading rounds from magazines, ready for the long, thirteen-hour flight on a heavily overladen Hercules to the Task Force.

The flight took off from Ascension in the middle of the night, at 2.45 a.m. The cargo hold was crammed with four huge fuel bladders and the eight SAS men resting on stretchers rigged above them, barely coping with the almost overwhelming stench of the aviation gas. Seven hours into the flight, the C-130 held a rendezvous at 17,000 feet with a Victor tanker. The transfer of 37,000 pounds of fuel took twenty minutes, with both aircraft flying 'downhill' until they reached an altitude of 2,500 feet. Then, contact was broken and the pilot, who had only undertaken this operation five times, pulled up the plane – one of only two recently equipped for aerial refuelling – to gain height and resume the epic journey. By the time they had entered the Total Exclusion Zone directly north of East Falkland and approached the RFA *Fort Austin* from the stern, the Hercules had dropped to 2,000 feet and was flying at 120 knots.

Parachuting into the South Atlantic in mid-winter would be sheer folly under any other circumstances. What looked easy on paper – picking up eight men from the sea by a Gemini inflatable – is very hard to pull off in reality, with the men, assuming they had survived the 1,200-foot drop, only able to survive for a few minutes in the water temperature of 4 degrees. Even with the benefit of their wetsuits, the rescuers had to race against the clock but without the advantage of clear vision.

These kinds of operations are practised in good weather off Poole Harbour with an air-sea rescue helicopter standing by, bearing little resemblance to the twenty-foot rollers of the grey Atlantic. Although the eight men had completed two drops into Studland

Bay on the Dorset coast, none had ever undertaken an operational jump. Down in the deep troughs, those aboard the rigid raider could only see the water towering around them. The coxswain was in radio contact with the bridge on the *Fort Austin*, where one observer had been assigned the task of watching a particular target. Light signals guided the boat's navigator, port or starboard, to the next figure floundering in the icy water. The drops were in a single line, but the Rigid Inflatable Boat (RIB), powered by outboard motors that had been known to fail at critical moments, had not found it easy to spot the figures in the water, even if they had all deployed their fluorescent orange lifejackets. The last of the swimmers to be scooped into the boat was signaller Lance Corporal Mick Fraser, a tough Gordon Highlander.

To complicate matters further, the usual procedures had been reversed, with the men being dropped first followed by a second pass with their stores. Normally, the equipment would go first, followed by the men, so there would be life rafts in the water in case anything went wrong. In the event, it had taken forty minutes to complete the pick-up, so the circling Hercules had been at the very limit of its endurance when it had finally received permission to make the second drop of the two 500-pound containers into which had been packed the patrol's rations, weapons, clothing, explosives and communications equipment. When the Hercules finally reached Ascension with its fuel tanks at a critical level, it had been aloft for just over twenty-four hours.

Once safely aboard the fleet replenishment vessel, the SAS men were given mugs of hot soup and the opportunity to wriggle out of their wetsuits and into their clothes – unpacked from the two containers, one of which turned out not to have been completely watertight. Consequently, all eight found their new clothes to be either damp or wringing wet. Only a few minutes later, they had clambered onto a Sea King helicopter for the brief cross-decking flight to the flagship, HMS *Hermes*.

Once landed on the carrier, mission leader Captain Andy Legg had been escorted to see the captain on the bridge who had broken the news that the next phase of the mission was scheduled for midnight that same night. Aghast, Legg had requested a delay, pointing out that his men were wet and cold, their equipment was damp and they still had not been issued with much in the way of maps. Captain Linley Middleton had agreed to request a 24-hour postponement.

After an uncomfortable night in a narrow companionway, no other accommodation having been made available, Legg and his men had been taken in the afternoon to the flight deck for a short cross-decking, five-mile flight to HMS *Invincible*, in preparation for the mission which had been rescheduled for the next evening. Legg had conferred with the Sea King aircrew about the route planned for the mission to the mainland. The distance involved was 325 nautical miles.

The traumatic journey to the Task Force had left all eight men physically and emotionally drained, and they had been secretly relieved when the news had circulated that there would be a 24-hour delay in the next phase of their mission, the helicopter flight to the mainland.

Their leader, Legg, was a former teacher from Manchester with a master's degree in mathematics from Reading University. He had passed out of Sandhurst and joined the Royal Hampshires in 1977. Recently married, Andy Legg was an unconventional SAS officer, but he was popular with his men, whom he had intended to take to Canada six weeks earlier. He had been scheduled to fly with B Squadron on 5 April to Alberta, to participate in an exercise at the huge Suffield live-firing training area. Instead, his squadron commander had cancelled the trip and mooted a role in what would become Operation MIKADO. He had gained support from one of the older men, Jake Vaughan, a senior staff sergeant from a Highland regiment who had seen action in Aden, Borneo and Dhofar. Vaughan had explained his doubts about the operation's viability to the officer, who was young enough to be his son. On that occasion, he remembered, Legg apparently turned pale but he had not pulled out.

The rest of the team included the weapons specialist, Neil 'Nasty' Gibson from the Royal Marines, who at an early briefing at headquaters had produced a Welrod 9mm silenced handgun, which had been made famous during the Second World War by SOE as an expedient for dispatching German sentries. Bolt action and loaded with six rounds, each of which had to be chambered individually, the Welrod unmistakably was an instrument of quiet assassination rather than a combat weapon. Appalled, Legg had stormed out of the meeting but later had been reconciled to the likelihood that such a gun might have its uses in Rio Grande. The problem of compromise by a civilian was always a challenge and no orders were ever given before an operation because split-second decisions of this kind can only be made by the man unexpectedly confronted by a stranger who has blundered into a patrol. It might be a child goatherd in the Radfan mountains or an innocent member of the public walking their dog in Northern Ireland. If a hide is exposed or a team put in jeopardy by such a chance encounter, one option will be a permanent solution, whatever the consequences. Under most circumstances, taking a prisoner is simply not viable. Whatever reservations Legg may have had about Gibson's choice of personal weapon, his companions knew that his special skills might come in handy.

Also on the mission were 37-year-old 'Taff' Townsend, formerly a Regimental Sergeant-Major in the Royal Signals; Corporal Peter Byng; Lance Corporal Stude Buch; and Sergeants Gwynne Davies and 'Danny the Rat' Ratowski. The final briefing had taken place at 1.00 a.m., ready for a take-off scheduled for just after 3.00 a.m.

One planned additional member of the team was to be D Squadron's Billy Ratcliffe, who was to act as escort for the aircrew after the helicopter had landed in Chile. A veteran of operations in Oman and Northern Ireland since joining the regiment in 1973, Ratcliffe was a Spanish speaker and had been briefed by his commanding officer Cedric Delves, but at the last moment he had been scrubbed from the mission to save weight. Since the helicopter crew had undergone escape and evasion training, it was considered that they probably would not need Ratcliffe and every extra ounce of weight was critical and translated into vital fuel.

The Sea King's pilot was Royal Marine Lieutenant Dick Hutchings, his co-pilot was Lieutenant Alan Bennett and the winchman was Peter Imrie. Having been brought as close as possible by *Invincible*, which had steamed west under cover of darkness at full speed and without radar, escorted by HMS *Brilliant*, the Sea King set off. Coincidentally, the date chosen was Argentine Navy Day, when the opposition might be expected to have relaxed their guard following a day of celebrations. Fully laden, with the SAS men all dressed in their Norwegian Arctic warfare gear and wearing immersion suits to keep them warm, the Sea King had attempted a horizontal take-off from the flight deck and, dangerously overloaded, only narrowly avoided plunging into the sea as the rotors gradually achieved lift. As soon as the helicopter was clear, *Invincible* and *Brilliant* had turned east towards the Exclusion Zone and a few hours later had put on a fireworks display of high-intensity Lepus flares, dropped from a pair of Harriers, as a decoy to distract the enemy's attention. In addition, *Invincible* had launched a dawn raid on Port Stanley and dropped six 1,000-pound bombs to demonstrate that the ship was still in the vicinity.

The remainder of the three hour and forty-five minute flight across the bitterly cold Atlantic was uneventful, but as the helicopter approached the target area twenty miles north-east of Rio Grande, the hand-held Omega radar warning receiver alerted Hutchings to a lock-on by a hostile radar. Then Bennett reported a flare some distance away towards the coast, not realising it was actually a burn-off from an offshore oil-production platform. After a quick consultation with Legg, it was agreed that the mission should continue but as they landed in dense fog fourteen miles north of Rio Grande, a second flare was seen much closer and those peering out of the rear windows believed they could also see headlights on a nearby road.

The patrol was already scrambling out of the sliding side door when, after an agonising few moments of crisis management, Legg announced that he was aborting the first stage of the mission, which, in his judgement, had been compromised and would opt for the second, emergency, drop-off point just inside the Chilean frontier a further dozen miles away. The whole scheme had depended upon surprise and his principal task was to avoid discovery and maintain a covert hide from which the Rio Grande base could be kept under surveillance. The prospect of being chased across the Pampas by well-armed Argentine troops was not part of the plan and the merest hint of a raid could transform a brilliant *coup de main* into a costly fiasco. Accordingly, Legg shook his head and called out to the two NCOs already on the ground, 'I'm sorry, it's Chile after all.'

Uncomprehending, Gwynne Davies made the memorable reply, 'Chilly… it's fucking freezing!'

They climbed back aboard the helicopter, and moments later Hutchings took it into a steep climb, heading west towards the border to fly above the heavy fog. However, this had been a calculated risk, for as soon as the aircraft reached the safety of 750 feet it attracted another danger. The warning receiver indicated that they had been acquired again by a hostile radar. The next sequence, anticipated by any competent aircrew, would be the equivalent of a death sentence – an audible confirmation that a fire control radar had engaged the target. Thereafter, there would be a missile launch or a burst of gunfire from a radar-directed weapon, such as the Rheinmetall 202s sited on the ground. Death would probably be instantaneous and none of those aboard would know anything about it.

The mission's fallback plan was to fly to neutral territory, so Hutchings took the helicopter on course to Chile, dropping the SAS team off in the empty wilderness before flying on towards a dirt track ten miles south of Punta Arenas on the last remaining drops of fuel.

For the three hours before dawn, the SAS team took a westerly compass route towards the Argentine border but made slow progress over the exposed, sodden ground, as challenging as any of the terrain in south Wales where the regiment underwent the most demanding training. Finally, they found a gully in which to conceal themselves during daylight, and Mick Fraser achieved a fix on the satellite orbiting just over the horizon and sent a 'mission aborted' signal to headquarters.

Meanwhile, a further thirty miles to the east, the aircrew set fire to the helicopter to destroy any incriminating evidence of their clandestine assignment and moved off by foot in what they hoped was the direction of Punta Arenas. According to their plan, Hutchings, Bennett and Imrie would try and live off the land until they gave themselves up to the Chilean authorities, claiming to have suffered a navigational error. While the trio waited patiently for a friendly Chilean, Legg was sheltering from the freezing rain and weighing up his options.

After the initial euphoria as *Invincible* had signalled the safe dispatch of the PLUM DUFF mission, the planners settled in to a period of quiet anticipation. The imposition of radio silence as part of the plan had ensured that Victor Charlie would not send periodic reports, and the operational orders for the pilot dictated that the communications ban could only be broken if the helicopter spotted the elusive carrier *Veinticinco de Mayo*.

PLUM DUFF had made satellite contact somewhat later than had been scheduled because the satellite phone proved not to have been completely waterproof, and the news was bad. Legg's patrol had been dropped in Chile, an estimated seventy miles beyond their target, and the weather conditions were described as quite appalling, a combination of sleet and freezing temperatures. Worse, Townsend had fallen ill and was running a high fever. Unimpressed, headquarters ordered Legg to complete his mission. He would eventually rendezvous with staff from the embassy in Santiago and the troop was exfiltrated without further incident.

The war Cabinet had also authorised another very secret operation, which remained entirely dependent on Chilean cooperation and had been negotiated in London with the Chilean air attaché, General Raúl Vargas del Campo – although a suspicion lingered that he may not have consulted his superiors before giving his consent. As well as providing access to the Chilean Air Force's radar plots taken from the station in Tierra del Fuego, Chile's air intelligence branch D-2 had also collaborated in the installation of a British mobile radar which had been flown down by an RAF Hercules painted in Chilean Air Force livery to Balmaceda and placed on top of the Andes overlooking Comodoro Rivadavia.

The S-259 radar station, manned by the RAF's 400 Signals Unit, was called 'mobile' only because its three components – the control cabin, the parabolic antenna array and the diesel generator – were air transportable on a Wessex helicopter. Manufactured by Marconi, the apparatus was really a copy of the American AN/UPS-1, a tactical search radar with a range of nearly two hundred miles, depending upon the terrain and physical environment, but devoid of any height-finding capability. Although subject to atmospherics and local weather conditions, the Marconi S-259 radar apparatus, which had been removed from the Shetland Islands, had helped to fill the gaps in the Chilean coverage of the Argentine airfields and had the range to track aircraft over Rio Grande once they had reached a certain altitude. The delivery of the equipment had been supervised by Wing Commander Edwards with General Matthei, who had served as air attaché in London and proved to be a great

Anglophile. Under his personal authority as a member of the ruling junta, Matthei had sponsored the delivery of the S-259 radar and provided technicians to man it. The installation at Balmaceda was reported by conventional radio to General Matthei's D-2 headquarters in Santiago, where the SAS supervised a satellite link direct to the Task Force.

The innovative satellite communications system had been supplied secretly by the Green Berets at Fort Bragg and consisted of half a dozen pioneering devices, which had been developed to their own demanding specifications. Small enough to fit into a Bergen knapsack, the apparatus opened an encrypted voice channel to a reactivated US Navy satellite. The sets had been distributed to HMS *Hermes*, Ascension, Hereford and the D-2 headquarters so that an early-warning message could be transmitted direct to the Task Force, thereby giving *Hermes* one hour's notice of an impending Argentine air-raid.

• • •

I completed *The Secret War for the Falklands* in record time and having listened to the American, Argentine and Chilean perspectives, attempted to tackle the most problematic of all, the JIC. This shadowy organisation is the fulcrum of the British intelligence community and sets the targets for MI6, GCHQ and Defence Intelligence, but very little has been written about it, and its composition was, in 1995, still considered secret – as was the identity of its chairman, a person who until Lord Franks's review committee had been a senior diplomat drawn from the Foreign Office. Clearly the JIC's reports on the potential threat to the Falklands would have been of crucial importance, and the Franks Report acknowledged that the threat had been underestimated, with armed conflict being the direct consequence. But while Lord Franks had been critical in his comments about the JIC, he did not identify its membership nor even explain the composition of the Current Intelligence Groups, which had the responsibility to monitor specified geographical areas and specific hotspots likely to impinge on British interests. Thus, the performance of the Latin America Current Intelligence Group (LATIG) was of crucial importance.

The classified annex to the 1983 Franks Report still remains under wraps, although eighty-four files of evidence submitted to the Cabinet Office have been deposited in the National Archives. This material includes submissions made by the JIC's assessment staff, GCHQ and MI6. Despite a robust defence of its pre-conflict reporting, assembled by a senior officer who drafted an internal 'lessons learned' document for MI6, the organisation came in for considerable criticism. In the best traditions of the Service, the annex will probably never be released for public scrutiny.

The first draft of my book was delivered to Admiral David Pulvertaft of the MoD's D-Notice Committee in early 1997, when negotiations were opened on what names or passages the relevant agencies wanted to remove. Surprisingly, the arguments were few, and the book allowed some of the participants to learn for the first time of the conflict's *sub rosa* dimensions.

CHAPTER XIV

GEORGE BLAKE

The experience of the defector is invariably a painful one, and the eleven Soviet defectors whom I encountered during my research of the Cold War – Stanislav Levchenko, Boris Yuzhin, Alexander Kouzminov, Oleg Gordievsky, Vladimir Kuzichkin, Albrecht Dittrich, Alexander Litvinenko, Stanislav Lunev, Viktor Makarov and the Rezuns – had chosen the most difficult of paths, but the problems they encountered were diminished when compared to those endured by George Blake.

I had written about Blake in *Seven Spies Who Changed the World*, a collection of case histories of interesting intelligence personalities.[1] My analysis of the Dutch national, born George Behar, drew on the evidence of his former MI6 colleagues, particularly Charles Seymour who believed that his claimed conversion to Soviet communism, as asserted to his interrogators Harold Shergold and Christopher Phillpotts, was nothing more than a sham. Phillpotts and Seymour believed that Blake had been a victim of British antisemitism and his decision to betray his adopted country had been a reaction against it. However, when I was to put this theory to Blake in person in his shabby apartment in Moscow, he denied it vehemently. His protests of a commitment to Marxism, at a time when Mikhail Gorbachev was dismantling the centrally planned economy, was so passionate that I had no doubt the elderly spy really believed in his version of events.

Blake had always claimed that he had switched sides and become an adherent to socialism while a prisoner during the Korean War and that it had been indiscriminate bombing by the Americans that had acted as the catalyst. He had also always insisted that while under interrogation in London it had been suggested that he had succumbed to coercion when he began spying for the KGB and he had given himself away inadvertently by protesting that he had been a willing conspirator. But did any of this sound likely?

According to Seymour, Blake had been offended when the father of the woman he had fallen for had tried to explain that there was absolutely no possibility of him marrying her. Phillpotts recalled that far from accidentally slipping up when he was being questioned, the key to his abject confession had been a report from a surveillance team, which had spotted Blake circling a telephone kiosk in Soho, apparently undecided about whether to make a call. Challenged soon afterwards, Blake could not think of an explanation and when caught in a lie about having tried to ring his mother, he had broken down and admitted that he had contemplated sending an emergency signal to the KGB asking to be rescued. But which version was true? When asked in Moscow, Blake was surprisingly vague and feigned no memory whatever of the beautiful MI6 secretary with whom Seymour had claimed he had fallen head over heels in love with.

Blake represented a special kind of egregious treachery that so offended his colleagues, and it was the nature of his duplicity that put him in a class of his own. Comparisons with other cases would be unhelpful, except that while there is an argument that Kim Philby did not inflict immense lasting damage to MI6 in operational terms and was selective about the material he passed to the Soviets, Blake did not discriminate. He compromised everything at a time when the KGB was MI6's principal adversary. Philby also fulfilled a role of reassurance for Moscow, insisting that – even after the establishment of Section IX in 1944 – MI6 was *studying* the NKVD but was not actively engaged in espionage against it. In contrast, for seven years Blake haemorrhaged *everything* to the KGB and effectively neutralised the careers of colleagues such as Peter Lunn. It had been a watershed moment when the Secret Intelligence Service realised it was no longer secret and that virtually every member of staff had been compromised. Indeed, a traffic light colour-coding system was introduced to indicate on personnel records the probability that an individual's MI6 role was known to Moscow.

To the public, Blake seemed like an oddball who had received a record 42-year prison sentence and had then escaped from Wormwood Scrubs in 1966. For MI6, he was an ingrate who had been embraced by the MI6 family and had deliberately set out to cause harm. All those affected remembered the moment they had received an encrypted two-part signal, the second of which was simply the name of the traitor: B L A K E. Many realised that their professional careers were over and their efforts hitherto had been for nothing.

Born in Rotterdam in 1922 with the surname Behar, Blake was the first (and only) MI6 officer to have been convicted of betraying his country. His background was fairly unusual. His businessman father, a Sephardic Jew originally from Turkey, had been granted

British citizenship after having fought in the First World War with the French Foreign Legion, claiming to have won a Croix de Guerre and a Military Cross.

When his father died in 1934, Blake was taken to Cairo to live with an aunt. During the Second World War, Blake was in the Netherlands and active in the resistance but eventually escaped through Spain to the UK in January 1943, where he was reunited with his mother and sister who were living in Northwood. He applied to join the Royal Navy but was found to be medically unfit. Instead, having Anglicised his name by deed poll, he was recruited by MI6 in August 1943. As well as his language skills, Blake had the advantage of having had first-hand experience of life under the German occupation. Having been accepted into MI6's Dutch section, designated A.2, he fell for MI6 secretary Iris Peake, who was the daughter of Sir Osbert Peake, later ennobled as 1st Viscount Ingleby.

Blake's A.2 colleague Charles Seymour would later recall that the young and inexperienced Blake had become infatuated with Iris but then turned resentful when her father had told him one evening after dinner at his mansion at Snilesworth in North Yorkshire that there was no future for him with his daughter. According to Seymour, this incident had the most profound effect on Blake who had not before experienced antisemitism in the UK. Blake confided in Seymour, who was something of a mentor for the younger man, and Seymour expressed the belief that Blake became resentful of the treatment he had received but concealed the depth of his anger. Semour asserted that Blake's subsequent career, including a posting to Hamburg and a Russian language course at Downing College,

Cambridge, had been driven by a desire to wreak revenge on what he perceived to be the hypocrisy of the British ruling classes.

Blake's second overseas posting was under consular cover to Seoul in South Korea in October 1948. However, eighteen months later the capital was seized by communist troops, and he was interned. He spent three years as a prisoner, during which time he was cultivated and then recruited by a KGB officer, Nikolai Loenko. By the time Blake returned to London in March 1953, he was fully committed to the Soviet cause and had already been introduced to his first handler, the KGB *rezident*, Nikolai B. Korovin.

Welcomed back by MI6, Blake was regarded by colleagues as something of a hero, having undergone three years of captivity. He was quickly assigned to an operational role and indoctrinated into GOLD, the clandestine Anglo-American construction of a tunnel into Berlin's Soviet sector to tap telephone cables. He was then transferred to MI6's Berlin station to work with Peter Lunn. During his period in Berlin, Blake compromised every classified document he could lay his hands on and did immense damage. Specifically, he betrayed at least eight MI6 assets in East Germany known to have been incarcerated in the notorious Hohenschönhausen Stasi prison. Among them were Hans Möhring, a 42-year-old state planning commission employee, who was released in 1976 and Colonel Robert Hofmann of the National People's Army, who may have been executed. A subsequent damage assessment suggested that another of his victims may have been GRU officer Major Piotr Popov, who had attempted to re-establish contact with the CIA by approaching a British officer. The message had been relayed through the MI6 Berlin station, and it was possible that Blake had alerted the Soviets. In any event, Popov had not survived the experience.

Blake's arrest in London in January 1961 after three days of interrogation was followed by a full confession, and he remained cooperative even after his conviction, apparently enjoying his conversations with Terence Lecky. Lecky was the MI6 officer assigned the task of identifying Blake's contacts, Nikolai Korovin, Sergei Kondrashev and Vasili Dozhdalev, and establishing how many of his colleagues were now flagged by the KGB as intelligence professionals. To facilitate these interviews, Blake was kept in Wormwood Scrubs long after he had been due to begin serving his sentence in a high-security, long-term prison. Accordingly, Blake had been free to mix with lower category inmates, some of whom were scheduled for imminent release. Among them were Sean Bourke, Pat Pottle and Michael Randle, who offered Blake their support and in October 1966 helped Blake to escape.

The escape, over a perimeter wall at night with the aid of an improvised rope ladder fashioned from knitting needles and string, resulted in a fractured wrist for Blake, who was sheltered by various accomplices until he was smuggled to East Berlin hidden in a camper van.

During my conversation with Blake, I asked him what, if anything, kept him awake at night, and he freely acknowledged that he feared the Kremlin, in developing better relations with the west, might send him back to the UK to complete his prison sentence. I was left with a poor impression of Blake and wondered how anyone abroad would have accepted him for a moment as an MI6 officer. He was so very different to the average MI6 officer, speaking

English with such a heavy accent, that he seemed an unconvincing representative for the organisation.

Blake's treachery towards his adopted country was all the greater because he had been welcomed by and married into an MI6 family. His father-in-law, Colonel Arthur Allan, well known as a Russian interpreter, had been in charge of MI6's telephone interception operations and both his daughters had worked as MI6 secretaries. The family consisted of MI6 insiders, yet Blake had betrayed them all.

As well as my interview with Blake, my other objective in Moscow was to escort defector Oleg Gordievsky's wife Leila and daughters Anna and Maria to London. When Gordievsky had made his escape in July 1985, his family had been on holiday in Azerbaijan, and when they returned to Moscow, his wife was not allowed to travel and had been kept under close supervision at the family apartment. Although the KGB suspected otherwise, Leila had known nothing about her husband's espionage and had played no part in his exfiltration to Finland. Accordingly, the trio had become de facto hostages and perhaps an embarrassment to the Soviet authorities. This was an issue I had raised in London with my KGB-appointed co-author Oleg Tsarev, and he had brokered what appeared to be a solution to a significant obstacle in the way of improving bilateral relations.

On the face of it, there appeared to be very little advantage for the KGB in releasing Leila, apart from showing weakness by undertaking a humiliating climb-down. My suggestion was that I would offer a guarantee, already approved by Gordievsky, that there would be no press conferences and no adverse publicity generated by what I preferred to portray as a magnanimous gesture. When

I arrived in Moscow, I visited the British embassy to confirm the arrangements but was met with scepticism. As it turned out, someone had changed their mind. The embassy's doubts were proved justified, and Leila remained in Russia until September 1991.

My conclusions about defectors were mixed. Blake was the only surviving British defector in Moscow and seemed to me to be living a miserable existence, even if he had the use of a dacha in the country and was well off by Soviet standards. My experience of Soviet defectors in the UK suggested that they were also unhappy individuals who were wretched about having broken with the motherland. Some lied about their motives or were thought to have told less than the truth, and a couple were psychiatric cases. A few, such as the Rezuns and probably Kuzichkin (or so he claimed) had been the victims of circumstance and had never planned to switch sides. Vladimir Rezun had been recalled to Moscow for bungling an operation relating to Arkady Shevchenko's son in Geneva and had not previously considered defection. Nor had his wife Tatiana, who was also a GRU officer. Kuzichkin said he feared disciplinary action after he had mislaid *rezidentura* documents, but MI6 suspected he simply wanted to start a new life without his wife.

Nor did Soviet intelligence defectors fare much better in the US, where resettlement programmes often failed to live up to the (often unreasonably elevated) expectations of their clients. The common denominator among all defectors is that they are exceptional individuals who have endured much and wrecked much more than their own lives, for not always the loftiest of motives.

Before my visit to Moscow to see Blake, I read everything in the public domain about him, which amounted to four biographies – *Shadow of a Spy* by E. H. Cookridge, *George Blake: Superspy* by H.

Montgomery Hyde, *The Greatest Traitor* by Roger Hermiston, *The Happy Traitor* by Simon Kuper – and one autobiography, *No Other Choice*.[2] These would inadvertently provide one source of amusement in an otherwise bleak landscape.

The first biographer had been E. H. Cookridge, previously the author of an important account of SOE's wartime operations, *Inside SOE*. Cookridge was the pen name of Vienna-born journalist and wartime refugee Edward Spiro, the author of several non-fiction books on espionage of somewhat dubious quality. In *Shadow of a Spy*, Cookridge acknowledged that although he had not been able to discover the real name of Blake's recruiter, he had found out that he was known as 'Gregory Kuzmitch', or 'Kuzma' for short.[3]

In fact, Cookridge's research had led him to *The Observer*'s war correspondent Philip Deane, who had been interned in the same camp as Blake in Korea. In his 1953 memoirs *I Was a Captive in Korea*, Deane recalled that he and his fellow prisoners had called their interrogator Kuzma Kuzmich, a fictional character from a Russian novel: 'We had nicknamed him Kuzma Kuzmich after a character who appears regularly in every new Russian novel – the convert to communism who still suffers from "survivals of capitalism"'.[4] Despite having conceded that he did not know Kuzmitch's true name, Cookridge claimed to have researched his past career. Reportedly, this had included spells under diplomatic cover in Ottawa, Washington DC and finally London where he had adopted the alias 'Kuznetsov', Cookridge revealed. At the end of the war in Korea, Gregory Kuzmitch defected to the Americans and was sent to Washington where he was employed for several years by Allen Dulles's CIA.[5]

Cookridge's qualification that 'Kuzmitch' was not a real name was missed by Blake's next biographer Hyde, who twenty years later referred to Blake's encounter with an interrogator by writing, 'His name was Gregory Kuzmitch.'[6] Hyde did not pursue the issue of whether Kuzmitch subsequently defected, but there is no record of any such Soviet intelligence officer defecting to the CIA anyway.

Thus, during the course of three books, a nickname had been transformed into a genuine identity. None of this would really matter if the same subject had not been addressed in 1990 by Christopher Andrew and Oleg Gordievsky, who stated in *KGB: The Inside Story*:

> Blake's recruitment seems to have begun in the autumn of 1951. According to the first MGB officer to interrogate him, Grigori Kuzmich, Blake quickly expressed disillusion with western policy in general and with Anglo-American intervention in Korea in particular, but did not at first betray the secrets of SIS.[7]

This passage is source noted to Hyde's book, which seems odd as 'Kuzmich' was the spelling adopted by Deane but *not* Hyde. Furthermore, the authors added in the source note, 'Kuzmich, the first MGB officer to interrogate Blake, later defected.'[8] This is a bogus assertion made by Cookridge alone. The implication of this is that the authors (one of whom was a KGB defector himself) must have relied on Deane (to adopt the same spelling) and Cookridge (for the defection canard) but had attributed the information to entirely the wrong book! This little literary puzzle is made all the more remarkable since it would seem to be based on the attribution of a previous paragraph about the MGB being given unrestricted access to western detainees ('among them George Blake'), which was attributed to Gordievsky alone.

The three certainties that emerged from the Blake literature were that the interrogator nicknamed Kuzmich never defected, he never served in the posts attributed to him by Cookridge and that Gordievsky knew nothing whatsoever about Blake's recruitment in Korea.

CHAPTER XV

VENONA

VENONA is a completely meaningless codename, which probably has more significance within the intelligence community than any other in the post-war era. It refers to a joint Anglo-American cryptographic attack on Soviet ciphers, which was conducted over a period of forty years against some 2,900 messages that had been intercepted between 1940 and 1948. Originally codenamed BRIDE, the project underwent many codenames including DRUG, SUEDE and DUVET until it became known as VENONA.

I had first learned of the background to this super-secret source in 1980 from David C. Martin's *Wilderness of Mirrors*, a ground-breaking account of the impact of counter-intelligence paranoia on the CIA and FBI during the Cold War.[1] Then in 1981, Arthur Martin, who had handled VENONA at MI5 from the outset, gave me a briefing on the subject from his perspective, having been the liaison officer responsible for dealing with the messages that referred to a spy in the Manhattan Project codenamed CHARLES and REST. Lengthy sleuthing by the FBI finally identified the spy as the German refugee Klaus Fuchs, and Martin had been the person at MI5 to take charge of what was then classified as a 'Y-Box file', the most secret MI5 category, considered too sensitive to be entrusted to the registry and retained with the counter-espionage branch. Access to Y-Box files was very restricted, and even MI5's interrogator Jim Skardon was not allowed to know the true nature of the original information about Fuchs that suggested he had been working for the Soviets continuously since 1941.

The VENONA cryptographic breakthrough had transformed Allied counter-intelligence investigations, even if the actual texts could never be used as evidence in a criminal prosecution because of the nature of the baffling methodology adopted by the codebreakers. No jury would be able to follow the process of transforming a complex cipher system and translation from Russian to English, which involved the reconstruction of a codebook. It was believed that defence attorneys would have a field day and easily discredit the material. Even after the codename had been disclosed, the subject remained highly secret. When I attempted to discuss the topic with the CIA's Bill Hood over lunch at the Players Club in New York, he froze and warned me never to mention the word outside a classified environment. 'Just because the word is in circulation doesn't mean it's been declassified,' he whispered.

It would not be until 3 October 1996 that the CIA sponsored a presentation at the National War College at Fort McNair in Washington DC, which marked the first release of declassified messages. The intercepted traffic included communications exchanged between Moscow and various *rezidenturas* across the globe between 1940 and 1948 but principally New York, Washington DC, London, Stockholm and Canberra. Only a tiny fraction of the total messages on these channels had been attacked and most of the individual cables were incomplete. In other words, the decryption process was more of an art than a science, and there was plenty of room for debate about the analysts' interpretation of the broken-out text. As I would learn, and as would be expected in cipher messages, the original Russian texts did not include paragraph or line breaks to guide the reader; they had been inserted after the Allied decryption process.

Although the individual texts were made available by the National Security Agency (NSA), there was a continuing ban on any discussion of *how* the original encrypted texts had been intercepted, and the so-called 'working papers' would never be released. This strict prohibition meant that intelligence community insiders asked no questions and the outsiders did not know what questions to ask.

Looking back on those exciting days, sifting through the paperwork that offered clues to the identities of hundreds of Soviet spies, I was struck by two important points. Firstly, although many academics and counter-intelligence professionals studied the VENONA material, very few of them actually knew the underlying cryptographic methodology. Secondly, only a tiny proportion of the total number of telegrams had succumbed to attack. In the end, 2,900 individual messages were translated, but judging from their serial numbers, this was only a small proportion of the total number of Soviet communications. They amounted to just under half of the NKVD's New York–Moscow circuit in 1944; 15 per cent of the 1943 traffic (about 200 out of 1,300); and only 23 of the estimated 1,300 telegrams sent in 1942, which represents only 1.8 per cent of the total. As for the Naval GRU, half was recovered from the 1943 Washington–Moscow channel but none for any other year. In 1940, for instance, the New York GRU is calculated to have sent 992 messages to Moscow, with 335 from the NKVD. In short, the messages were gold dust, but there were comparatively few of them, and no amount of technical resources would ever provide more.

The secret behind the 'methodology' lay in three truckloads of old Soviet bills of lading, stored in a Department of Commerce warehouse in upstate New York and discovered there by the FBI's John Larkin. These cargo manifests, on what became known as the trade channel, had been encrypted on the same cipher system used for NKVD, GRU, Naval GRU, diplomatic and consular communications. Although it must have seemed an impossibly tedious task, a team of cryptanalysts matched the transmission dates to particular bills of lading. Having achieved that cleartext, a comparison was made to find a duplication in any of the non-trade traffic.

At the heart of the operation was the breathtaking realisation that, for reasons unknown, the Moscow codemakers had adopted the expedient of duplicating individual pages of their one-time pads (OTP) and repaginating them to insert into other OTPs. Why had this happened? No satisfactory answer was ever discovered, partly because the Soviets themselves always refused to admit an error had been made, but also because the few western cryptographers who knew about the blunder were never in a position to pose the question to anyone who might have known what had gone wrong. In these circumstances, the working assumption was that as the Wehrmacht approached Moscow, desperate measures were called for and duplicate OTPs were mixed in with original pages to create 'new' OTPs, ready for operational use.

The intrinsic flaw in the new system was that the fundamental integrity of the OTP principle had been undermined. Doubtless someone somewhere had taken a gamble that the duplication would never be spotted and the contamination was so minimal that it would be almost impossible to exploit it. Both assumptions were wrong. By the end of the Allied VENONA project, about 16,000 duplicate pages had been found. This was estimated to be about half of the total, representing an OTP production of around three to six months. Some of the earliest duplicates dated back to July 1940, when it might be assumed that the deteriorating international situation might have placed an extra, unanticipated burden on Soviet communications and created a demand for OTPs.

Prolonged study of the traffic was undertaken by Cecil Phillips's team of cryptanalysts, who had recently broken the Japanese weather codes employed in the Pacific theatre to report meteorological data. Together, they made a series of important discoveries. Firstly, they noticed the number 7 was disproportionately represented in the traffic. If the OTPs had contained truly random five-figure groups, no one single number would stand out. Secondly, general study of the traffic suggested that all the various Soviet organisations operating abroad and reliant on cables used the same system. Bizarrely, it seemed that the NKVD, diplomatic, consular, military intelligence (GRU), naval intelligence (Naval GRU) and trade (or commercial) branches all shared the same OTP system. This meant that the cryptanalysts had to overcome the challenge of sorting the irrelevant messages, such as the consular or trade telegrams, from the material that was likely to be much more interesting, generated by the NKVD and GRU.

The BRIDE cell's understanding of Soviet procedures was hugely enhanced at the end of July 1946 when a telegram from Moscow – signed by the NKVD's foreign intelligence chief Pavel Fitin, dated 10 August 1944, addressed to the *rezident* at the New York consulate, Stepan Apresyan – was broken. The topic of the telegram was cipher systems and was of great interest because it mentioned specific book titles employed for book codes. It was also highly relevant because it referred to HARRY, the codename of Jacob Epstein, a key NKVD agent in Mexico City who was known to communicate in a book code with New York over his plot to free Trotsky's convicted assassin Ramón Mercader from prison.

No. 1142
Your No. 3502

1. In accordance with a decision of the HOUSE [The Communist International] SISKIN and KARLOS [Christian Casanova] before departure from TYRE [New York] were instructed in the use of a reciphered code which they were to (46 groups unrecoverable) alphabet and in addition SISKIN was to write in English and KARLOS in Spanish. We cannot establish whether the pads for the codes were sent home since they were entered under the heading 'SISKIN's Business' and 'KARLOS's Business' (4 groups unrecovered) there are no inventories. From TYRE no enciphered letters were sent by [or to] SISKIN and KARLOS. Both codes ended up in STOCK's [Mikhail A. Shalyapin] hands.
2. For correspondence with ARTHUR a book in the Spanish language 'Una Excursion a Los Indios Ranqueles' was used as a code.
3. For correspondence with ALEKSANDR the books 'My Sister Eileen' and 'Defense Will Not Win War' were used as codes.

4. For correspondence with MARGO [Margarita Nelken] the book 'Opera' which was sent to you in accordance with your instructions, was used.
5. For correspondence with GARRI [Jacob Epstein], JUAN [Juan Gaytan] and ANITA books were used whose titles were not kept since they were destroyed after the departure of LUKA [Pavel Klarin] to the COUNTRYSIDE [Mexico].
6. In a sample cipher square TWAIN [Semyon Semyonov] trained (34 groups unrecoverable) … ZUL, PAUL which were destroyed and for STAFFMAN which we are dispatching to you by the next regular post.

This single telegram, which was obviously an NKVD channel, illustrated the value of eavesdropping on the most private conversations conducted by the most senior Soviet intelligence officers. Furthermore, because the FBI had interdicted some letters exchanged between Epstein and his courier Lydia Altschuler in New York, considerable research had been undertaken already on the likely true identification of Soviet personalities mentioned in the traffic. The breakthrough had been the catalyst for many years of cryptographic research, and some of those involved had gathered at the War College to learn more about what they had accomplished.

While sitting through the presentation at the National War College, I was a witness to the scope for error. My neighbour was Meredith Gardner who, as the NSA's former chief Russian linguist, had been one of the original architects of the project. A Russian Federation intelligence officer was part of the proceedings, but her English was poor, and a call went out for a translator. I noticed that

Gardner had not volunteered to help, and half in jest, I suggested he help out. He shook his head, explaining, 'I can read and write Russian, but I can't speak it.'

Another invitee was Morton Sobell, the Soviet spy who had spent seventeen years in prison after he had been implicated in the Rosenberg network in 1950. He read the references to his own case and pointed out that the NKVD codename attributed to him, RELAY, was demonstrably wrong. RELAY was mentioned as having a prosthetic leg, whereas Sobell, as he proved by rolling up his trousers, had two perfectly good legs. Additionally, RELAY was described in a decrypt as living in Philadelphia, whereas Sobell lived in Brooklyn. Sobell turned out to be right. The correct identification had been the Los Alamos physicist Philip Morrison who had been afflicted with childhood polio and wore callipers. There is no word in Russian for 'callipers' or, as Americans would say, 'braces'. All artificial limbs are simply known in Russian as *prosthes*.

• • •

As well as compromising Fuchs and later Donald Maclean, VENONA had indicated the existence of more than three hundred other GRU and NKVD agents in the US, Britain, Sweden and Australia, most of them protected by codenames, which raised the possibility that careful analysis of the often-fragmented texts would reveal clues to the spies' identities. Of assistance to the molehunters was the misplaced confidence of the Soviet intelligence personnel in the integrity of their communications, which led them to select some surprisingly transparent codenames for their sources. Thus Julius Rosenberg, who had trained in the US Army Signals Corps as a radio expert, was codenamed ANTENNA and Harry Dexter White, a lawyer, was JURIST. While it was rumoured that VENONA held the answers to many mysteries of the Cold War and even provided proof of Alger Hiss's guilt, nobody outside the small circle of people indoctrinated into the traffic with the highest security clearances knew for sure, and they were obliged to remain silent.

VENONA had become a political issue in the US where Senator Daniel Patrick Moynihan lobbied the Clinton White House to declassify the texts. Much to his surprise, the NSA agreed to release the material in 1996, and when the texts were read, they had immediate impact. Attention was keenly focused on the degree to which they incriminated senior figures in Roosevelt's administration, such as Harry Dexter White and Lauchlin Currie.

In the UK, the reaction was muted because the most familiar names to be compromised were Klaus Fuchs, Ursula Kuczynski and Donald Maclean, who were already well known as spies. However, I was drawn to the few VENONA texts from the London–Moscow circuit during 1940–41 and concentrated on what was referred to as the X GROUP, a GRU network headed by a hitherto unknown spy codenamed INTELLIGENTSIA with help from two subordinates codenamed NOBILITY and RESERVIST. Intriguingly, the true identities of these three traitors were known but their names had been redacted in the released texts, apparently at the insistence of the British government. Evidently, this spy-ring had operated in London undetected, and it was not until GCHQ began reading some of the London GRU traffic in the mid-1960s that the breathtaking scale of the organisation and the social status of its membership was understood. But who were they? The clues were contained in the actual texts, and I attempted to repeat the exercise that must have been conducted by MI5's molehunters when the VENONA texts had become available for study.

The first target was NOBILITY, and of the six texts that referred to him, only one looked promising. That appeared to be a report by the GRU *rezident* in London, Colonel Ivan Sklyarov, on a visit made by his spy to a military site in Denham, Buckinghamshire on 29 October 1940, occupied by the 339th Battery of the 26th Searchlight Regiment of the 1st Anti-Aircraft Division. The following day he reported:

1. In a regiment there are four batteries, each of four troops. A troop consists of two detachments. Each detachment constitutes a self-contained unit with an establishment of 12–13 men, one searchlight, one sound locator, one diesel generator and one Lewis gun. In all there are 350 men and 24 searchlights in a battery. The officers (one group unrecovered) territorial troops; they received a special type (1 group unrecovered) beginning of the war.
2. A detachment occupies a site 25 metres in diameter. The distance between detachments is 2.5–9 kilometres. The searchlights are automatically directed onto the targets by means of the data from the sound locator. The searchlight beams are effective up to a height of 5,000 metres. Detachments are linked to battery and battery is linked to regiment and to Sector Operations Room from which information about the enemy is sometimes received. The battery commander stated that during the last fortnight two SAUSAGE-DEALERS [Germans] had been shot down by machine-gun fire.
3. BRION No. 324[2]

In the footnotes to this VENONA text, the analysts referred to NOBILITY as an 'unidentified covername'. Significantly, there are no redactions whatsoever in the text.

As well as making these rather routine observations that were of value to both the Soviets and presumably their German allies, NOBILITY also acted as a link for other CPGB (codenamed CORPORATION in the messages) members anxious to convey classified information to the Soviets. On 20 December 1940, Sklyarov reported to Moscow that:

> Through NOBILITY the X GROUP has passed material (12 groups unrecovered) received from a member of the CORPORATION who has been working on technical work in intelligence departments [40 groups unrecovered].[3]

Only on one occasion, on 16 October 1940, was there a clue to the kind of technical intelligence data NOBILITY had encountered. On that date, Sklyarov signalled that:

> NOBILITY has reported the following information on the SAUSAGE-DEALERS air-raid on FILTON 10 days ago. 30 SAUSAGE-DEALER bombers and 30 fighters used a radio beam to fly from Northern France, they passed over PORTLAND straight to BRISTOL from where they turned on to the FILTON Aircraft Factory. All the bombs were dropped in a ring of smoke laid above the factory by one of the SAUSAGE-DEALERS. Three shelters were destroyed by a direct hit, killing 81 people and injuring 300–500. The damage to production was slight. British fighters appeared after the raid.[4]

The contents of this message might on first glance seem relatively inconsequential, with the Luftwaffe launching raids on southern England on a daily basis. However, the assertion that the aircraft had been guided to their target by a 'radio beam' was supposed to be a closely guarded secret. As Air Ministry scientists had discovered through a combination of eavesdropping on PoW aircrew, interrogation of prisoners and inspection of wreckage, the Germans had developed a navigational aid to assist their bombers in finding their targets. Pilots who were already used to assistance from devices designed to aid night landing had received training on a more sophisticated apparatus codenamed KNICKERBEIN (crooked leg), which guided them along an invisible pathway, deviation from which produced an audible warning in the form of pulses. Manufactured by Lorenz, the system took the plane to its target, identified the moment to release its bomb and then guided the crew home. At the time of Sklyarov's message in October 1940, the Soviets were still supporting the Nazis under the terms of the Molotov–Ribbentrop Pact, so the GRU *rezidentura* in London was likely sharing its information with its German counterparts, thus making the issue a major counter-espionage priority.

So, who was NOBILITY? I traced the war diary of the 26th Searchlight Regiment and spotted that on the date of NOBILITY's visit, Tuesday 29 October 1940, it had received a visit, sponsored by the Ministry of Information, of officially accredited war correspondents. Among the journalists on the tour was a name that almost jumped out of the page, for the person concerned had a title, the Honourable Ivor Montagu. Could he have been NOBILITY?

Educated at Westminster School and King's College, Cambridge, Montagu was the younger son of Lord Swaythling, head of an immensely rich family of bankers. He was also a lifetime CPGB member, becoming the party's president, and was the *Daily Worker's* war correspondent, part-time employment that gave him access to privileged, restricted military information. His 1970 autobiography *The Youngest Son* covered his life until 1927 and describes how he was influenced by a visit to the Soviet Union in 1925:

> When I came back from the USSR, though deeply impressed, above all, by the sense of comradeship there and, in the current cant phrase, the evidence of the wind of change, I still did not join the Communist Party of Great Britain. I still did not know enough about Communism or Marxism. I admired both Lenin and Trotsky, and could not understand the issues between the Soviet Party and Trotsky which were then reaching the surface. I did join the scientists' trade union (the National Union, now the Association, of Scientific Workers) as soon as it was formed and, as a trade unionist, the Minority Movement. I consorted with Communists and found among them the only political friends of like approach.[5]

Montagu never concealed his leftist ideology and in 1940 published *The Traitor Class*.[6] He served on the editorial board of *Labour Monthly* with Rajani Palme Dutt and another CPGB zealot, Robin Page Arnot. Undoubtedly, Montagu's Communist Party credentials would have made him a candidate for recruitment as a Soviet spy, and the familiar use of the semi-transparent codename, so characteristic of the VENONA traffic, convinced me that Montagu had been NOBILITY.

Ivor's older brother Ewen was a barrister, but during the war he had worked in the Naval Intelligence Division and represented the Admiralty on the Twenty Committee, which supervised MI5's double-agent operations. In 1953, he wrote *The Man Who Never Was*, an account of the celebrated wartime strategic deception scheme Operation MINCEMEAT, which involved planting a corpse on the Spanish coast intended to mislead the Germans about Allied plans.[7] Clearly, he was wholly oblivious to his brother's espionage on behalf of the Russians. As I learned when I questioned Ivor's relatives, none of the family realised that he had been engaged in espionage but the revelation did not come as a great shock to his closest relations, who regarded him as a talented black sheep easily capable of working enthusiastically for the Soviets.

Even though there were only six VENONA texts referring to NOBILITY, his importance to the GRU could be seen from the fact that Sklyarov's deputy Simon Kremer used him as a conduit to the X GROUP, apparently because, as he reported on 6 September 1940, 'INTELLIGENTSIA lives in the provinces and it is difficult to contact him.'[8] So, who was INTELLIGENTSIA?

The very first VENONA text to mention INTELLIGENTSIA is dated 25 July 1940 from Kremer in London. Reporting an initial meeting, Kremer stated, 'He [INTELLIGENTSIA] had been detailed to organise work with me, but he had not obtained a single contact. I came to an agreement with him about the work and pointed out the importance of speed.' Kremer went on to say that INTELLIGENTSIA reported the following:

1. Hitler's speech will not make a great impression here. The press has taken it unfavourably. He considers that the SAUSAGE-DEALERS were given their answer earlier by Churchill since

the SAUSAGE-DEALERS' conditions passed to the British through KHOSKHOR and [Sir Horace] Wilson proved unacceptable. Halifax's speech was not only an additional answer to the SAUSAGE-DEALERS but also the outline of a political programme. The slogan 'For Christianity' is similar to one of the conditions in Roosevelt's declaration on the freedom of religion, will also impress Pétain, Franco and the Pope and has an anti-Fascist edge to it. INTELLIGENTSIA considers that there is an anti-SAUSAGE-DEALER mood in the army and the knowledge of this is so strong that the Conservative Party is afraid of risking talking about peace. They might start talks if Britain were to suffer some serious defeat or the SAUSAGE-DEALERS start effective bombing. Churchill continues to stay the main figure of the war in the SAUSAGE-DEALERS' eyes but he intends (corrupt text) but is supporting Chamberlain's group so as to give the anti-SAUSAGE-DEALER mood no chance of developing into a movement of the left.

2. Generals IRONSIDE and GORT were removed from the leadership because at a parliamentary secret session on the question of the cause of the defeat in Flanders the Minister of Supply proved with documents that the Expeditionary Force was supplied 100 per cent in accordance with the instructions of these generals who are personally responsible for the development of the mechanised armies.
3. No. 200 BARCh.[9]

There is little in the text to suggest INTELLIGENTSIA's true identity, although it would appear that hitherto he had not been active and had failed to make a single contact. As far as the political analysis is concerned, relating to Churchill, Chamberlain and the British Expeditionary Force's defeat, it does not seem particularly insightful.

The second telegram, dated 16 August 1940 and numbered 895, was also sent from London:

1. INTELLIGENTSIA has not yet found the people in the War Office finance department. He has been given the address of one officer but he has not found him yet. He has promised to deliver documentary material from Professor Haldane who is working on an Admiralty assignment concerned with submarines and their operation. I have taken the opportunity of pointing out to the X GROUP that we need a man of a different calibre and one that is bolder than INTELLIGENTSIA.
2. MARTHA has handed over material on experience gained from using artillery in France. The material is in French and we are looking for a translator. In view of MARY's departure I request permission to put DICK or MARK in touch with MARTHA.
3. A Lieutenant Hein of the Czechoslovakian army has presented himself at the METRO [embassy]. He (1 group unidentified) that in October 1939 when he was in an internment camp near Kamenets-Podolski, he was recruited by somebody for special work. His covername is BAUER and he has been instructed to look for Kolarky. BAUER is now in the Czechoslovakian camp near Malpas. The total number of Czechoslovakian troops in Britain is about 4,000 other ranks and up to 700 officers. He himself is on the reserve for the time being. In France there was only one Czechoslovakian division. He has confirmed that up to 600 Czechs have been removed from the camp and

> sent somewhere or other because of their left-wing views. Czechoslovakia has no weapons. Send instructions at once.[10]

Only the first part of the message related to the X GROUP, but two issues arise. Firstly, there is the complaint that INTELLIGENTSIA is insufficiently bold to carry out his GRU duties, and secondly, there is a direct reference to the celebrated scientist Professor J. B. S. Haldane, the implication being that he is someone different to INTELLIGENTSIA. In reality, it may be that the author of the message was employing a rather primitive ruse to remind the recipient that INTELLIGENTSIA was Haldane who, by way of explanation for his failings, was working at an Admiralty underwater research establishment – which indeed Haldane was in 1940. The individual's apparent inability to find an officer's address could be interpreted to mean that INTELLIGENTSIA was unconnected or unfamiliar with the military or the War Office.

The other two paragraphs, concerning MARTHA and Lieutenant Hein, have no bearing on the X GROUP and so are of no consequence, beyond showing that that the message was quite routine, covering several unrelated topics, and that the author, perhaps a member of the GRU *rezidentura* subordinate to Sklyarov and Kremer, was seeking Moscow's guidance. A further telegram, dated 6 September 1940 and sent to Moscow by Kremer, devoted a single paragraph to INTELLIGENTSIA:

> INTELLIGENTSIA has handed over a copy of Professor Haldane's report to the Admiralty on his experiments relating to the length of time a man can stay underwater. However, he does not deny the main point that for a month he has not been in

> touch with the British Army colonel picked out for work with us although the latter does come to London. I have told the X GROUP via NOBILITY to give us someone else because of this. INTELLIGENTSIA lives in the provinces and it is difficult to contact him.[11]

Again, Kremer has adopted the ruse of using an agent's real name, in this case Haldane, so as to separate him from a cryptonym, in this case INTELLIGENTSIA. The ploy appears elsewhere in the VENONA collection. For example, messages about Klaus Fuchs supplying the NKVD with one of his own Manhattan Project reports were not attributed to CHARLES, Fuchs's own codename. In short, Kremer is going through the motions of pretending that someone else who had access to Haldane's submarine survival research for the Admiralty had betrayed it to the GRU. In reality, of course, that person was Haldane himself.

In terms of further clues to the true identity of INTELLIGENTSIA, described as living 'in the provinces', it is worth noting that in 1940 Haldane lived in Rothamsted in Hertfordshire. Montagu, codenamed NOBILITY, stayed at a flat in Kensington Court and evidently it was easy for Kremer to contact him personally.

In a message from Kremer to Moscow dated 18 October 1940, he returned to the issue of the British Army colonel first mentioned on 6 September as having been 'picked out for work with us':

> 1. BARCh [Simon Kremer] had a meeting today with one of the members of the X GROUP. This was an artillery colonel who had been in the British Expeditionary Force, but who at

present is out of active service and doing a job at the Ministry of Supply because he was seriously wounded. He thinks he will be returning to service in the regular army in two months' time. RESERVIST has agreed to work with us. He has promised to bring to the next meeting in a fortnight's time his notes on the campaign in France and information on how the British Army is organised.

2. RESERVIST reports that the progress of reorganising the army continues. The organisational structure of the Home Forces command, army corps, division. There are individual garrison districts which are directly subordinate to the C-in-C Homes Forces, e.g. the Dover garrison which includes two infantry brigades and one tank division. The composition of an infantry battalion is: two infantry companies, one machine-gun company consisting of two heavy machine-gun platoons and one anti-tank defence platoon. A brigade consists of three battalions. Each brigade deployed in a war zone has its own independent defence sectors and divisional reinforcements are placed under the command of brigades.
3. Tanks are the main item of the work of the Ministry of Supply. The following are in mass production: 14-ton cruiser tanks and 25-ton ARMSTRONG-WOLSELEY MK-8's armed with one 37 mm gun and two Browning machine-guns (it has been suggested that a machine-gun be tried on the turret for anti-aircraft fire). There were five tank divisions in the British Expeditionary Force in France; he does not know how many tank divisions there are now. 300 light tanks are expected to arrive from SASHA. A battalion of light tanks consists of three

companies with 30 tanks per company. A battalion of 25-ton tanks is 40 strong. The different kind of organisation can be explained by the shortage of officers.

4. In France the British had 25 and 36 mm anti-tank guns. They proved to be too light against the German tanks and were replaced by 75 mm French guns which were successful in action. The arming of units with 49 mm anti-tank guns is now beginning. Anti-tank units are now being brought together into a brigade for training.
5. Artillery batteries are armed with 18 and 25-pounder guns. The London air defence is now using new 6-inch guns as well as the 4.5-inch A.A. guns. They are experimenting with new 4.9-inch A.A. guns.
6. He considers that the War Office is not making the slightest use of the experience of the French and the coastal defence is based on a network of blockhouses that are weak in design with no allowance made for the manoeuvrability or strong artillery and tank equipment of the SAUSAGE-DEALERS.[12]

Close examination of this text revealed that it is not entirely accurate, as no six-inch gun was ever used as anti-aircraft artillery. The explanation probably lay in poor transliteration, of the type that is bound to occur when converting to or from metric measurements. For instance, the 25mm gun referred to is undoubtedly the Hotchkiss, while the 36mm gun is most likely the ineffective two pounder, and the fourteen-ton cruiser tank is better known as the Matilda.

So, the question remained, who was INTELLIGENTSIA?

Undoubtedly, INTELLIGENTSIA was remarkably well connected

and enjoyed a very wide circle of friends. On 2 October, the *rezidentura* reported to Moscow that:

> INTELLIGENTSIA has reported that the X GROUP has reported to him that a girl working in a government establishment noticed in one document that the British had broken some Soviet code or other and apparently she noticed in a/the document the following words 'Soviet Embassy in Germany'. I stated that this was a matter of exceptional importance and he should put to the group the question of developing this report further.[13]

On 11 October 1940, Sklyarov reported on INTELLIGENTSIA's knowledge of techniques for rendering enemy munitions safe: 'INTELLIGENTSIA confirms that the British really do render delayed-action bombs safe by freezing the bombs' exploder mechanism.'[14]

On 15 October, Sklyarov reported to Moscow on a conversation INTELLIGENTSIA had engaged in with 'an officer of the Air Ministry':

> The shortage of trained night navigators is confirmed by the fact that the SAUSAGE-DEALERS have not used strong forces of aircraft in night air-raids on Britain. He stated that the British pilots who fly by night over Germany have an extra four months' training in addition to the usual six months' training. Apparently when there has been no anti-aircraft fire the SAUSAGE-DEALERS have been bombing from a height of 5,000 metres and at a speed of 290 kph, and from 6,000–7,000 metres at a speed of 400 kph when there has been no firing. He considers that the SAUSAGE-DEALERS proceed towards the target along a radio beam.[15]

Even if INTELLIENSIA had limited access to the War Office, he demonstrably had an indiscreet source in the Air Ministry and had not experienced any problems in acquiring a copy of Haldane's report for the Admiralty. Accordingly, on the admittedly limited evidence available, I drew up a profile of a highly intelligent individual, perhaps an academic, who lived in the provinces and had not been entirely proficient at dealing with military personnel, who nevertheless occasionally mixed in circles that had given him access to information about the enemy's radio beams and the measures taken to render detonators safe. In addition, he had strong CPGB connections. Given that the Soviets had always relied heavily upon CPGB volunteers, I concluded that the GRU had co-opted the author of *The Inequality of Man* and chairman of the editorial board of the *Daily Worker*, Professor J. B. S. Haldane.

Like his close friend Ivor Montagu, who had also trained as a geneticist, Haldane was a campaigning political radical but came from a very conventional background and had been educated at Eton and New College, Oxford. The two men met in Cambridge in 1923 while studying biochemistry and maintained their friendship thereafter. Haldane did not formally join the CPGB until 1942, but he may have been a member of an underground cell. His popular journalism on scientific subjects made him a household name, and he was also trusted to work on classified projects. He contributed to the official inquiry into the loss of HMS *Thetis* which had sunk in Liverpool Bay with the loss of ninety-nine lives in June 1939. In 1940, he was designing midget submarines for the Admiralty.

During the First World War, Haldane had served with the Black Watch battalion with distinction, gaining a reputation for innovation and inventing weapons to harass the enemy without the need for costly, frontal infantry attacks – although his fellow officers commented in the Black Watch's regimental history that some of his devices were 'stove-pipes almost as dangerous to their users as to the enemy'. Field Marshal Douglas Haig had described him as 'the bravest and the dirtiest officer in my army'.

Haldane, a nephew of Lord Haldane, then Lord Chancellor and later Secretary of State for War, was encouraged to take an interest in the development of countermeasures for the clouds of chlorine gas deployed by the enemy at Ypres in April 1915. He would be wounded during the Festubert offensive and transferred to Béthune before being posted to the Nigg Bombing School near Aberdeen.

In October 1916, he accompanied his battalion to Mesopotamia, where he was injured again in an accident on a Royal Flying Corps airdrome. He spent the remainder of the conflict in India, where he trained Indian troops at the Mhow Central Bombing School. In 1918, Haldane joined the staff at University College, London and became overtly political, campaigning for the Association of Scientific Workers and writing feature articles for the *Daily Worker*.

In February 1935, Haldane made the first of three visits to Spain, and in December 1936 he was appointed the principal gas adviser to the Republican forces, although the weapon was never used by either side. Nevertheless, Haldane campaigned for the communists and took the opportunity to study the effects of the aerial bombardment of the civilian population by the Luftwaffe's Condor Legion. He made numerous visits to the frontline trenches and became quite a celebrity, commentating on every aspect of the conflict.

Soon after the outbreak of the Second World War, Haldane moved out of his London home to the Rothamsted agricultural experimental station at Harpenden in Hertfordshire. Nevertheless, he was in London frequently and regularly attended the *Daily Worker*'s editorial board, as was recalled by Douglas Hyde, the Roman Catholic journalist who later broke with communism. He would take 'little part in the discussion and absent-mindedly doodle in Greek as the Dean of Canterbury held forth at length'.[16]

Haldane's commitment to Marxism is beyond doubt, but his zealotry made him stand out from other CPGB members who harboured doubts about the increasingly intolerant and ruthless Soviet leader, whose destructive purges were hard to ignore. Haldane made no attempt to conceal his politics, although he probably was not a card-carrying member at this stage. His willingness to suspend his critical faculties on political grounds was exposed by his wife Charlotte Franken, who was also a Communist International agent. Born in London to German Jewish parents, Charlotte had been a *Daily Express* journalist who had fallen for the geneticist while interviewing him at Cambridge in 1924. They were married two years later, and in 1928 they travelled to Moscow at the invitation of Professor Nikolai Vavilov, one of the world's leading plant geneticists. Although it is not known when Haldane was recruited as a spy, his wife became a member of the CPGB's underground in 1937, and her son by a previous marriage, Ronnie, became the youngest member of the British Battalion of the International Brigades in Spain.

Haldane's connection with Montagu had developed through politics and the *Daily Worker*, as Montagu recalled in his memoirs:

> I lost sight of him for a time after leaving Cambridge, and ran into him again only after he started his *Daily Worker* contributions in

> the thirties. When I first knew him Haldane had not yet become a Marxist; he had seen the fallacies in what Marxists call 'mechanical materialism' and been inclined to what they call 'God-building'. It was encountering Engels, whom he valued above Marx, that changed this attitude, and he found in dialectical materialism as outlined by Engels a view adequate to unify the disclosures of processes and reality achieved by science. The thirties, with their sense of gathering storm and the patent incompetence of the course followed by the statesmen, intensified his sense of social responsibility – as they did that of so many other intellectual workers in the most diverse fields. He asked himself how he might bring his special qualifications to participate in the fight against fascism and the coming war.[17]

Among Haldane's many areas of specialist knowledge was aerial bombardment, the strategy pioneered in the Spanish Civil War by the German Condor Legion. This was a novel form of warfare – the indiscriminate destruction of civilian areas to create panic in the population – and Haldane made himself an expert on the subject. He was at the forefront of the 'deep shelter' campaign, intended to persuade the British government to build sufficient underground accommodation to protect the city dwellers – a cause that became highly politically charged. His skill as a journalist attracted the attention of John Hilton, director of home publicity at the Ministry of Information, and Haldane's knowledge was used to support civilian morale through the distribution of several articles on semi-scientific subjects.

If Haldane and Montagu had been spies, why had they escaped prosecution? Doubtless, MI5 had decided that the chances of either making any admissions would have been negligible, as neither had enjoyed access to classified information for many years. When the VENONA texts became available, the Security Service probably had judged it pointless to conduct an investigation and then maybe prepare a case for trial. A successful prosecution would almost certainly require a confession and both men were still hardened, sophisticated Marxists who could simply decline to be interviewed. VENONA was not evidence that could be adduced at a criminal trial but rather a counter-intelligence instrument that provided leads for further investigation. In the absence of admissible testimony, perhaps from an eyewitness, no lawyer would be able to advise the Attorney General that there was more than a 60 per cent prospect of a conviction. Charlotte Haldane, whom J. B. S. had divorced in 1945, had left the CPGB in 1941 and had written about her husband's secret work for the party, but even she had been excluded from the private gatherings in her home.

After the war, Haldane remained on the *Daily Worker*'s editorial board and wrote *They Want to Geld* [sterilise] *the Poor*, the last of some three hundred articles, in August 1950. Three months later he announced his departure from the CPGB, having been obliged to resign from two government committees because his security clearance had been withdrawn. In July 1957, Haldane moved to India with his second wife Dr Helen Spurway, renounced his British citizenship, and died of cancer in December 1964.

My analysis of the declassified texts was published in 1999 as *VENONA: The Greatest Secret of the Cold War* and competed with several other titles on the same subject released in the US. However, this was the only one to emphasise that the operation had been a joint Anglo–American undertaking, with proper credit going to

Wilfred Bodsworth and Nigel de Grey, the two senior project pioneers at GCHQ, as well as the NSA's cryptographers Cecil Phillips and Meredith Gardner.

• • •

The identification of Montagu and Haldane would become more complicated a decade later, when, in 2009, Christopher Andrew's authorised centenary history of MI5, *The Defence of the Realm*, included a new release of the redacted 25 July 1940 text and identified INTELLIGENTSIA as Montagu and rejected NOBILITY as Haldane – almost the reverse of my conclusion.[18] This surprise, apparently unilateral intervention left NOBILITY as 'a journalist'.[19] Remarkably, the author acknowledged, 'The Security Service devoted no significant further resources to unravelling either the connection between Montagu and the rest of the X Group, or the identity of NOBILITY, which remains unknown.'[20]

This reluctance to delve deeper might seem strange, but there was a further oddity. The authorised history cited just one four-line extract from the new, unredacted version of the text as evidence that Montagu was INTELLIGENTSIA:

> [The Honourable] Ivor Montagu brother of Lord Montagu, the well-known communist, journalist and lecturer. He has [*several words not decrypted*] contacts through his influential relations. He reported that he had been detailed to organise work with me, but he has not yet obtained a single contact.[21]

At first glance, the choice of this passage seems entirely reasonable and uncontentious. But when it is compared to the text of the version sent to the National Archives, it is slightly different in two respects. Firstly, the square brackets [The Honourable] are not in the original, and neither is [*several words not decrypted*], which should read [1 group unidentified]. This has rather a different meaning, and a cipher group is not necessarily 'several words'. One is bound to ask, who edited the original and added the italics, and why?

It could be argued that these are issues of little or no consequence, but I would maintain that official or 'authorised' historians should not edit documents to suit their purpose.

The controversy was subsequently exacerbated by the publication of two new biographies, written by academics. *Comrade Haldane is Too Busy to Go on Holiday: The Genius Who Spied for Stalin* by Gavan Tredoux, and *Codename Intelligentsia* by Russell Campbell, both published in 2018.[22] During my research, I had spoken to Geoffrey Sudbury, formerly GCHQ's principal Russian linguist, who had worked on the X GROUP decrypts. He had given me an interview at his home in Cheltenham where he lived with his wife, a local GP who had no idea about the nature of her husband's employment. He told me that he had concluded that the best candidate for INTELLIGENTSIA was Haldane and that NOBILITY had been his friend Montagu.

Demonstrably, MI5, GCHQ et al. had conceded that Haldane had been a Soviet spy and member of the X GROUP. Despite this general acceptance of Haldane as a spy and despite his rejection of Haldane as INTELLIGENTSIA, Tredoux did not mention what he thought Haldane's codename had been in his book and even claimed that 'the VENONA intercepts certainly showed that Ivor headed an espionage ring called the X Group'.[23] Although he declined to disclose what he thought had been Haldane's codename, Tredoux insisted, based on the MI5 release in 2009, 'This settles the identification of INTELLIGENTSIA as Montagu rather than Haldane.'[24] Thus, Tredoux concluded that while the issue of Haldane's codename was settled, there remained a mystery about NOBILITY who was evidently a senior member of the X GROUP. It is tempting to assign this name to Haldane himself – he was not really nobility but the Russians could easily have taken him to be such, given his uncle's career – but this suggestion is made improbable, though not impossible, by the construction of the reports. Haldane features in it explicitly under his own name and is not linked in the text to NOBILITY, who seems to be a separate individual.

This convoluted explanation amounts to a Byzantine effort to insist that Haldane was a spy but was neither of the spies codenamed NOBILITY or INTELLIGENTSIA. In other words, Tredoux is convinced that Montagu was INTELLIGENTSIA, but he does not suggest a true name for NOBILITY… even though he acknowledges that NOBILITY was a journalist.

Campbell, Montagu's biographer, also relied on the mistaken interpretation of the 25 July 1940 VENONA text and so incorrectly identified Montagu as INTELLIGENTSIA. As for NOBILITY, Campbell explains, 'The identity of NOBILITY mentioned a number of times in the VENONA intercepts remains unknown. He was a journalist.'[25] Perhaps realising the inherent contradiction and improbability of identifying the *Daily Worker* journalist Montagu as INTELLIGENTSIA, and not even speculating on Haldane's codename, Campbell acknowledges that Haldane was a member of the X GROUP and was passing classified information to 'his old friend from Cambridge', Montagu.[26]

So, why is it that MI5 asserted that Montagu was INTELLIGENTSIA and NOBILITY remains unknown, when there is another body of opinion that says Montagu is NOBILITY and Haldane is INTELLIGENTSIA? There are two arguments for this view. Firstly, there is a very ambiguous decrypt dated 25 July 1940 where there is allegedly a parenthetical reference to the spy: 'He (INTELLIGENTSIA) reported the following'. The context implies that 'he' is Montagu, who is mentioned in the previous two sentences. That impression is given partly because of the analyst's choice of a line break, but in the original messages there was no such editing. It could equally be argued, as I do, that the correct reading of the text is that the message is a report about a meeting with 'representatives' of the X GROUP, with emphasis on the plural. The first participant is obviously Montagu, but the second is a separate personality codenamed INTELLIGENTSIA.

The critical sentences read, 'I came to an agreement with him about the work and pointed out the importance of speed. He (INTELLIGENTSIA) reported the following:' and is followed by the line break inserted gratuitously by the analyst. However, if the line break is placed between these two sentences, the text makes better sense and introduces the second of the two X GROUP representatives. Thus, the first half of the message describes Montagu and the second deals with someone else, a co-conspirator codenamed INTELLIGENTSIA.

When this particular decrypt was released in 1995, it had been heavily redacted to conceal forty-five words in the text and mask the footnoted identification of INTELLIGENTSIA as Montagu. For whatever unexplained reason, the unredacted version was only released in 2009 and this was the version reproduced by Tredoux.

In short, this particular decrypt can be interpreted either way, so one needs to look for collateral. One place to start is the decrypt dated 30 October 1940, which records NOBILITY's visit to the anti-aircraft site in Denham. Montagu was on the tour in in his capacity as the *Daily Worker*'s war correspondent, which rather suggests that he was indeed NOBILITY, especially as Haldane was not there.

The second argument put forward by those who adhere to the Montagu as INTELLIGENTSIA preference is that Haldane cannot be INTELLIGENTSIA because he is referred to in the messages by name as a third person. This, as previously mentioned, is a not uncommon characteristic in the VENONA material and may have been a rather lame internal security precaution to avoid linking a source to a compromising cryptonym. Whatever the Soviet motive for adopting this style, which can also be seen in a reference to Klaus Fuchs in another decrypt, it is hardly exculpatory.

The alternative solution, as endorsed by Sudbury, solves the puzzle that has defeated the two authors and means that NOBILITY was probably chosen as a highly appropriate codename because Montagu was the son of a peer and INTELLIGENTSIA accurately describes Haldane, one of the leading scientists of his era. It means too that there are no gaps to be filled in a search for Haldane's codename or a candidate for NOBILITY.

There is no obvious explanation for this curious course of events, especially when one considers that both Haldane and Montagu were long dead by 1995, so there were no issues about protecting their privacy when VENONA was declassified. This suggests that during the declassification process, in the months leading up to the 1995 release in the US, MI5 and/or GCHQ analysts realised there had been a gaffe and the redactions were intended to avoid future misidentifications. However, by 2009, those in the know might have moved on, or retired, or the institutional memory simply failed.

Why is any of this important? It matters because GCHQ has not worked out who was betraying its secrets in May 1941. There have been attempts – eminent cryptographers Nigel de Grey and Wilfred Bodsworth devoted several years of their professional lives to tracking down BARON, a mystery member of the GRU's X GROUP in London. At one moment, Czech spy Karel Sedlacek was considered a possible match, but the search continues. None of the suspects were interviewed before they died, so there remains a danger that these GRU moles and any successors they cultivated may go undetected. In the meantime, any amateur sleuths will have to discriminate between fact and fiction in the hope of arriving at the truth.

Assuming, as we should, that both Montagu and Haldane were major traitors, there is some wry, perverse comfort to be taken from their stature. The British certainly produce colourful spies – the Cambridge Five, for example, spring to mind. Haldane and Montagu were in the same mould: one an unrepentant Marxist who was an inspirational scientist, the other a film producer and critic and championship table tennis player. Both wrote autobiographies but neither even hinted in them of their secret adherence to the Red Army's intelligence organisation. They led astonishing lives. In comparison to an earlier biography of Haldane by Ronald Clark, Tredoux lifted every stone to show the many facets of an essayist, pamphleteer, campaigner and Eton- and Oxford-educated geneticist, widely regarded as one of the most influential figures of his era. Montagu too was a multi-talented intellectual who counted Charlie Chaplin among his friends. Ultimately, it seems there was yet another dimension to their very public careers, which may require even further investigation.

CHAPTER XVI

GUY LIDDELL

Guy Liddell was an exceptional intelligence officer in every way as his extraordinary wartime diaries demonstrate, a twelve-volume document that was declassified by MI5 in November 2002 and which I edited for publication in 2005.

In retrospect, it is hard to think of anyone who so dominated the international security and intelligence scene in anything like the way Liddell did over such a long period in the twentieth century. He may only have achieved the military rank of captain but for the latter half of his professional career, until his resignation in 1953, he maintained close personal relationships with his Allied counterparts, was universally respected and was almost completely unknown outside his chosen sphere. Over the years, a few Cabinet ministers learned of his existence and influence, but his name was never mentioned by the media, and he never appeared as a witness in any prosecution. And yet, he routinely talked to his contacts in Whitehall and Buckingham Palace and – perhaps the greatest paradox – kept a daily diary for the last fourteen years of his employment by MI5.

In many ways, Liddell was the personification of the consummate intelligence professional: wise, unassuming, considered trustworthy by colleagues, occasionally enigmatic and always anxious to prevent others from drawing the Security Service into some nefarious enterprise that would damage the organisation's reputation or bring it into controversy.

Liddell died in December 1958 at the age of sixty-six, and we never met. However, I did talk to dozens of his closest friends, subordinates, colleagues, family and staff, including his wartime personal assistant Anthony Blunt and his long-serving assistant director, Dick White. When I learned that we shared the same birthday (albeit fifty-nine years apart) and had lived on the same London street, I began to develop an affinity for a truly remarkable individual and true public servant, devoid of party politics, who developed an intense understanding of national security and the national interest.

For all of his praiseworthy professional attributes, it is essentially his longevity in post for which he will be most remembered, for he is the common denominator in literally hundreds of security investigations conducted between 1919 and 1953. During the period from 1919 to 1931, he was employed as an analyst at Scotland Yard and thereafter he worked for MI5 for twenty-two years until his resignation, by which time he had been deputy director general since 1946. If the thousands of original MI5 files stored in the National Archives are any guide, and that is virtually the only source for them, Liddell signed off or contributed to most of them, one way or another. Accordingly, he appears as a constant thread across individual case histories relating to espionage and subversion over more than three decades. His continuous role was to advise subordinates, direct investigations, suggest new leads to be followed up, write memoranda and act as a link with Whitehall and chief constables.

In short, Liddell's interwar and Second World War experiences in his chosen field were unrivalled and amount to a living encyclopaedia or the embodiment of an institutional history. Considering that the essence of security work is the acquisition, retention and timely distribution of valuable information, Liddell performed precisely that function, for longer than anyone else. Indeed, Liddell's prodigious memory, combined with his carefully cultivated Allied liaison relationships, allowed him to remind his staff that there was rarely anything completely new in the cases that MI5 dealt with. Whenever an enthusiastic case officer claimed some astonishing new development, perhaps the recruitment of a new source or the observation of some suspicious behaviour, Liddell would wisely refer the subordinate to any case that had manifested a similar trajectory.

Liddell's background was conventional. He was the son of an army officer and probably would have become a professional musician if his studies in Germany had not been interrupted by war in 1914. He joined the army as a private soldier and was commissioned from the ranks. Like his two brothers, he was decorated with the Military Cross while serving with the Royal Field Artillery. In 1919, he joined Sir Basil Thomson's Directorate of Intelligence, a short-lived organisation that the ambitious and colourful Thomson, a former Prime Minister of Tonga and governor of Dartmoor Prison, had created under the auspices of the Metropolitan Police and with the authority of the assistant commissioner to study and investigate the ongoing political extremism that threatened to escalate into widespread civil unrest. Even the police went on strike in

1918 and 1919, and Liddell became very conscious that some Special Branch detectives with whom he had daily contact had supported the strikes.

Thomson's plans for his Directorate of Intelligence would be thwarted by an absence of political support, concerns about Thomson himself and some astute lobbying by MI5's shrewd chief, Vernon Kell. Eventually, Thomson would be forced to resign in 1921, supposedly because he had been held responsible for an incident at Chequers where Irish republicans had entered the estate and daubed slogans on the walls of the Prime Minister's country home.

Liddell's first major participation in a Soviet counter-espionage investigation occurred in 1924 and involved radical *Daily Herald* journalist William Ewer, who was also an overt CPGB member. Ewer, known as 'Trilby', ran a freelance correspondent's bureau in London, the Federated Press of America (FPA), in partnership with another office in Paris managed by George Slocombe. The pair came to MI5's notice because of an advertisement published on 24 November 1924 in the *Daily Herald*:

> Secret Service: A Labour group carrying out investigations would be very glad to receive information and details from anyone who was connected with the intelligence department or its operations. Write to the following address: Post Box 573, Daily Herald.

The advertisement was traced to Ewer, who was placed under surveillance by MI5. The watcher service soon reported that Ewer was also being kept under observation by another group of professional watchers, among them three former Special Branch detectives:

Hubert Ginhoven, Charles Jane and Walter Dail. Further investigation showed that one of the opposition watchers had visited the Soviet embassy in London accompanied by Rosa Edwards, a policeman's daughter employed as a secretary at the FPA's office in the Outer Temple. Two other detectives linked to Ewer, Albert Allen and Walter M. Homes, had been dismissed from Scotland Yard after the strike because they had organised an illegal police union.

The MI5 investigation had taken a sinister turn when an agent had been introduced to Ewer to gain his confidence and establish an inside source. Suddenly, as the operation appeared to be progressing well, it collapsed when Ewer severed the connection without explanation. Evidently, he had been tipped off by someone close to or even inside the investigation.

Despite the FPA's suspected involvement in Soviet espionage, no action was taken against either Ewer or the former Special Branch detectives. Ewer moved abroad and the FPA closed down in March 1928, doubtless because the Soviets believed mistakenly that the network had been compromised or even penetrated. Nevertheless, MI5 maintained its interest and in August 1928 established contact with Allen, who had fallen on hard times. He became MI5's principal source of information about Ewer and the FPA, confirming the Soviet links and disclosing that there were still two undetected individuals leaking material to Ewer.

On 11 April 1929, Ewer's inside sources, Detective Inspector Hubert Ginhoven and Detective Sergeant Charles Jane, were both arrested but never faced criminal charges. Instead, they were dismissed without a pension by a police disciplinary board, and received little support from their colleagues. More information from Allen and the interrogation of the suspects revealed that although

Ewer had closed down the FPA, he had continued his activities through the commercial front of another group, the Featherstone Typewriting Bureau.

The Soviet penetration of Scotland Yard and, in particular, Special Branch had a profound impact on Liddell who previously may not have fully appreciated the counter-intelligence threat to the British intelligence establishment. The fact that the Soviets had employed a journalist of Ewer's stature and had deployed Scotland Yard detectives to run surveillance operations was astonishing and encouraged Liddell to move to MI5 when the opportunity arose. Doubtless he knew too that there was lingering sympathy for Ginhoven and Jane and plenty of resentment towards MI5.

Liddell's first major counter-espionage case began in March 1927 when a well-connected Lloyd's underwriter, George Monckland, reported to MI5 that he had been approached by a young acquaintance, Wilfred Macartney, for sensitive commercial information about shipments of weapons to Finland. Macartney was a well-known political activist and occasional contributor to the *Sunday Worker* newspaper, with a criminal record for petty crime.

Under Kell's direction, Monckland offered Macartney a genuine classified document, albeit largely obsolete, a manual entitled *Regulations for Training the Flying Personnel of the Royal Air Force*. Macartney took the bait and was observed to pass it on to one of 233 Soviet employees of the Soviet Trade Delegation. The Home Secretary then approved a search warrant for the entire building. On the afternoon of 12 May 1927, Liddell was present when 100 uniformed policemen, accompanied by thirty Special Branch detectives, sealed off the premises and conducted a raid. Although the search disclosed a large collection of documents and a long list of foreign addresses, thought to be members of the Communist International, the RAF handbook was not recovered. However, the episode resulted in the publication of a government white paper to provide translations of some of the material seized and concluded with a suspension of diplomatic relations with Moscow.

Liddell and his team of analysts remained on the staff of Special Branch until October 1931 when, following the 1931 Statute of Westminster, they were all transferred to MI5 where Liddell acted as deputy to the director of the counter-espionage branch, Brigadier Jasper Harker. Ostensibly, the official reason for the transfer was the Statute's division of responsibility for global security and intelligence between MI5, which embraced the British Empire, and MI6, which was to operate in the rest of the world. Unofficially, Liddell had been appalled by the penetration of Special Branch and realised that all his work at Scotland Yard was likely to be compromised by corrupt or politically motivated detectives.

Following his twelve years' experience at Scotland Yard, Liddell would always be wary of Special Branch detectives and he was dismayed in 1940 when the decision was made to bring six of them inside the Security Service. He believed this was a terrible mistake, but at that stage had neither the seniority nor influence to change minds. In the event, Liddell came to trust Leonard Burt, who after the war would return to Scotland Yard and in 1946 be appointed to head Special Branch, a post he held for twelve years. When Liddell was promoted to direct MI5's B Division, he ensured that the police contingent was separated from the rest of the organisation and was deployed not on investigations but on liaison with provincial police forces. Liddell never lost his distrust of the police or his assumption that the Yard was inherently corrupt, although he did develop a genuine friendship with Burt, who shared Liddell's view that any information shared with detectives would leak to the press.

Liddell's home life certainly suffered because of his commitment to work. Having married the Hon. Calypso Baring in 1926, he separated from her in 1943. She later went to live in California with her half-brother Larry and thus isolated Liddell from his four children, Peter, Gay, Lucy and Juno. Liddell was a lonely figure whose work absorbed him and who found solace in the cello, an instrument in which he excelled as one of the country's most gifted amateur players.

In the pre-war period, MI5's B Division undertook a programme of counter-intelligence operations based on the principle of investing in the recruitment of young, part-time agents who were deployed to infiltrate potential adversaries. For example, the CPGB prided itself on being virtually immune to hostile penetration because of the party's comprehensive vetting procedures, which included background checks on membership candidates conducted either by the mysterious control committee or by party branches. The only way to join the party without these intensive inquiries was to join the Young Communist League (YCL), membership of which transferred automatically to the CPGB at the age of eighteen. Accordingly, MI5 took measures to identify and recruit a group of youngsters who joined YCL in the hope of later being accepted by the CPGB.

It was the penetration of the League Against Imperialism, a CPGB front, by Olga Gray in 1931 that would pay immense dividends. After working assiduously to be accepted by the League, she was invited by the CPGB leadership to act as a courier and make contact with the banned Communist Party of India. Gray accepted the assignment and reported to MI5 that one of her tasks was to deliver a particular edition of *Treasure Island* to India as this was the key to a book code used to encrypt messages transmitted to Moscow covertly.

The identification of *Treasure Island* was a breakthrough of immense proportions because the same key had been employed to encipher the CPGB's clandestine wireless channel with Moscow, based on a transmitter in Wimbledon operated by a trusted CPGB member who was an experienced ship's telegraphist. Thereafter, from March 1935 until January 1937, the CPGB channel was monitored by MI5 and decrypted by John Tiltman, a celebrated Government Code and Cipher School cryptanalyst. These messages were examined by MI5 and many of the decrypts were distributed in Whitehall by MI5 under the codename MASK.

Although the MASK source lasted less than two years, it demonstrated that the CPGB was not by British standards a legitimate political party but was actually a branch of Soviet intelligence, directed from Moscow. Having facilitated MASK, Gray maintained her contact with the CPGB through its national organiser Percy Glading, who would be arrested on espionage charges in 1938. A former employee of the Royal Arsenal at Woolwich, Glading had controlled a spy-ring of his former colleagues who passed him classified blueprints to photograph and deliver to the Soviets. At his trial at the Old Bailey, Glading had been stunned to recognise a prosecution witness, identified only as 'Miss X', as his confidante, Gray. Glading would be convicted and sentenced to six years' imprisonment.

Together, MASK and the Royal Arsenal case proved to Liddell that the Soviets posed a potent threat to British interests. His concern about foreign espionage extended to Germany too. MI5 became aware of a developing German espionage offensive when several retired army officers reported in 1933 that they had answered advertisements in *The Times* for people with military experience to proofread articles contributed to various unnamed academic journals. One of the retired officers approached to undertake this kind of work was colourful RAF pilot Major Christopher Draper, who was interviewed by Kell and Harker and agreed to play the role of a double agent by appearing to assist the Abwehr.

Draper was given a post box address in Hamburg with which to correspond, and this immediately became a target for interception by the General Post Office (GPO). All mail sent to this address was extracted, photographed and then returned into the regular post for delivery to Germany, a technique that had been refined during the First World War. This procedure revealed that several other Abwehr assets used the same post box and one of them was a hairdresser in Dundee, Jessie Jordan. Monitoring her letters led MI5 to one of her correspondents in New York who signed himself 'Kron'. This information was shared with the FBI in January 1938 when Liddell visited Washington DC to brief the director, J. Edgar Hoover. The FBI quickly identified 'Kron' as US Army deserter Sergeant Guenther Rumrich, and he was arrested in February 1938. Under interrogation, Rumrich made a comprehensive confession and implicated several other Germn spies active in the US. The case was a significant triumph for the FBI and Hoover took the credit for having broken up a major spy-ring. Although Liddell was anxious to protect Draper from being identified as the double agent who had given the tip about the Hamburg post box, which had initiated MI5's investigation, his name was mentioned at Rumrich's trial, causing MI5 considerable embarrassment.

Although Draper's role was compromised by the disclosures in the US, his usefulness as a double agent had already come to an end because his German controllers simply lost interest in him. To sustain the deception, MI5 had asked the Air Ministry to authorise the release of information that would be of value to the Germans but nobody was prepared to take that responsibility. Thus, Liddell came to understand that successful double-agent operations required military authorities at a high level to sanction the release of material that would keep the attention of an adversary. The advantage of such a strategy was the confidence that if a double agent appeared to be satisfying an appetite for useful material, their handlers were unlikely to embark on other recruitment attempts. Perhaps predictably, Draper's failure to keep the Abwehr supplied with useful information had caused him to be dropped.

The Rumrich case also demonstrated that the FBI had very little experience of espionage or counter-intelligence and as a law enforcement body under the Department of Justice, was primarily interested in arrests and successful prosecutions. The US had no central intelligence organisation. The OSS would not be formed until 1942 and the CIA did not come into existence until after the war in 1947. Accordingly, Liddell's main pre-war contact with the Americans was through Herschel Johnson, a first secretary at the US embassy in Grosvenor Square who was acting as a conduit for the exchange of intelligence. Thus, Liddell became, on his own initiative, the main channel for the exchange of intelligence with Washington.

During his visit to Washington, Liddell had taken the opportunity to visit Ottawa to encourage the Royal Canadian Mounted Police (RCMP) to devote more resources to dealing with the threat of Soviet and German espionage. On Liddell's initiative, an MI5 officer was posted to Ottawa to liaise with the RCMP Special Branch. This collaboration proved to be the foundation of a long, fruitful era of cooperation between the Canadian authorities and the Security Service, which lasts to this day and pre-dated the 'Five Eyes' cooperation, which had developed originally in the cryptographic field in 1943.

Liddell's wartime contribution is most eloquently detailed in his diaries, which reflect his preoccupation with nurturing the double agent project, from its infancy with a handful of agents to its maturity as a sophisticated vehicle conveying strategic deception to the Axis. As well as keeping a guiding hand on the double agents, he supervised numerous counter-espionage cases, several of which have failed to attract the attention of historians. Take, for example, the German spy Ludwig Warschauer who would be pursued by one of Liddell's protégés Harry Lee, a young solicitor who had experienced childhood polio and therefore was unfit for combat. Before hostilities broke out, Warschauer had been the senior electrical engineer at Siemens, but he was also an Abwehr spy posing as an authentic Jewish refugee together with an accomplice, Leon Bergl. Aged forty-one and originally from Posen, Warschauer had been recruited by the Abwehr in 1938 for a mission to Poland but instead was sent to the UK in June 1939 accompanied by his assistant Elisabeth Kohsen, who became his wife. He was sent to the country ostensibly to represent the Mannesmann recording equipment through his firm WAF & Co. Ltd.

Warschauer had some intelligence experience in his background, having served in 234 Flight, an aerial reconnaissance unit, during the First World War. His activities in London, as he canvassed government departments for opportunities to sell his patented apparatus, caught MI5's attention. Potential purchasers were warned off accordingly. In 1940, Warschauer was designated an enemy alien and interned in Douglas on the Isle of Man, where he was periodically interrogated about his intelligence connections. Finally, in August 1943, MI5's persistence paid off and he provided Harry Lee and John Noble with a signed, fifty-page confession, implicating his former accomplice, Max Betram, who had returned to Germany just before the outbreak of hostilities.

Warschauer was not 'turned' into a double agent, nor hanged as a Nazi spy, and appears in none of the official histories of British intelligence, but nevertheless his case is an interesting manifestation of the Abwehr exploiting a Jewish refugee. This very unusual case is but one of hundreds of individual investigations mentioned by Liddell in his diaries. It is only by studying the collection of loose-leaf, ring binder pages that one can appreciate the depth of Liddell's knowledge, his sense of humour and the breadth of MI5's interests and influence. The diaries themselves were never intended for outside scrutiny and, codenamed WALLFLOWERS, were secured in the director general's personal safe.

The end of Liddell's MI5 career came unexpectedly in May 1953 when he retired to become security adviser to the Atomic Energy Authority. His resignation had been prompted by his unsuccessful application to succeed Percy Sillitoe as director general and by the decision to appoint his protégé Dick White instead. Of course, White was the younger man and was closely associated with professional success as the case officer who had run the pre-war German diplomat Wolfgang zu Putlitz, the architect of Allied security and intelligence in the Middle East and as chief of SHAEF's counter-intelligence staff, which had traced and neutralised all the enemy stay-behind networks after D-Day. Whitehall was so anxious to be rid of Liddell that he suffered the indignity of being eliminated during the very first round of interviews chaired by the Home Secretary, David Maxwell Fyfe.

Unquestionably, Liddell was quite the best-qualified of those who had put their names forward. He was the pre-eminent counter-intelligence officer of his generation, respected by his adversaries and admired by his subordinates. He had an unrivalled reputation for discretion and developed an intuitive talent for handling the most difficult cases in a highly politically charged atmosphere with constant interference from Whitehall officials and interventions from senior politicians. Liddell's great triumph was that he had guided Britain's counter-intelligence agency through these minefields during a war which lasted nearly six years without much scandal. Yet, apart from his closest staff, and subsequently the readers of his diaries, few had any idea of what he accomplished. There is a strange irony in that the secrecy which he advocated and enforced should have mitigated against his chances of being director general. Quite simply, Liddell had ensured that almost nobody outside MI5 knew of him or his achievements.

By the same token, there were aspects of White's professional and private life which were unknown outside 'the office'. Although his affair with his secretary or his marriage to a former CPGB member would not have excluded him from the top job, what should have was the fact that he had contemplated resignation in 1950 after he had been singled out for blame by Sillitoe who had lied to the

Prime Minister over the investigation of Klaus Fuchs, based on a thoroughly misleading brief which had been prepared by White in anticipation of his meeting scheduled for 3 March. Sillitoe had been infuriated that Liddell, Hollis and White had persuaded him to reassure Attlee that MI5 had never suspected Fuchs of espionage, whereas Fuchs's file showed very clearly that during a background check on the atomic physicist in December 1947, MI5 officers Michael Serpell and James Robertson had both suggested Fuchs was likely a spy and should be investigated. Indeed, Liddell had mentioned the issue on 9 December in his diary:

> I had a talk with Dick White, Roger Hollis and Martin Furnival Jones on the case of Klaus Fuchs who is employed on atomic research. The question of this man's establishment has come up. It was agreed that, although our information was entirely negative, we should tell Atomic Research what we know, and express the opinion that the information does not really amount to anything. The alternative was to say nothing, which seemed to me to be undesirable – the more so since Henry Arnold, the security officer at Harwell, would be putting in his comments which might be somewhat unbalanced.[1]

White had ignored the recommendation and three years later had been castigated by Sillitoe, who had gathered his staff into the Leconfield House canteen to vent his anger. Liddell confided this to his diary on 17 March 1950:

> The D-G called a meeting for the purpose of conducting a post-mortem on the Klaus Fuchs case. He began by

> congratulating all those concerned in bringing Fuchs to justice within the short space of six months. He said that he had satisfied the Prime Minister on the brief which was given to him when he visited the latter on 3 March, but at that time he had not seen the file. Had he done so he would have been extremely apprehensive, and had an inquiry been ordered he felt that he would probably have lost his job and the department would have been split from top to bottom. He then criticised the action during the earlier stages of the inquiry. He drew attention in particular to a minute by James Robertson which had expressed the view that Fuchs might well be a spy, and also to one by Michael Serpell expressing the view that both Fuchs and Rudolf Peierls might well be spies. He could not understand why, in the light of these minutes, more had not been done to investigate the case, beyond the imposition of a Home Office Warrant for a period of two months. He also criticised a letter by Garrett in which it was suggested that details of the slight suspicion against Fuchs should not be communicated to the Americans.[2]

Liddell then went on to describe a further encounter with Sillitoe and couched his account in Whitehall mandarin:

> The D-G had made the point during the meeting that he had never been informed at the time the Fuchs case was re-examined in 1947. I said that I accepted responsibility, but that he must realise that the case as it appeared then was only one of a very great number which might have been held to be of equal or greater importance. The D-G subsequently made it clear to Dick White that he did not wish to imply in any of his remarks that the brief

> which had been put up to him when he visited the Prime Minister was in any way intended to be inaccurate or misleading.

The translation of this, for those unfamiliar with mandarin, is Liddell had observed that White had given the director general an inaccurate and misleading version of the background to the Fuchs investigation, but the deception had not been *intentional*, which almost made the offence all the more egregious.

Immediately after the unprecedented humiliation inflicted by Sillitoe, White had sought Liddell's advice in contemplation of resignation. Liddell had advised White to stay and simply accept the criticism. Would the Home Office appointments panel have opted for White in 1953 if it had known about this episode? Or if it had known of the blunder on the night of the Burgess and Maclean defection? White had been assigned the task of flying to France to intercept Maclean when his ship, the *Falaise*, docked at St Malo but had discovered too late that his passport had expired and he was unable to travel – a mishap of monumental proportions and thereafter MI5's senior management perpetuated a cover-up to protect White's carefully nurtured reputation for swift, silent efficiency. Would the panel have chosen White if it had known about this particular skeleton? Few knew the truth, and of those that did, none talked.

One of the mysteries that arose following Liddell's death in December 1958 was the controversy over Anthony Blunt, the Soviet mole who had been recommended to Liddell in 1940 by Victor Rothschild and who Liddell appointed as his personal assistant. He also tasked Blunt with drafting an assessment of the performance of the Watcher Service and chose him to supervise the highly sensitive TRIPLEX, the joint operation with MI6, which discreetly plundered the diplomatic pouches of neutral embassies in London. Perhaps even more embarrassing was Liddell's selection of Blunt to research and prepare the monthly reports on MI5's activities, which were shown to the Prime Minister by the director general from April 1943. This particular duty ensured that he could enter every office, requisition every file and demand a briefing on MI5's every secret undertaking. Liddell's account of the aftermath of the Burgess and Maclean defections on Friday 25 May 1951 makes for difficult reading, as does this entry in November which refers to Philby by his codename, PEACH:

3 November 1951

I dined with Tommy Harris and his wife last night. We did not get on to any discussion of office matters until after dinner when Tommy expressed anxiety about Anthony Blunt's indiscretions.

Anthony had told Tommy that the American, Bernard Miller, was returning to this country to study and that he intended to resume touch with him. Tommy had told Anthony that he considered this most unwise. He said that he had never been wholly satisfied with the peculiar story of Bernard Miller, who had become acquainted with Guy Burgess on board ship, had visited Geneva, been present when Burgess was packing his clothes to depart, and had returned to America immediately afterwards. Tommy thought it quite conceivable that Miller might have played some part on behalf of the Russians, or, alternatively, that he might have been an agent of the FBI. Even if he were wrong in both of these assumptions, it was quite possible that Miller might now be acting for the FBI, and that information detrimental to

Anthony might go back to them. On all these grounds he had strongly advised Anthony to have nothing to do with Bernard Miller and had told him that if he, Anthony, had no objection he thought of mentioning the matter to me and asking my advice.

I told Tommy that he could tell Anthony that I entirely agreed with his, Tommy's, view, and I was sure that if Anthony did not pull himself together he might well be jeopardising the whole of his career.

We then talked about Anthony's relations with Jackie Hewit. Tommy, of course, knew about the latest incident and had strongly advised Anthony to break with Hewit and not to go on visiting him in St. Mary's Hospital.

This led to a discussion about Guy Burgess, and of a hunch which Tommy had just after his disappearance that he might have gone behind the Iron Curtain. He recalled that he mentioned this at my first interview with him and Anthony, that I had asked him what made him think so, and that he had been unable to give any concrete reasons. I had then told him and Anthony that Burgess and Maclean had been traced to France. It was clear to me that Tommy now felt rather confirmed in his original belief, although he had always been worried by the idea that, whatever his potentialities, nobody could have seriously employed an individual who was so notoriously unreliable. He felt that if this had been a smoke-screen to cover up more sinister activities, Burgess was a far cleverer man than he had ever believed him to be.

During the whole evening PEACH was hardly mentioned and no reference was made to his dismissal. Tommy did say at one point of the conversation: 'I suppose you have seen PEACH and got all the information you want from him?'. It was quite clear to

> me that the idea that there could be anything wrong with PEACH had never entered the head of either Tommy or Hilda.
>
> As I was going away, Tommy took me out to the car. I told him that we had no positive evidence of the whereabouts of Burgess or Maclean, but that there were a number of points where I thought he might be able to help us, I could not go into them now, as Dick had a good many of the details. Could he spare the time to look in on us one day next week? He readily accepted and we fixed 11 o'clock on Monday.
>
> In the course of this final conversation, Tommy did mention that he had driven Benes about at the request of Burgess and that this was in 1939 when Burgess was working for Section D of SIS.
>
> During the whole of our discussion I could detect nothing that would suggest that Tommy was not being wholly frank and genuine.[3]

How much did Liddell really know about the defections earlier in the year? Did he ever have any suspicions about Blunt's loyalties? These are just two of the many questions that could or should have been put to him. Curiously, the secrecy over these events continues to this day, with a large part of Liddell's diary entry for Monday 28 May redacted and Maclean's name unmentioned until Tuesday 29 May, three days after his escape. Why has MI5 concealed Liddell's comments on the day Maclean was reported missing?

It is undeniable that Liddell's links with Burgess and Blunt cast a permanent shadow over an extraordinary career, and it may be that while so much of the 'Third Man' debate continued, it would have been impolitic to promote Liddell. On the other hand, as shown here, White was hardly a safer pair on hands in which to entrust the defence of the realm.

CHAPTER XVII

THE MOSCOW ARCHIVES

All credit for opening the KGB's archives to external scrutiny should go to the late John Costello, the controversial Cambridge-educated historian who died suddenly while returning home to Miami from London in August 1995. Five years earlier, he had knocked on the door of the old KGB headquarters in Dzerzhinsky Square and asked to see someone, anyone, who could speak English. This brazen approach resulted in an extraordinary agreement made between Vladimir Kryuchkov of the Russian Federation Foreign Intelligence Service's (SVR) FCD and Crown Books, a division of Random House, to authorise a group of western historians' access to the former Soviet intelligence archives, under the supervision of a genial Georgian, Yuri Kobaladze.

Costello, who had graduated from Fitzwilliam College, Cambridge, had published *Mask of Treachery*, a biography of Anthony Blunt in 1988, and then began to research Rudolf Hess's flight to Scotland in May 1941.[1] While working on *Ten Days that Saved the West* he met Oleg Tsarev, a former member of the KGB in London who had spent seven years under journalistic cover as the *Soviet Industry* correspondent.

Tsarev received permission to collaborate with Costello on another project based on the NKVD's operational files. This project would be about Alexander Orlov, who had headed the *rezidentura* in Barcelona during the Spanish Civil War.[2] Orlov had defected in 1938 and fled to the US, where he declared himself in a 1953 *Life* article. Thereafter, he was interviewed by the FBI and moved under federal protection to Ann Arbor, Michigan. The FBI believed that Orlov, who died in March 1973, had been entirely candid about his NKVD career. However, in their 1993 collaboration *Deadly Illusions*, Costello and Tsarev revealed that according to Orlov's personal file, he had been the illegal *rezident* in London in 1935 and had kept silent about the many recruitments he had supervised, among them Kim Philby. When Orlov had defected he had written to Stalin and head of the NKVD Nikolai Yezhov to promise that he would remain silent about his clandestine work if no action was taken against his family. The files suggested that Orlov had kept the bargain.

Deadly Illusions was a significant publishing breakthrough because of the cooperation between Costello and Tsarev, a serving Russian intelligence officer. A further contract was made with Crown Books to allow access to the KGB files relating to post-war Berlin, the Cuban missile crisis, the Communist Party of the United States of America and the Third Department FCD files concerning the London *rezidentura* up until 1960. Selected western authors would be assigned KGB co-authors, and soon work was underway by David Murphy and Sergei Kondrashev on *Battleground Berlin*, Tim Naftali and Aleksandr Fursenko on *One Hell of a Gamble*, and Allen Weinstein and Alexander Vassiliev on *The Haunted Wood*.[3]

My only involvement with the project at that stage was to be brought in as a consultant to authenticate the handwriting of Donald Maclean and Kim Philby, who over the years had written hundreds of messages to their Soviet controllers. The American publishers had become anxious about the progress made by its team of historians, and Costello was instructed to produce some samples from the files so the money men in New York could be reassured that the project was on schedule and that the KGB had supplied genuine texts.

All appeared to be going well until Costello's visit to the south of France in August 1995 when he became unwell. He returned to London overnight and then caught a flight to Miami but died while still in the air. Nobody had planned for such an eventuality, and I was invited by Random House in London to visit Moscow and assess whether the project remained viable. However, no date for my visit was arranged, and when I called to settle the travel arrangements a week later, I was told that the entire project had been scrapped and that Jim Wade, the supervising Crown Books editor in New York, had been sacked. Stunned by this news, I spoke to Tsarev in Moscow, who had not been informed of Random House's decision. He was justifiably angry, but also puzzled. The SVR had been paid a large fee and the six other authors had received their advances. All would be astonished by Random House's behaviour. The following day, Tsarev called back with a proposal. Would I take over Costello's current book, *Deadly Illusions*, and find a replacement publisher for the other authors too? One conversation over breakfast in the Savoy with the mercurial Eddie Bell committed HarperCollins to a seamless takeover of eight authors and four books that had been paid for already.

Over the next two years, I made several trips to Moscow to

sift through the material already selected from the KGB files by Costello and to look at the huge quantity of papers that had to be assessed. Tsarev and I shared an office in the street neighbouring the SVR headquarters, which contained Felix Dzerzhinsky's suite of carefully preserved rooms from which he had run the Cheka. Our only obstacle was the lack of photocopying facilities, as the Xerox machine on our floor had not been serviced for years and broke down frequently. This meant smuggling secret documents out of the building to the ultra-efficient business centre in the new Marriott Hotel and then secreting them back into our office. However, the real challenge was taking the authorised, declassified documents through customs at Sheremetyevo Airport, where the Russian word for 'declassified' was something of a misunderstood novelty. To ensure safe passage, I insisted that Tsarev, armed with his magic red KGB identification card, should accompany me through all the security procedures.

In retrospect, it might seem odd that someone of my political background should have participated in this exercise, but the opportunity to read even selected excerpts from the KGB's archive was too good to ignore. There were dozens of other historians who would have seized the chance and at least I was already well briefed on what to look for. As we worked together, Tsarev and I developed a system of sifting the paperwork. He would hand me each page, and I would decide whether the item was worth copying. When the KGB had changed a codeword and substituted a replacement, Tsarev was allowed to tell me, although he could not tell me the deleted original. Usually, he himself did not know the original.

The KGB files were fascinating for several other reasons. None of the Cambridge Five had spoken Russian at the time they were active spies, so the information they had delivered to their contacts in London had been written in English. Secondly, there had been a severe shortage of paper in Moscow in 1942, so many of the *rezidentura* reports had been typed on the back of redundant papers taken from other files. Accordingly, it became advantageous to read both sides of a sheet in case the reverse inadvertently contained something interesting that, theoretically, had not been through the declassification procedure.

In due course, the books were completed and all contained fascinating new information which appeared to silence the academic critics, such as the American scholar Amy W. Knight who feared that we had become KGB dupes, peddling a pro-Soviet perspective. While it is true that the KGB management only allowed us to see the documents that had already been scrutinised by the KGB, who obviously had an agenda, propaganda was not one of the organisation's motives – they were rather more motivated by the money. Knight claimed that we had been naïve and that we had deliberately overlooked the vile nature of the regime but we pointed out that our co-authored book *The Crown Jewels* contained references to Stalin's purges and to the murderous nature of his regime. While Knight acknowledged that *The Crown Jewels* revealed the existence of an Oxford group of spies headed by an agent codenamed SCOTT, she complained that this disclosure had been made 'without giving any names' of its membership.

In retrospect, with the benefit of a couple of dozen other books devoted to the Cambridge spies whom the British media found so beguiling, *The Crown Jewels* represented a major step forward in understanding the traitors of the 1930s and 1940s and explained the crucial talent-spotting and recruiting roles of the illegal *rezidents*

Alexander Orlov and Arnold Deutsch. It also revealed the contribution made by the NKVD recruiter Edith Suschitzky. Judging from the reaction of her brother, the celebrated cinematographer Wolfgang Suschitzky, whom I interviewed at his flat overlooking the Regent's Canal, he thought the KGB had been rather too candid.

The Soviets were justifiably proud of what their spies had accomplished, but from a counter-intelligence viewpoint, the book's value lay in the London *rezidentura*'s shifting assessments of their agents and the personality profiles drawn up about each of them. Indeed, it is fair to say that until this opportunity to dip into the files came, no person and no agency in the west had the slightest idea of what Stalin's 'Ring of Five' (the Cambridge Five) had actually betrayed. The picture that emerged in *The Crown Jewels* gave an entirely new insight into the Cambridge Five. It also shed light on the roles played by some hitherto unknown Soviet agents, such as William 'Trilby' Ewer and Peter Smollett and revealed Burgess's offer to murder Goronwy Rees. Another gem was the explanation in 1950 for the VENONA compromise of Klaus Fuchs. According to Philby, the Anglo-American cryptographers had relied on the misuse of one-time pads and the innovative employment of a machine 'which in one day does the work of a thousand people in a thousand years'.[4] The only embarrassment was the large KGB file devoted to MOLIERE/LISZT, who was revealed to be John Cairncross. Where he had sought to minimise his involvement in espionage and had flatly denied having spied after the war, his file told a very different story. The Moscow file detailed Cairncross's industrial-scale espionage and the KGB management belatedly realised that rather too much relating to Cairncross had been released. In particular, the file showed that Cairncross had concentrated on atomic issues both during and after the war and in June and July 1951 (within weeks of the defection of Burgess and Maclean), he had passed 1,339 Whitehall documents to his Soviet contact. In this particular case, it was the Soviets who had demonstrated some naivete, for it was learned subsequently that he had been infuriated by the contradiction and had even demanded some financial compensation (which was never paid).

After *The Crown Jewels* had been broadly welcomed by the academic community, it was clear that there was plenty more material available from the archives, comprising original documents stolen by the Cambridge spies. The excess material included such gems as Philby's contribution to MI6's post-war reorganisation and Blunt's 1943 assessment of neutral embassies in London. These were important files, which the spies had selected themselves for onward delivery to Moscow. There, the analysts had been overwhelmed by the sheer industry of their agents in London and had not even attempted to guide the spy-ring to the subjects of greatest interest to the Kremlin.

However, two important issues arose: reproduction of these original MI5 and MI6 documents might constitute an infringement of Crown copyright. On the other hand, the Crown would have to admit their authenticity to bring a successful legal action alleging infringement. In other words, if the British authorities wanted to suppress the material, it would have to declare it authentic. In these circumstances, the two organisations decided that expediency dictated that no action should be taken in terms of injuncting the papers – to be included in my book entitled *TRIPLEX* – if the book included a statement indicating that the government had not acknowledged that the documents were genuine. Indeed, it turned out that because of the busy 'weeders' who had destroyed so much of MI6's registry, the book contained material that had long disappeared from MI6's own archive. The title *TRIPLEX* was a case in point. It had been the MI5 and MI6 codeword for a highly secret joint operation to access the diplomatic pouches of neutral missions based in London. The MI5 officer selected to liaise with his MI6 counterpart David Boyle had been Anthony Blunt. Thus, it was probably fair to say that this super-sensitive material, from a top-secret source, was read in Moscow as soon as it was ready for its very limited internal distribution in Whitehall. Other TRIPLEX operations were conducted in special laboratories set up in Bermuda and New York and maybe Trinidad too.

All the KGB collaborations would make important contributions to our understanding of the Cold War. For example, Tim Naftali and Aleksandr Fursenko's 1997 account of the Cuban missile crisis detailed the deployment of the three November-class submarines, each armed with a pair of nuclear-tipped torpedoes, that had been sent to the Caribbean. The first anyone had known of this episode was when a conference on the crisis had been held at Hawks Cay, Florida in March 1987 and had been attended by Russian scholars, who had taken advantage of the Kremlin's policy of *glasnost* to disclose previously secret information.

The other book which changed perceptions was *The Haunted Wood: Soviet Espionage in America – The Stalin Era* by Allen Weinstein and Alexander Vassiliev. Together, they trawled the FCD's Moscow archive and concentrated on NKVD networks in the US. Importantly, they were able to identify particular agents to whom there had been references in the VENONA material. Vassiliev, while working on the project, had made copious notes in a series of notebooks, which he subsequently brought to London in 1996. These then became the basis of a further book, *Spies: The Rise and Fall of the KGB in America*, which arguably remains the most comprehensive study of Soviet espionage before, during and after the VENONA era.[5]

CHAPTER XVIII

ST ERMIN'S PRESS

In July 1996, I received a letter from a New York banker named Geoffrey Elliott, recently retired from Morgan Stanley, who asked if I had any knowledge of a wartime SOE mission to Yugoslavia codenamed DISCLAIM. It so happened that DISCLAIM had been mentioned in my book *Secret War: The Story of SOE* and was the first deployment of an SOE liaison team to the Yugoslav partisans, sent from Malta in February 1942. The mission had been led by Major Kavan Elliott, but he and his men had been captured within hours of their arrival in Croatia. Geoffrey was Kavan's son and was keen to learn more about his father's activities. Indeed, he only knew the bare minimum about his father's past but had documented a pre-war career in the Balkans perhaps as a representative of Unilever, an expulsion from Budapest in October 1948 on charges of espionage and his retirement in Jamaica with a new young family. Kavan had been an unreformed scoundrel and as postmaster in the Wiltshire village of Chilton Foliat had robbed his own shop in 1966. He had died in London in July 1977.

We met in New York in September 1998. Geoffrey explained that he had spent much of his life in the City and had recently retired.

He was now intent on pursuing some of his interests, one of which was an ambition to research his father's rather remarkable career. Within a few months, Geoffrey had produced a manuscript based on his father's papers and I added material from the National Archives, which had begun to receive the SOE records which had previously been under MI6's protection. The result was *I Spy*, the very first of the titles to be published by our joint venture, St Ermin's Press, in association with Little, Brown & Co.[1] Our firm was so-called because of the St Ermin's Hotel in Westminster, which had accommodated several MI6 offices during the war. Our initial plan was to create a partnership to publish two books, Geoffrey's biography of his father and then my *Counterfeit Spies*. However, as the business developed it became clear that there was room in the market for a niche publisher concentrating on titles that would not at first glance attract the mainstream publishing houses but were nevertheless gems, with some less than obvious advantage that would make them a marketing success.

Elliott was no stranger to the intelligence world. He was of Russian Jewish heritage and had spoken Russian at home to his grandparents. Later, when he had been called up for National Service, he had been elected for language training at RAF Crail and had been deployed as a voice intercept radio operator, eavesdropping on Soviet troops in Germany.

During the past ten years, I had encountered a growing number of non-fiction titles that purported to be authentic accounts of wartime espionage, but as I had learned with *A Man Called Intrepid*, there were plenty of books that were downright frauds. Over a period, I had accumulated the offending books and then forensically analysed them with the benefit of what had become known more recently about wartime clandestine operations. Unfortunately, the likelihood of a defamation action was considered too high for a mainstream publisher to participate in the project, but Geoffrey had deep pockets and was personally quite affronted by some of the bogus SOE memoirs in circulation. Like so many of those associated with SOE, often through family connections, Elliott was contemptuous of the fakers. His father may have been a rogue in his private life, but he had been a brave agent, opting to drop blind into hostile territory. Accordingly, I edited *I Spy* and he backed *Counterfeit Spies*. Both books were released in 1998... and nobody sued.

The third book published in that debut year was the official history of the British Security Co-ordination, a document sponsored at the end of the war by the organisation's director Sir William Stephenson, who had employed members of his staff to draft particular chapters and then passed the finished document to the Cabinet Office, which seems to have lost it. Only twenty copies were printed by Stephenson, who kept one for himself. The Cabinet Office agreed to the St Ermin's Press edition on condition a disclaimer was included to confirm that it had not been officially endorsed by Her Majesty's Government. The copy that we relied upon was kindly supplied by Bill Hood of the CIA's counter-intelligence staff who, as an OSS veteran, was keen to have the embellishments and inventions of *A Man Called Intrepid* dealt with authoritatively, once and for all. Alas, Stephenson had succumbed to dementia at his home in Paget, Bermuda in January 1989 and never knew the book had been released.

The next book to be released was Roger Fleetwood-Hesketh's *FORTITUDE: The D-Day Deception Campaign*. Fleetwood-Hesketh had battled Whitehall for years to negotiate permission to publish, but he had been fobbed off with the excuse that Sir Michael Howard had been commissioned to compile an official history of deception and this project had been delayed by Thatcher's government, which was having second thoughts about the wisdom of releasing Harry Hinsley's multi-volume series. As a former MP, Fleetwood-Hesketh understood the labyrinthine manoeuvres of the Cabinet Office mandarins, but he was frustrated to hear that other authors had been allowed access to his very impressive, large-format book. In particular, he suspected that a subordinate, Colonel Noel Wild, had passed a copy to Sefton Delmer, who had used the draft as the basis of his own book, *The Counterfeit Spy*.

Fleetwood-Hesketh died in November 1987, but his son Rob was determined to see his father's book published at last. The version used by St Ermin's Press, released in 1999, was the unredacted draft that had escaped the Cabinet Office scissors. At long last, Roger Fleetwood-Hesketh received the long-overdue credit for his role as architect of the D-Day deception campaign.

In 1999, St Ermin's took on an exceptionally challenging proposal, which was based on a manuscript written by Kim Philby's widow Rufina and her husband's old friend, Michael Lyubimov, formerly of the KGB London *rezidentura*. Rufina had saved Philby's life in Moscow by getting his alcoholism under control and her story covered the later period in his life after his arrival in the Soviet Union in January 1963. They had met in Moscow in 1970, having been introduced by George Blake, and were married the following year. They remained together until his death in May 1988, and her perspective on their life together was fascinating but would require a heavy edit to make it acceptable to western readers.

One solution to the problem was to find an expert on Philby with all the necessary skills, and St Ermin's settled on Colonel Hayden Peake, a serving CIA officer who was a renowned bibliophile and a world-acknowledged expert on Cold War counter-intelligence. Peake was intrigued by the project and the prospect of gaining access to a cache of Philby's private papers, so we travelled to Moscow to accomplish the impossible and persuade Rufina that her manuscript had to be completely rewritten and restructured. We dined together at the grill room of the new Marriott Hotel, and halfway through the meal I noticed that Rufina and Peake had been in earnest conversation for quite some time and were ignoring the rest of the table. Peake later explained that during their conversation, Rufina discovered his birthday and realised they had both been born on the very same day. Russians, of course, are highly superstitious and Rufina was instantly convinced that here was a man she could trust completely. Thereafter, they became firm friends and her judgement proved entirely accurate. She took all his advice regarding the book, which was now retitled *The Private Life of Kim Philby: The Moscow Years.*[2] It combined Peake's academic research over several decades with Rufina's unique insight into her time living and traveling with Philby.

These first titles established a certain reputation, which attracted offers from across the world. One such contact was Zeev Avni, a Soviet spy who had penetrated Mossad and then served a long prison sentence in Israel. Avni, who died in January 2007, had been arrested in April 1956 but released from a fourteen-year sentence in 1965. His story was quite remarkable because although he had been ideologically drawn to the NKVD (and later the KGB), he had eventually confessed all to Shin Bet, Israel's internal security service. Even more remarkably, his autobiography *False Flag* included a postscript written by Yehuda Prag, his Shin Bet interrogator, and a detailed account of his role in a notorious operation conducted in West Germany, which had been intended to identify German scientists working on an Egyptian ballistic missile development programme.[3] Avni had masqueraded as a Federal German intelligence officer seeking information from the former Nazi technicians based in Cairo and they were perfectly willing to cooperate, unaware that Avni was operating under a classic false flag. Having identified the German scientists working in Egypt, Mossad initiated a campaign of intimidation to persuade them to abandon the project.

Avni, who had started his espionage career for the Soviets while serving in the Swiss Army in 1942, had been tried in secret in 1956 and his entire case was considered an Israeli state secret – even in May 1998 when I visited Tel Aviv to negotiate a few excisions in return for permission to publish from the military censor. The entire experience was delightful, and Avni proved to be a very engaging host who had persuaded himself at least that the discussions with Mossad's senior management were a mere formality. He may have been right but it did not seem so at the time.

The next big project was a chance discovery in the Public Record Office of an SOE headquarters file relating to the preparation of the organisation's official history, completed in 1948 by a Scottish academic, William Mackenzie. At that time, there had not been any intention to publish as the Foreign Office, MI6 and the Cabinet Office were all agreed that the contents were too secret for public consumption. Whitehall's institutional memory remained conscious of the retribution meted out in 1940 to the patriots in

Belgium and Luxembourg who had received British decorations for their clandestine roles during the German occupation in the First World War. Improbable as it seemed, this was the principal argument deployed to prevent wider circulation of wartime Allied intelligence operations.

Instead, a mildly aggrieved Mackenzie acknowledged his authorship by mentioning the title in his *Who's Who* entry but was powerless, under the terms of his contract with the Crown, to have any further interest in the matter. He had been paid a straight fee for his work and enjoyed no further rights, thus allowing Whitehall to bury the potential embarrassments revealed in its 814 pages. He had died in August 1996 at the age of eighty-seven, so he never knew his book would eventually be released.

Public awareness of SOE developed from 1960 when a parliamentary campaign was initiated to discover the fate of some forty women agents sent by SOE into Nazi-occupied France. A formidable combination of Dame Irene Ward MP and the author Jean Overton Fuller had been determined to lift the veil on the fate of SOE's women agents. The furore led Secretary of State for War Jack Profumo to announce that an official history, *SOE in France*, had been commissioned to put the tragic losses into an acceptable context.[4] The historian selected to undertake the research was M. R. D. Foot, who had himself served with the Special Air Service regiment in France after D-Day as a liaison officer. However, he was also contracted by the Cabinet Office, which imposed some unusual conditions. Foot agreed not to mention MI6 and not to interview any SOE personnel. His book was to be written entirely from the files… and to lean heavily on Mackenzie's history.

Conveniently, the Crown had abandoned claims to copyright

on most of its archive collections and embraced a policy under the Waldegrave Initiative, which espoused 'open government' and the wholesale declassification of secret papers. From our viewpoint, this meant huge tranches of Whitehall shelves relating to MI5, SOE, the Political Warfare Executive and the Joint Intelligence Committee (JIC) would be opened for public scrutiny at Kew. Better still, we would be able to copy what we wanted and then publish it ourselves. Thus, Mackenzie's *The Secret History of SOE* became the first of several in the genre.[5] Accordingly, Foot was invited to contribute a foreword to the book. Others included M. R. D. Foot's magisterial *SOE in the Low Countries* and *The Secret History of PWE: The Political Warfare Executive 1939–45* by David Garnett, who had died in February 1981.[6]

Also associated with this series was *Invasion 1940*, which was a translation of *Informationsheft GrossBritannien*, the plan and arrest list for the imminent Nazi occupation of Great Britain. The original document, drafted as part of Operation SEALION, was to have been distributed as a handbook to help the occupation authorities understand Britain and the British population. Of particular interest was a chapter entitled 'The Intelligence Service', which supposedly had been based on information supplied by Sigismund Payne Best and Richard Stevens after their abduction at Venlo in November 1939. The version in the Imperial War Museum library was not allowed to be copied, apparently because the intelligence content was all too accurate, but I tracked down another copy at the Hoover Institution in California, and it was published in full in 2000, with an added introduction by John Erickson.

By 2000, St Ermin's Press had attracted another foreign writer, a KGB First Chief Directorate officer named Igor Damaskin who offered a biography entitled *Kitty Harris: The Spy with Seventeen Names.*[7] Although he had not been a party to the original Crown Books agreement with Vladimir Kryuchkov, Damaskin had somehow gained access to the NKVD file on Kitty Harris, who had been Donald Maclean's handler (and lover) in pre-war London and wartime Paris. As well as operating in Europe as a Soviet illegal (hence the seventeen names), she had been born in London and brought up in Canada before she moved to Chicago and was the mistress of Earl Browder, general secretary of the Communist Party of the United States of America. She had also been assigned a secret mission in China.

Damaskin's manuscript was translated by Geoffrey Elliott and proved a revelation, clearing up at least one mystery. The name of Maclean's NKVD contact, dealing with his pre-war management and acting as an intermediary with the illegal *rezident* Grigori Grafpen, had been sanitised to protect the true identity of a courier codenamed ADA. Unfortunately, there had been no clue as to ADA's real name, but now it was revealed to be Kitty, and what a tale Damaskin had to tell!

The last category of St Ermin's Press publications is those written by a group of CIA officers, among them Dick Walters, David Doyle and Dick Holm. The most senior of this trio was General Vernon 'Dick' Walters who had been deputy DCI between 1972 and 1976 during the Watergate era and was widely credited with having saved the CIA when the organisation was under pressure from Congress and seemed likely to be closed down. A gifted linguist, fluent in Portuguese, German, French, Italian, Russian and Spanish, Walters had served as ambassador in Paris, Bonn and the United Nations. Educated in the UK, he was a devout Roman

Catholic and an enthusiastic Knight of St Columba. His wish to have his memoirs *The Mighty and the Meek* published by St Ermin's Press was a huge endorsement and probably influenced some of his colleagues to follow his example.[8] Another great CIA Anglophile, who carried a British passport undeclared to the CIA, was David W. Doyle, whose *True Men and Traitors: From the OSS to the CIA, My Life in the Shadows* covered much of his career, including a controversial posting to Elisabethville in the Congo, but omitted his clandestine role in Asia under non-official cover (NOC) as a magazine journalist.[9]

Doyle eventually retired to a very pleasant academic life in Honolulu and was married to Hope Doyle, a former CIA counter-intelligence officer who had previously been married to KGB defector Yuri Rastvorov, by whom she had two daughters. Years later, their children discovered their father was not a Czech tennis coach, as they had been led to believe, but a Soviet intelligence professional who had deserted the KGB *rezidentura* in Tokyo. Worse, they learned that he had been married in Moscow to a famous ballerina… and that they had a half-sister.

The third CIA officer to write his memoirs, *An American Agent: My Life in the CIA*, for St Ermin's was Dick Holm, whose career began in Laos and led to his appointment as station chief in Paris, a post from which he was eventually expelled. According to the French authorities, Holm had authorised the deployment of an NOC against an Élysée Palace official from whom the agent had tried to extract economic information. Holm, who had been responsible for organising the capture of the terrorist 'Carlos the Jackal' in Khartoum in 1994, publicly took the blame for the fiasco but was later decorated.

In 1998, the British historian Gordon Brook-Shepherd tipped off St Ermin's to the existence of an FBI special agent who had retired to Lexington, Kentucky but had spent much of his operational career as a counter-intelligence specialist responsible for the security of the most senior Soviet officer ever to have defected to the US, Alexander Orlov. The FBI and CIA had debriefed Orlov fairly continuously since he had revealed himself in a series of 1953 *Life* articles in which he described how he had fled Barcelona in 1938 and had lived in America under several aliases. While the FBI had been embarrassed to learn that a fugitive from the NKVD had been living in the US without its knowledge, the pragmatic CIA counter-intelligence staff had attempted to extract as much information from him as possible and was reasonably satisfied that he had been squeezed dry. It had been John Costello and Oleg Tsarev who had disclosed Orlov's reticence and his discretion over such sensitive issues as his mission as illegal *rezident* to pre-war London. Orlov may have been a defector, fearing for his wife and daughter when he was recalled to Moscow in 1938, but nevertheless he had remained loyal to the Soviets until his death in Cleveland, Ohio in March 1973.

The FBI had assigned Ed Gazur, an FBI officer of Hungarian heritage, as Orlov's bodyguard in April 1955. The two men had developed a strong bond, to the degree that Gazur had been appointed the executor of Orlov's estate after his death. I flew to Kentucky in August 1998 to meet Gazur and over four days of negotiation agreed to publish two books: *Secret Assignment: The FBI's KGB General*, which was partly Gazur's own autobiography combined with new material from Orlov, and then in 2004, Orlov's memoirs *The March of Time*, which he had completed shortly before his death.[10] Happily, *Secret Assignment* included a foreword by Gordon Brook-Shepherd, who had made the original introductions.

Gazur was a remarkable individual who had won Orlov's friendship and had been entrusted with some secrets, such as the location of a huge cache of gold which had been removed from the Bank of Spain in October 1936 to be shipped by the Republicans to the Soviet Union through Cartagena. Officially, the consignment, carried aboard four freighters destined for Odessa, had been in payment for Soviet weapons, but unofficially, the vaults had been looted of bullion vastly more valuable than any deliveries of contraband. Significantly, while most of the gold arrived safely in Moscow, one lorry load had been diverted on the journey and the cargo buried in a churchyard near the border with France. This was intended by Orlov to be his personal insurance policy and early retirement fund but he never had the opportunity to enjoy it. Instead, he had confided enough details of the church's location to convince Gazur to devote several annual vacations to a treasure hunt. When we met in August 1998, he was preparing for yet another expedition to find the right church. Gazur never did find Orlov's gold, but upon his death in March 2013, he instead bequeathed his papers to Georgetown University in the hope that someone one day would work out the clues…

St Ermin's Press proved to be a wonderful experience for the authors and publishers alike, and apart from the acrimony over John Cairncross's memoirs, which would be so comprehensively contradicted by his voluminous KGB file in Moscow, the books produced were generally important contributions to intelligence literature. I was proud to be associated with such titles as *They Arrived by Moonlight*, an account of an SOE mission to Belgium undertaken in August 1943 by Captain Jacques Doneux. Very little had ever been written about SOE's 'T' Section, most likely because of the hideous casualty rate it endured. Of 163 agents sent to Belgium, ninety-three were either arrested or killed.

Of all the books considered for publication by St Ermin's, the strangest was a thin volume entitled *Blowing Up Russia*, which was offered in June 2001 by two authors, Alexander Litvinenko and Yuri Felshtinsky. According to their version of events, the Russian Federal Security Service (FSB) had been responsible for detonating bombs in four apartment buildings in Buynaksk, Moscow and Volgodonsk in September 1999, killing over 300 and injuring over 1,000 – atrocities that hitherto had been attributed to Chechen separatists. Indeed, the Kremlin had cited the incident as one of the triggers of the Second Chechen War. The slim, 200-page book had been written largely by Felshtinsky, a well-respected academic. When the two co-authors made a presentation to St Ermin's, Litvinenko came across as slightly deranged and it was far from clear that he was an intelligence defector. He had just been granted political asylum, having made his way to London in November 2000. We learned that as well as working for MI6 as a consultant on Russian organised crime, he was also on Boris Berezovsky's payroll as a security adviser. The book was clearly intended to be part of a political campaign, which did not suit St Ermin's. Accordingly, no offer to publish was made. In November 2006, Litvinenko died of polonium-210, a deadly radioactive toxin that had been administered three weeks earlier in a London hotel by two of his former FSB colleagues.

By far the most ambitious St Ermin's publication was *Agents for Change: Intelligence Services in the 21st Century*. The book was based on the proceedings of an intelligence conference at St Antony's College, Oxford in September 1999. The event centred around Jim Woolsey, Bill Clinton's former CIA director; Vadim Kirpichenko and Oleg Tsarev on behalf of the KGB; and Daphne Park and Gerry Warner representing MI6. The event's coordinator was Professor Harry Shukman, and other notable people present included Michael Herman, formerly secretary of the JIC, and Marrack Goulding of the United Nations. For two days, these illustrious attendees debated the role of intelligence agencies in the modern, post-Soviet era, and the individual papers submitted were combined into a single hardback book, which was released the following year. The experience was truly a meeting of minds, although it was also something of a revelation. It turned out that Kirpichenko, famous for his role as the veteran head of the KGB's illegal intelligence gathering directorate, had been especially close to the chief of the Italian Secret Intelligence Service. Neither spoke each other's language, so they shouted at each other across the auditorium in very poor French.

St Ermin's Press was a pathfinder in terms of finding newly declassified material in the archives and acting as intermediary for intelligence professionals who wanted to negotiate permission to release their memoirs. Its success was all the more remarkable as it only employed two part-time staff and maintained no permanent office!

CHAPTER XIX

MOLEHUNTING IN THE TWENTY-FIRST CENTURY

It might have been imagined that the problems of keeping an intelligence agency's successes and failures secret in an unprecedented era of recorded intelligence history would be challenging, especially when institutionalised declassification programmes in the UK and US have been embraced, with a commitment to official histories as demonstrated by MI5, MI6 and even GCHQ. Indeed, GCHQ's former director Sir David Omand always insisted that while the two other services had opted to publish official histories, his own organisation was so secret that nothing useful could ever be published. Yet, the history of GCHQ *Behind the Enigma* was written by Canadian historian John Ferris and was released in 2020.[1] In the meantime, Omand himself would write *Securing the State* in 2010, *Principled Spying* in 2018, *How Spies Think* in 2020 and *How to Survive a Crisis* in 2023.[2]

These exercises in open government set an example that has been followed, at least in Australia, with a three-volume history of the Australian Security Intelligence Organisation (ASIO). The final book included a chapter entitled 'Looking for Moles: Counterintelligence and the Penetration of ASIO 1975–89', which revealed that a molehunt had been initiated on a tip from an unknown source (actually Oleg Gordievsky) who had mentioned that the Canberra *rezident* Geronti Lazovik had been decorated for an operational success involving a major recruitment during his five-year posting from 1971.[3] On any assessment, this was likely to be a penetration of ASIO, perhaps implying a compromise of 'Five Eyes' material. As the authors observed:

> While the secret of success in the espionage business is keeping one's successes and failures secret, secrecy for secrecy's sake can on occasion prove counterproductive. It is possible that many of ASIO's efforts may have been compromised through revelations to the Soviets in the 1970s and 1980s. Thousands of hours of covert surveillance aimed at exposing Soviet espionage operations had been for nought because of the penetration of the Organisation.[4]

This was an astonishingly candid assessment of the penetration problem and demonstrated a typically robust Australian approach to the issue, even if the agency itself had utterly failed to run a successful molehunt.

According to Gordievsky, who had provided the first confirmation that Lazovik had been the Canberra *rezident*, Lazovik's two successors Gennadi Nayanov and Lev Koshlyakov had also enjoyed what had been considered in Moscow to be very successful postings to Australia. The inference was, of course, that both men's careers had benefitted from the mole. Gordievsky's Third Department insider gossip, which directly impacted on his own prospects for promotion, was supported by Oleg Kalugin who knew that ASIO had been penetrated by more than one mole. He had recalled in his 1994 autobiography *SpyMaster* that when the *rezident* had received an anonymous letter from an ASIO benefactor, he had invited Kim Philby to validate the attached authenticating documentation. Kalugin described how:

> [I] asked Philby for advice on operational matters and sought his opinion on whether certain 'volunteers' who had come to us were genuine or not. In one case, an Australian sent a letter to our embassy in Canberra, enclosing top secret documents and requesting that payment be made to a post office box in the capital. The anonymous volunteer promised to supply more information if we sent the money. Fearing a setup by Australian security services, we debated whether to send the cash. Finally, we decided there was no harm in transferring the funds anonymously to a post office box. Thus began a fruitful relationship in which the volunteer (apparently someone in the Australian intelligence agency) supplied us with extremely useful information about the Australian Secret Intelligence Organisation and its American and British partners. At some point, I showed Philby the Australian's letters and the classified material he had supplied us. I had blacked out references to the country, to protect the security of the operation, but Philby quickly surmised that the volunteer was from Australia and was genuine. Eventually our Australian began passing on so much material that we set up a series of dead drops similar to

> those used by Walker. Although I lost touch with the operation after 1980, I don't think the Australian ever was caught.[5]

Thus, according to Kalugin, the mole inside ASIO had emulated the tradecraft practiced by the US Navy spy John Walker who had successfully sold huge quantities of classified material to the KGB from 1968 until his eventual detection in 1985, having employed a complex but secure system of signals and dead drops for their communications. Walker believed that this precaution had prevented the KGB from learning his name. Evidently, Kalugin thought that the ASIO mole had done much the same. Later, Kalugin asserted that in his role as chief of Directorate K, he had ordered Lazovik to find out the mole's true identity, a task he had accomplished by placing a dead drop under surveillance and then following the person who had serviced it. For Kalugin there was a fundamental principle at stake, and he was not prepared to deal with a source whose true identity was not known to him.

Significantly, Kalugin had asserted that the KGB 'had productive moles in Australian intelligence who passed us documents from the CIA and British intelligence, as well as providing us with information on subjects as varied as the peace movement and the Australian military'.[6] While he may not have explicitly stated that the KGB had run more than one source inside ASIO, the implication was that Five Eyes material had leaked from 'Australian intelligence'. On the basis that the Soviets almost always tasked their agents to provide personality profiles of potential candidates for recruitment, it should be assumed that JABARU, the codename given to the mole by ASIO, acted as a talent-spotter and Kalugin's use of the plural referred to other spies in ASIO.

Another reliable source on the subject of the ASIO mole was the defector Vasili Mitrokhin who in 1992 added two important clues to the investigation: the mole had retired in 1983 and his wife had also been employed by ASIO, perhaps as a secretary. Yet another KGB officer with a knowledge of JABARU turned out to be Vitaly Yurchenko, the KGB officer who had defected to the CIA in August 1985. Unfortunately, he had been debriefed by Soviet spy Aldrich Ames, who had deliberately omitted the defector's remarks about the Australian mole from his report. It would be a further seven years before the CIA compared Ames's reporting to the actual audio recording of the conversation, and this was when Yurchenko's comments were discovered. Quite why Ames took it upon himself to suppress information about an ASIO mole remains a mystery. It may be that he simply saw himself as generally helping Moscow's cause.

Yurchenko had been an important source, even though he would redefect to Moscow in October 1985 after only two months in American hands. Nevertheless, before he changed his mind, Yurchenko confirmed that Gilles Brunet had been the long-sought Soviet mole in the Royal Canadian Mounted Police (RCMP) Security Service, as was already suspected, and identified Ron Pelton as a spy in the National Security Agency. Brunet had died in April the previous year, having been dismissed from the RCMP in 1973 for misconduct. Pelton would be arrested in November 1985 and subsequently was sentenced to three life terms plus ten years.

When the CIA realised Ames's mischief, the FBI's deputy assistant director for intelligence was sent to Canberra to make a personal apology to ASIO's chief. An abject grovel was certainly required, for if Yurchenko's debriefers had been more disciplined,

Ames would not have been able to suppress the defector's references to an Australian mole and ASIO would have been able to mount a timely investigation. Instead, the failure to reconcile Ames's version of the interviews with the original recording put ASIO at a disadvantage and allowed JABARU seven years of peaceful retirement.

Clearly the mole, with access to other Five Eyes information, was of immense importance to the Soviets and represented considerable embarrassment for successive Australian governments, who were appalled that ASIO had been unable to find the man codenamed JABARU. When I researched the issue for *Spy Swap* in 2021, I was already aware of a closely knit collection of FCD officers who called themselves GROUP NORTH and had been responsible for supervising spies such as Aldrich Ames and Robert Hanssen who had approached the Soviets and offered to sell their agencies' secrets.

In the case of JABARU, the culprit turned out to be former Royal Australian Air Force Spitfire pilot Ian G. Peacock, who had contacted Lazovik at the Canberra *rezidentura* in 1977. Lazovik had taken a considerable risk in accepting the anonymous traitor's packages of classified information because he could not be absolutely certain that the exercise might prove to be nothing more than a deliberate provocation intended to expose the *rezidentura* and embarrass the embassy. However, the quality produced by the source codenamed MIRA by the Soviets would prove its authenticity, and he was assigned a dedicated and experienced handler, Yuri Shmatkov. Reportedly, Peacock had avoided ever meeting any KGB officers and passed his information through dead drops located in Sydney's Centennial Park. MIRA's pay was couriered to Canberra in cash under the codename TOBACCO.

Originally from Hobart and educated at Geelong Grammar School, Peacock had joined the RAAF in 1941 and then ASIO in 1950, soon after his father's suicide. He had started his professional life using the work name BIRDMAN at the small field office in Tasmania, where he remained for ten years before joining a surveillance unit deployed against suspected Soviet agents in Sydney. In 1969, he was posted to the embassy in Rome as a liaison officer for four years and was then sent to headquarters in Kirribilli, New South Wales as head of registry. In 1972, he was transferred to B1, the section dealing with the infiltration of unions and was appointed the section head in 1977. That same year he headed B2 and finally, in 1980, was promoted to head of the 'E' (espionage) branch. His alcoholic wife Dorothy had also worked for ASIO in Rome, but it is thought that she had no knowledge of her husband's double life, which may have extended beyond his retirement in 1983. According to Oleg Kalugin, the mole, now known to his former colleagues as REGATTA, had been paid $50,000 to recruit his successor. However, nobody in ASIO had reported a recruitment pitch, so a young officer who had once served as Peacock's subordinate became the focus of attention. Known as 'Ken', he drove a Porsche and seemed to have unexplained wealth, but the investigation terminated with his death from a long-standing health condition. Allegedly, Ken had been asked by Peacock if he would be willing to pass privileged information to a group of American investors keen to trade on insider tips. He had declined the offer but had not reported it.

Peacock died in October 2006, having spent much of his retirement playing golf at the Balgowlah Golf Club on Sydney's north shore where he was elected to the management board. When finally confronted by ASIO, Peacock denied having been the mole, declined an offer of immunity and refused to cooperate with the investigation.

The JABARU molehunt was concluded in June 2023, not by yet another ASIO molehunt but by a private contractor, a respected colleague, who was hired to solve the mystery that had eluded ASIO for more than thirty years. With his knowledge of the KGB and its retirees, a single investigator was able to acquire the testimony that concluded the case.

It should be acknowledged, of course, that the Australians are not alone in seeking to tie up the loose ends of incomplete molehunts. In the US, speculation has been generated recently by Robert Baer about the existence of a 'fourth man' after the convictions of Aldrich Ames and Robert Hanssen and the defection in 1985 of Edward Howard.[7] When Ames was arrested in March 1993, it was realised that he could not have been responsible for all the losses previously attributed to him. Some senior counter-intelligence analysts have concluded, having studied cases known to have been betrayed to the Russians, that a few examples could not be attributed to the exposed spies, thus raising the spectre of another, as yet unidentified traitor.

Over the past thirty years, a small number of specially indoctrinated CIA and FBI officers have engaged in a search for a spy sometimes referred to as 'the fourth man', a hitherto unidentified mole most likely a former member of the Agency's Counter-Intelligence Center (CIC), who operated in parallel with, but isolated from, Howard, Ames and Hanssen. The search began in June 1994, when deputy director for operations Ted Price asked a small group of analysts, known as the Special Investigations Unit (SIU), to take a closer look at certain events which seemed to suggest the existence of a source who had evaded suspicion. This unknown individual was held to be responsible for, among other crimes, tipping off the KGB to Oleg Gordievsky's role as a British asset inside the London *rezidentura* in May 1985... on a date *before* Ames had started haemorrhaging secrets to his Soviet contact. Although Ames discovered Gordievsky's true identity, concealed by the codename NOCTON (but known within the CIA as AE/TICKLE), he has always denied responsibility for the betrayal. Secondly, in March 1986, CIA case officer Michael Sellers had been ambushed in Moscow while on his way to meet a local KGB recruit, Sergei Vorontsov, codenamed GT/COWL. The molehunters concluded that neither Ames, who was then in Rome, nor the FBI's Hanssen could have learned about Sellers's mission.

Another puzzle was that of Sergei Bokhan and Leonid Poleshchuk. Bokhan was a GRU officer exfiltrated from Athens at the end of May 1985, a fortnight *before* Ames had reportedly delivered his name to the KGB in Washington DC on 13 June. What had prompted Bokhan's summons to Moscow, dated 21 May, on the bogus pretext of dealing with a family problem? While Ames admitted that he had visited the KGB *rezident* Victor Cherkashin on 15 May, the chronology did not seem to accommodate the attribution of blame to him. Codenamed GT/WEIGH, Poleshchuk had been recruited in Nepal in 1974, and was recalled to the Soviet Union from Lagos in May 1985. Upon his return to Moscow he was tried and executed. Similarly, Gordievsky had been suddenly asked to fly back to Moscow in a cable dated 26 May 1985 and had taken the flight two days later, after hurried consultations with MI6. Thus, there were three clear examples of the KGB's intervention at a time when Ames had not yet made his big 'dump' of classified material.

This is the background to the 'fourth man' mystery, part of which became known to Baer. He was a controversial officer who had been accused by Bill Clinton's national security adviser Tony Lake of encouraging the Kurds to assassinate Saddam Hussein, as he had described in his book *See No Evil.*[8] However, Baer played a peripheral role in the molehunt, learning many of the details from former subordinate Laine Bannerman, who later worked as a CIA analyst. Based largely on Bannerman's memory, Baer recounted the SIU's inquiry, which reported in November 1998 and suggested that the accumulated evidence pointed towards a senior CIA officer, Paul Redmond. Redmond was a no-nonsense, plain-speaking officer and confirmed curmudgeon, who had argued with his colleague John Stein about the likelihood of a penetration in the months before Ames was caught. A former deputy director of operations (DDO) and inspector general, Stein had rejected the idea of a mole, suggesting the failures were explicable by poor tradecraft and security lapses. It had been Redmond who had insisted that the evidence was unambiguous, and he had turned out to be right.

Baer may not have been a counter-intelligence professional, but during his career he had learned a lot about molehunts. One key element to the search was Aleksandr Zaporozhsky, the CIA's crucial asset inside the KGB. Zaporozhsky had quietly retired from the KGB and moved with his family to the US but in 2000 had been lured back to Moscow and imprisoned. A decade later, he had been freed as part of the Vienna spy swap in June 2010. Formerly a member of the KGB's secretive Coordination Committee, he was one of the handful of trusted officers assigned to the single task of penetrating the US intelligence community, and he had proved his value when he provided the tip that ultimately compromised Ames. He had also alerted the CIA to the espionage of CIA operations officer Harold Nicholson, arrested in November 1996; FBI special agent Earl Pitts, arrested in December 1996; and NSA analyst David Boone, arrested in October 1998. As they say in the molehunting business, it takes a spy to catch a spy.

Over the years, Zaporozhsky's information had led to the successful prosecution of four American traitors; so when Baer reported that the Russian had actually claimed there had been a 'fourth man', someone who attended senior staff meetings, the assertion was taken seriously but not by everyone. Joe Augustyn, the CIA officer responsible for having resettled him, has cast doubt on this particular claim, pointing out that Baer has not specified exactly where or when Zaporozhsky made the charge. The DDO Mike Sulick dismissed the defector's testimony as an 'exaggeration' motivated by a wish 'to remain relevant in the eyes of the Agency', a not-unfamiliar characteristic of deserters who fear outliving their usefulness to their host country. Augustyn observed, in a review of Baer's book, 'I believe it is likely the KGB conducted its own investigation of Gordievsky, Bokhan and Poleshchuk without the help of a CIA mole.'[9] However, he does not dispute Baer's central thesis that the CIA had stalked a mole but had not yet run it to ground.

Delving further into the past, the very first FBI molehunt into the spy codenamed UNSUB DICK is also unresolved. The case had been triggered by KGB officer Aleksei Kulak, who in 1962 had approached the FBI in New York to reveal the existence of a mole apparently serving in the New York field office's surveillance unit. According to Kulak, later codenamed FEDORA, the FBI mole was controlled by the KGB *rezidentura* in the permanent mission to the United Nations. More than a hundred FBI special agents were investigated in the search for UNSUB DICK, but the principal suspect, whose son became a senior FBI officer, defeated three interviews and at the time of his death had maintained his denials.

Another Soviet mole who has thus far escaped any public attention is GARMASH, a senior DST (French Security Service) officer who would be appointed first deputy to the director Marcel Chalet in 1976. The elder of two brothers who joined the DST soon after the war, GARMASH had headed the DST regional office in Marseilles, and after his retirement he ran the DST pensioners' association. He is still blamed for having betrayed an important source in the KGB, Vladimir Vetrov, who was arrested in Moscow in 1981. Although the defector Anatoliy Golitsyn knew GARMASH's codename and that he had been recruited by the Soviets at the end of the war, he did not offer enough information to the DST to justify a full-scale investigation.[10]

GARMASH was held in such high regard by the KGB that Oleg Kalugin travelled by car from Switzerland to hold a clandestine overnight meeting with him in the Soviet Trade Delegation offices in Paris. Whereas some intelligence agencies show no appetite to open old wounds, the French have shown no inclination even to contemplate hostile penetration.

Closing counter-intelligence files, a task accomplished these days by assiduous pursuit of pensioners and access to dusty archives, is immensely gratifying and serves the cause of accurate history. It seems unconscionable that the British authorities still conceal the true identities of the GRU spies MINISTER and BARON, allow a muddle over INTELLIGENTSIA and NOBILITY to be perpetuated, and have not repudiated the 1955 White Paper on Burgess and Maclean, nor acknowledged the disastrous nature of MI5's advice given to Thatcher in November 1979 on the topic of historic hostile penetration.*

Molehunts may be politically embarrassing; they may even create tension within western liaison relations, but they are essential if complacency is to be avoided and legacy issues are not to return to undermine an agency's integrity. If these organisations are unwilling to keep their own house in order, there will always be room for the dedicated amateur.

* Admittedly, the VENONA evidence relating to MINISTER and BARON is very limited but nevertheless is surely too important to be overlooked. The texts show that BARON had been active between at least March and August 1941 as a member of the GRU's X GROUP and had access to original Enigma decrypts. This description, amounting to an early penetration of Bletchley Park, was never pursued exhaustively. Likewise, even less is known about MINISTER, apart from the provocative codename. Both cases remain unresolved.

NOTES

INTRODUCTION

1 *Ringside Seat* by James Allason (London: Timewell Press, 2007)
2 *The Spy Who Came in from the Cold* by John le Carré (London: Penguin, 1963)
3 *The Faber Book of Espionage* edited by Nigel West (London: Faber & Faber, 1993); *A Small Town in Germany* by John le Carré (London: Heinemann, 1968)
4 *The Israeli Secret Service* by Richard Deacon (London: Hamish Hamilton, 1977); *'C': A Biography of Sir Maurice Oldfield* by Richard Deacon (London: Macdonald, 1985)
5 *Operation Blunderhead* by David Gordon Kirby (London: The History Press, 2015)
6 *A Spy Has No Friends* by Ronald Seth (London: Andre Deutsch, 1952)

I. THE VENLO INCIDENT

1 *The Venlo Incident* by Sigismund Payne Best (London: Hutchinson, 1951)
2 *Invasion 1940* by Walter Schellenberg (London: St Ermin's Press, 2000)
3 Ibid.
4 Payne Best, p.45
5 *The Two Bills: Mission Accomplished* by Dick Ellis (unpublished manuscript)
6 *The Quiet Canadian* by H. Montgomery Hyde (London: Hamish Hamilton, 1962)
7 *A Man Called Intrepid* by William Stevenson (London: Macmillan, 1976)
8 *Madeleine* by Jean Overton Fuller (London: Pan, 1957)
9 Stevenson, p.xix
10 *Cynthia* by H. Montgomery Hyde (New York: Farrar, Straus and Giroux, 1965)
11 *History of the British Secret Service* by Richard Deacon (London: Taplinger, 1969); *My Silent War* by Kim Philby (London: MacGibbbon & Kee, 1968)
12 *British Agent* by John Whitwell (London: William Kimber, 1966)
13 *The Double-Cross System of the War of 1939–45* by J. C. Masterman (Yale: Yale University Press, 1972); *The Game of the Foxes* by Ladislas Faragó (New York: David McKay, 1972)
14 *Mirror of Deception* by Günter Peis (London: Weidenfeld & Nicolson, 1977)

II. *SPY!*

1 *The British Connection* by Richard Deacon (London: Hamish Hamilton, 1979)
2 Rudolf Peierls's MI5 file is at KV2/1658 and KV2/1659, National Archives
3 *Spy! Six Stories of Modern Espionage* by Richard Deacon and Nigel West (London: BBC Publications, 1980)

4 Hyde, p.76
5 *The Storm Petrels* by Gordon Brook-Shepherd (New York: Harcourt Brace Jovanovich, 1977)

III. TATE AND THE DOUBLE AGENTS

1 *Bodyguard of Lies* by Anthony Cave Brown (New York: Harper & Row, 1975)
2 *The Ultra Secret* by F. W. Winterbotham (London: Weidenfield & Nicholson, 1974)
3 See *The Scott Report* (HMSO, 1996) and *The Unlikely Spy* by Paul Henderson (London: Bloomsbury, 1993)
4 *Ashenden* by W. Somerset Maugham (New York: Doubleday, 1941)
5 *Greek Memories* by Compton Mackenzie (London: Chatto & Windus, 1939)
6 *Water on the Brain* by Compton Mackenzie (London: Chatto & Windus, 1954)
7 *All's Fair* by Henry Landau (New York: Putnam's, 1934)
8 *Secrets of the White Lady* by Henry Landau (New York: Putnam's, 1935); *The Enemy Within* by Henry Landau (New York: Putnam's, 1937); *Spreading the Spy Net* by Henry Landau (New York: Putnam's, 1938)
9 *Philby: The Spy Who Betrayed a Generation* by Bruce Page, David Leitch and Phillip Knightley (London: Penguin, 1969)
10 *George Blake* by E. H. Cookridge (Princeton: Vertex, 1970)
11 *Spy/Counterspy* by Duško Popov (London: Weidenfeld & Nicolson, 1973)
12 *The Philby Affair* by Hugh Trevor-Roper (London: William Kimber, 1968)
13 *Secret Service Rendered* by Lilly Sergueiew (London: William Kimber, 1968)
14 *The Real Eddie Chapman Story* by Eddie Chapman (London: Library 33, 1966)
15 *SOE in France* by M. R. D. Foot (London: HMSO, 1966)
16 *MI9: The Escape and Evasion Service* by M. R. D. Foot & J. M. Langley (London: Little Brown, 1988)
17 *The Cartland File* by Jeremy Cartland (London: Linkline, 1978)
18 *Never Judge a Man by his Umbrella* by Nicholas Elliott (Wilton: The Chantry, 1991); *With My Little Eye* by Nicholas Elliott (London: Michael Russell, 1993)
19 *John Moe: Double Agent* by Jan Moen (Oslo: Aschehoug, 1986)
20 *The Big Network* by Roman Garby-Czerniawski (London: George Ronald, 1961)
21 *Moonlight on a Lake in Bond Street* by Stephen Watts (London: Bodley Head, 1961)
22 *Sunday Telegraph*, 25 November 1979
23 *Elusive Rothschild* by Kenneth Rose (London: Orion, 2003)
24 HC Debs, 21 November 1979, col. 403
25 *MI5: British Security Service Operations 1909-45* by Nigel West (London: Bodley Head, 1981), p.336
26 HC Debs, 9 November 1981, col. 40

IV. MI5 AND *A MATTER OF TRUST*

1 Philby (1968), p.111
2 See *Climate of Treason* by Andrew Boyle (London: Hutchinson, 1979). At the time of his death in April 1991, Boyle had embarked on a biography of Dick White, a project completed by Tom Bower as *The Perfect English Spy* in 1995 (London: St Martin's Press).

V. THE HUNT FOR GARBO

1 *The Double-Cross System in the War of 1939–45* by J. C. Masterman (London: Yale University Press, 1972)
2 Masterman, p.114
3 *My Silent War* by Kim Philby (London: MacGibbon & Kee, 1968), p.122
4 *The Counterfeit Spy* by Sefton Delmer (London: Hutchinson, 1975), p.62
5 Philby, 1968
6 *A Game of Moles* by Desmond Bristow (London: Hutchinson, 1990)

7 *British Intelligence in the Second World War: Security and Counter-Intelligence* (Volume 4) by F. H. Hinsley and C. A. G. Simkins (London: HMSO, 1993)
8 MI5's file is at KV2/40, National Archives
9 *The Times*, October 1985

VI. CABINET WAR ROOM 2

1 *Their Finest Hour* by Winston Churchill (London: Cassell, 1949)
2 MI5's Operation HEGIRA file is at KV4/211, National Archives
3 *Beneath the City Streets* by Peter Laurie (London: Penguin, 1974)
4 The PADDOCK file is at CAB21/1068, National Archives

VII. ADMIRAL CANARIS'S MISTRESS

1 Erich Vermehren's MI5 file is at KV2/956, National Archives
2 Ibid.
3 *On Her Majesty's Secret Service* by Christopher Andrew (New York: Viking, 1985), p.557
4 *British Intelligence in the Second World War* (Volume 1) by Harry Hinsley, p.50
5 *MI6* by Keith Jeffery (London: Penguin, 2011), pp.380–82

VIII. *SPYCATCHER*

1 *Spycatcher* by Peter Wright and Paul Greengrass (New York: Viking, 1987)
2 *New Lies for Old* by Anatoliy Golitsyn (New York: Dodd, Mead & Company, 1984)
3 *Their Trade is Treachery* by Chapman Pincher (London: Sidgwick & Jackson, 1981)
4 *One Girl's War* by Joan Miller (London: Brandon, 1986)
5 *Inside Intelligence* by Anthony Cavendish (New York: Granta, 1998)

IX. GREVILLE WYNNE

1 *MI6: The History of the Secret Intelligence Service 1909–1949* by Keith Jeffery (London: Bloomsbury, 2010)
2 *No End of a Lesson* by Anthony Nutting (London: Constable, 1967)
3 *The Penkovsky Papers* by Oleg Penkovsky (London: Collins, 1967)
4 *The Man from Moscow* by Greville Wynne (London: Hutchinson, 1967)
5 *Daily Express*, 27 March 1985
6 Ibid.
7 *The Man from Odessa* by Greville Wynne (London: Robert Hale, 1981)
8 *Secret Service: The Making of the British Intelligence Community* by Christopher Andrew (New York: Viking, 1985), p.557; *MI6* by Keith Jeffery (London: Penguin, 2011), pp.380–2.

X. BILL CASEY

1 *The Secret War Against Hitler* by William Casey (New York: Regnery, 1988)
2 *Fortitude: The D-Day Deception Campaign* by Roger Fleetwood-Hesketh (London: St Ermin's Press, 2000)
3 *Wilderness of Mirrors* by David Martin (New York: HarperCollins, 1980)
4 *The Kennedy Conspiracy* by Anthony Simmers (London: Sphere, 1992)
5 Testimony made to the Tower Commission by Tom Twetten, https://www.cia.gov/readingroom/docs/CIA-RDP89G00643R001300120001-9.pdf, p.211
6 *Taken on Trust* by Terry Waite (London: Hodder & Stoughton, 1993)

XI. FARZAD BAZOFT

1 *Instant Empire* by Simon Henderson (London: Mercury House, 1991)
2 Henderson, p.23

3 *The Outsider: My Life in Intrigue* by Frederick Forsyth (London: Penguin Random House, 2015)
4 *Burn Before Reading* by Stansfield Turner (New York: Hyperion, 2006), p.100
5 *Secrecy and Democracy: The CIA in Transition* by Stansfield Turner (Boston: Houghton Mifflin, 1985)

XII. THE FIFTH MAN

1 *KGB: The Inside Story* by Christopher Andrew and Oleg Gordievsky (London: Hodder & Stoughton, 1990), p.272
2 *MI5: British Security Service Operations 1909–45* by Nigel West (London: Triad Books, 1983), p.335
3 *The Crown Jewels* by Nigel West and Oleg Tsarev (London: HarperCollins, 1998), p.234
4 *The Enigma Spy* by John Cairncross (London: Century, 1997), p.124
5 Cairncross, p.127
6 West and Tsarev, p.222
7 Ibid., p.223
8 Ibid., p.223
9 Ibid., p.223
10 Ibid., p.226

XIII. THE FALKLANDS CONFLICT

1 *The Franks Committee Report* (London: HMSO, 1983). At CAB 292, National Archives
2 *The Downing Street Years* by Margaret Thatcher (London: HarperCollins, 1993)
3 *Looking for Trouble* by Peter de la Billière (London: HarperCollins, 1994)
4 *The Falklands War* by Martin Middlebrook (London: Penguin, 2001)
5 *My Secret Falklands War* by Sidney Edwards (London: Book Guild, 2014)

XIV. GEORGE BLAKE

1 *Seven Spies Who Changed the World* by Nigel West (London: Secker & Warburg, 1991)
2 *Shadow of a Spy* by E. H. Cookridge (London: Leslie Frewin, 1967); *George Blake: Superspy* by H. Montgomery Hyde (London: Constable, 1987); *The Greatest Traitor* by Roger Hermiston (London: Aurum, 2014); *The Happy Traitor* by Simon Kuper (London: Profile Books, 2021); *No Other Choice* by George Blake (London: Jonathan Cape, 1990)
3 Cookridge, p.112
4 *I Was a Captive in Korea* by Philip Deane (London: Hamish Hamilton, 1953), p.167
5 Cookridge, p.114
6 Hyde, p.39
7 *KGB: The Inside Story* by Christopher Andrew and Oleg Gordievsky (London: Hodder & Stoughton, 1990), p.334
8 Ibid., p.628

XV. VENONA

1 *Wilderness of Mirrors* by David C. Martin (New York: Harper & Row, 1980)
2 VENONA, 30 October 1940
3 VENONA, 20 December 1940
4 VENONA, 16 October 1940
5 *The Youngest Son* by Ivor Montagu (London: Lawrence & Wishart, 1970), p.61
6 *The Traitor Class* by Ivor Montagu (London: Lawrence & Wishart, 1940)
7 *The Man Who Never Was* by Ewen Montagu (London: Evans Bros, 1953)
8 VENONA, 6 September 1940
9 VENONA, 25 July 1940. The first (redacted) version is available from www.nsa.gov. This was released in 1995, and it had been heavily redacted to conceal forty-five words in the text and mask the footnoted identification of INTELLIGENTSIA as Montagu. The second, unredacted version of the text was placed in the National Archives in 2009 at HW 15/43.

10 VENONA, 16 August 1940
11 VENONA, 6 September 1940
12 VENONA, 6 September 1940
13 VENONA, 2 October 1940
14 VENONA, 11 October 1940
15 VENONA, 15 October 1940
16 *I Believed* by Douglas Hyde (London: Heinemann, 1950), p.97
17 Ivor Montagu, p.97
18 *The Defence of the Realm* by Christopher Andrew (London: Allen Lane, 2009), p.381
19 Ibid., p.926
20 Ibid., p.926
21 At HW 15/43, National Archives
22 *Comrade Haldane is Too Busy to Go on Holiday* by Gavan Tredoux (London: Encounter Books, 2018); *Codename Intelligentsia* by Russell Campbell (Stroud: History Press, 2018)
23 Tredoux, p.106
24 Ibid., p.106
25 Campbell, p.339
26 Ibid., p.340

XVI. GUY LIDDELL

1 Diary of Guy Liddell, May–December 1947, held at KV 4/469, National Archives
2 Diary of Guy Liddell, January–December 1950, held at KV 4/472, National Archives
3 Diary of Guy Liddell, January–December 1951, held at KV 4/473, National Archives

XVII. THE MOSCOW ARCHIVES

1 *Mask of Treachery* by John Costello (London: Collins, 1988); *Ten Days that Saved the West* by John Costello (London: Bantam 1991)
2 *Deadly Illusions* by John Costello and Oleg Tsarev (New York: Crown Books, 1993)
3 *Battleground Berlin* by David Murphy and Sergei Kondrashev (New York: Yale University Press, 1997); *One Hell of a Gamble* by Tim Naftali and Aleksandr Fursenko (New York: W. W. Norton, 2001); *The Haunted Wood* by Allen Weinstein and Alexander Vassiliev (London: Random House, 1999)
4 West and Tsarev, p.182.
5 *Spies: The Rise and Fall of the KGB in America* by John Earl Haynes, Harvey Klehr and Alexander Vassiliev (Yale: Yale University Press, 2009)

XVIII. ST ERMIN'S PRESS

1 *I Spy* by Geoffrey Elliott (London: St Ermin's Press, 1998)
2 *The Private Life of Kim Philby* by Rufina Philby, Hayden Peake and Michael Lyubimov (London: St Ermin's Press, 1999)
3 *False Flag* by Zeev Avni (London: St Ermin's Press, 1999)
4 *SOE in France* by M. R. D. Foot (London: HMSO, 1966)
5 *The Secret History of SOE* by William Mackenzie (London: St Ermin's Press, 2000)
6 *SOE in the Low Countries* by M. R. D. Foot (London: St Ermin's Press, 2001); *The Secret History of PWE: The Political Warfare Executive 1939–45* by David Garnett (London: St Ermin's Press, 2002)
7 *Kitty Harris: The Spy with Seventeen Names* by Igor Damaskin (London: St Ermin's Press, 2002)
8 *The Mighty and the Meek* by Vernon A. Walters (London: St Ermin's Press, 2001)
9 *True Men and Traitors: From the OSS to the CIA, My Life in the Shadows* by David W. Doyle (London: St Ermin's Press, 2001)
10 *Secret Assignment: The FBI's KGB General* by Edward P. Gazur (London: St Ermin's Press, 2001); *The March of Time* by Alexander Orlov (London, St Ermin's Press, 2004)

XIX. MOLEHUNTING IN THE TWENTY-FIRST CENTURY

1 *Behind the Enigma* by John Ferris (London: Bloomsbury, 2020)
2 *Securing the State* by David Omand (London: Hurst, 2011); *Principled Spying* by David Omand (Oxford: Oxford University Press, 2018); *How Spies Think* by David Omand (London: Penguin, 2021); *How to Survive a Crisis* by David Omand (London: Viking, 2023)
3 *The Secret Cold War: The Official History of ASIO 1975–89* by John Blaxland and Rhys Crawley (Sydney: Allen & Unwin, 2016)
4 Ibid., p.422
5 *SpyMaster* by Oleg Kalugin (London: Smith Gryphon, 1994), p.137
6 Ibid., p.138
7 *The Fourth Man* by Robert Baer (London: Hachette, 2022)
8 *See No Evil* by Robert Baer (London: Arrow, 2002)
9 Joe Augustyn, 'The Fourth Man and the Hunt for Proof', review of *The Fourth Man* in *The Cypher Brief*, June 2022, https://www.thecipherbrief.com/book-review/the-fourth-man-and-the-hunt-for-proof
10 *Checkmate* by Anatoliy Golitsyn (unpublished autobiography)

GLOSSARY

AFIO	Association of Former Intelligence Officers
ASIO	Australian Security Intelligence Organisation
ASIS	Australian Secret Intelligence Service
BfV	Federal German Security Service
BSC	British Security Coordination
CIA	Central Intelligence Agency
CPGB	Communist Party of Great Britain
DCI	Director of Central Intelligence
DDO	Deputy Director of Operations
DST	French Security Service
FBI	Federal Bureau of Investigation
FCD	First Chief Directorate
G-2	Irish Intelligence Service
GCHQ	Government Communications Headquarters
GRU	Soviet Main Intelligence Directorate
JIC	Joint Intelligence Committee
KGB	Committee for State Security
MI5	Security Service
MI6	Secret Intelligence Service

NKVD	People's Commissariat for Internal Affairs
NSA	National Security Agency
OSS	Office of Strategic Services
PCO	Passport Control Officer
PIIC	Public Interest Immunity Certificate
PLO	Palestine Liberation Organisation
RCMP	Royal Canadian Mounted Police
SAS	Special Air Service regiment
SAVAK	Iranian Intelligence Service
SHAEF	Supreme Headquarters Allied Expeditionary Force
SIU	Special Investigations Unit
SOE	Special Operations Executive

INDEX

INDEX

INDEX

BOOKS BY NIGEL WEST

Spy! (with Richard Deacon)

MI5: British Security Service Operations 1909-45

MI6: British Secret Intelligence Service Operations 1909-45

A Matter of Trust: MI5 1945-72

Unreliable Witness Espionage Myths of World War II

Operation GARBO (with Juan Pujol García)

GCHQ: The Secret Wireless War

The Friends: Britain's Postwar Secret Intelligence Operations

Molehunt: The Search for the Soviet Spy in MI5

The Illegals

The Secret War for the Falklands

Counterfeit Spies

Crown Jewels (with Oleg Tsarev)

VENONA: The Greatest Secret of the Cold War

The Third Secret: Solidarity, the CIA and the KGB's Plot to Assassinate the Pope

MASK: MI5's Penetration of the Communist Party

The Guy Liddell Diaries: 1939–42

The Guy Liddell Diaries: 1942–45

TRIPLEX: Secrets from the KGB Archives

MI5 in the Great War

At Her Majesty's Secret Service

Double Cross in Cairo

The Kompromat Conspiracy: The Truth About the Trump Dossier

Cold War Spymaster

Churchill's Spy Files

Codeword OVERLORD

Spy Swap

Hitler's Nest of Vipers: The Rise of the Abwehr

Hitler's Trojan Horse: The Fall of the Abwehr